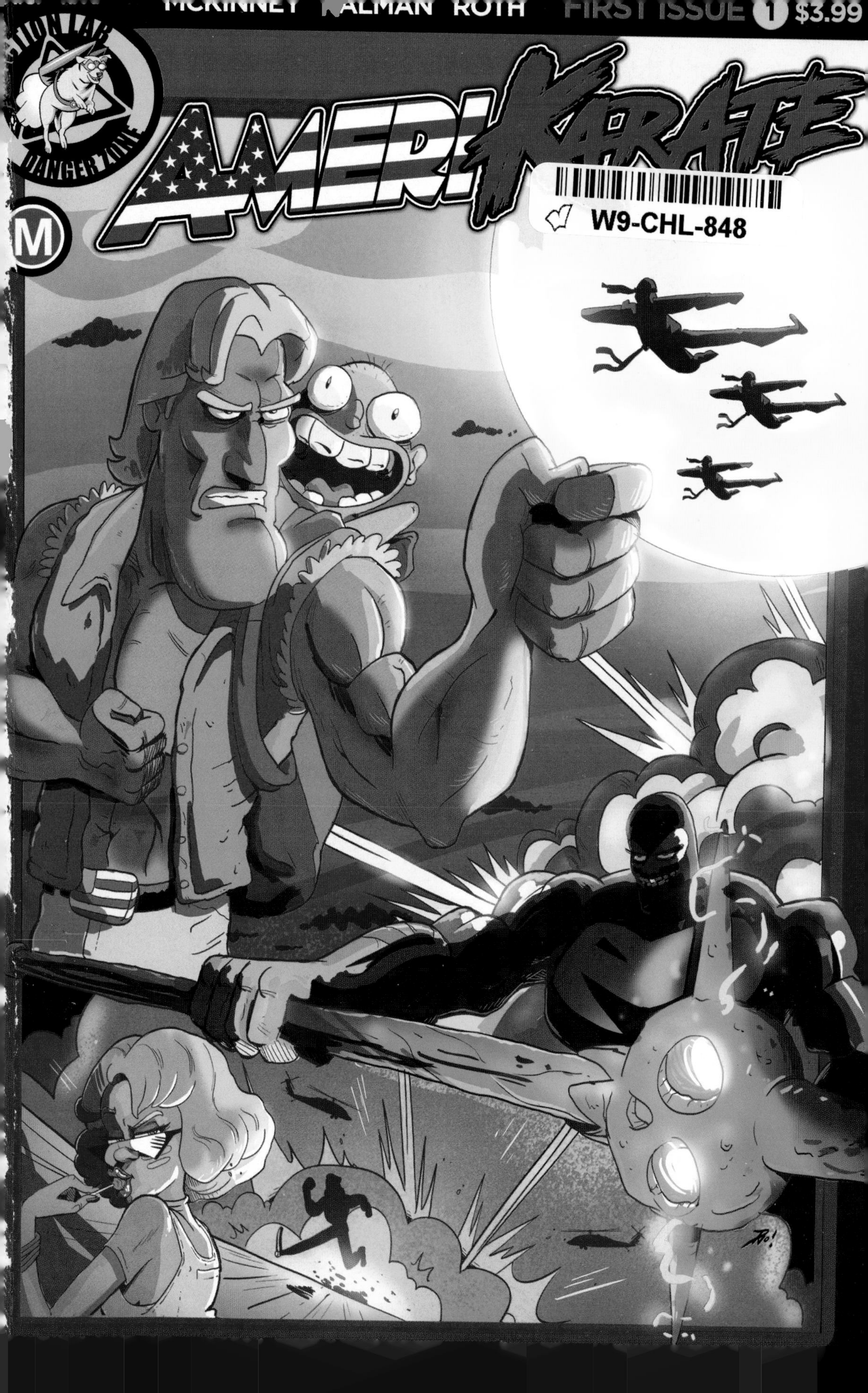
MCKINNEY
ROTH
FIRST ISSUE 1 $3.99
DANGER ZONE
M
AMERIKARATE

ACTION LAB: DANGER ZONE PRESENTS

In a world that outlawed karate, one man fights for his right to fight karate for America. With karate.

AMERIKARATE

WRITTEN BY
COREY KALMAN & BROCKTON McKINNEY

ILLUSTRATED BY
DEVIN ROTH

LETTERS BY
DAVE DWONCH

MATURE READERS MCKINNEY KALMAN ROTH
FIRST ISSUE 1 $3.99
AMERIKARATE

Kalman and McKinney REGULAR
Devin Roth

MATURE READERS MCKINNEY KALMAN ROTH
FIRST ISSUE 1
AMERIKARATE

April O'Neil PHOTO VARIANT
Limited to 1500

MATURE READERS MCKINNEY KALMAN ROTH
FIRST ISSUE 1
AMERIKARATE

Bill McKay ARTIST VARIANT
"Explosive Threesome"
Limited to 1500

MATURE READERS MCKINNEY KALMAN ROTH
FIRST ISSUE 1
AMERIKARATE

Sam Ellis ARTIST VARIANT
"Deathstare"
Limited to 1500

MATURE READERS MCKINNEY KALMAN ROTH
FIRST ISSUE 1
AmeriKarate

Daniel Arruda Massa ARTIST VARIANT
"Kickloose"
Limited to 1500

AMERIKARATE #1 March 2017.

Published by Action Lab Comics.

Printed in Canada.
First printing.

ACTIONLABCOMICS.COM

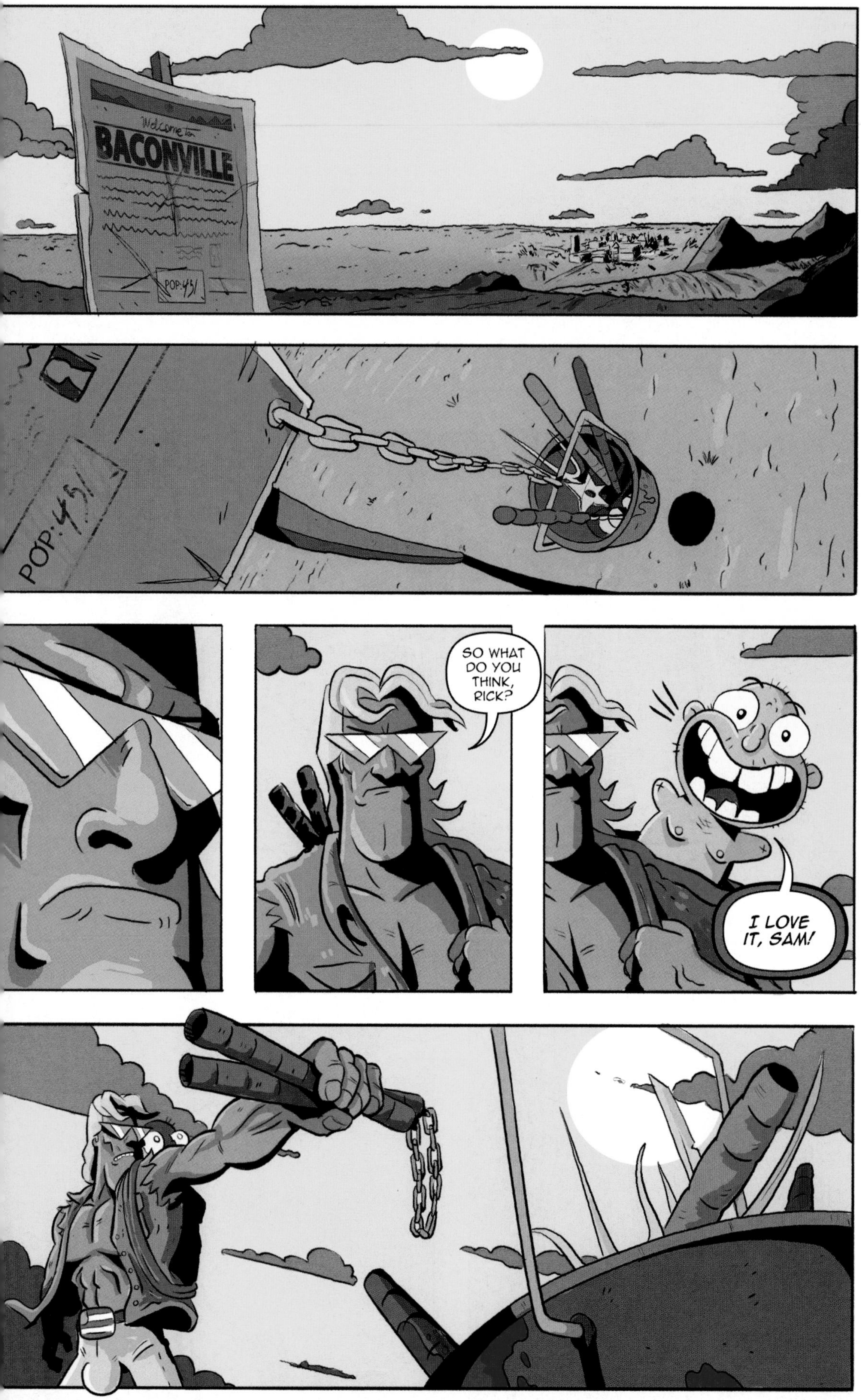
Welcome to
BACONVILLE
POP: 451
SO WHAT DO YOU THINK, RICK?
I LOVE IT, SAM!

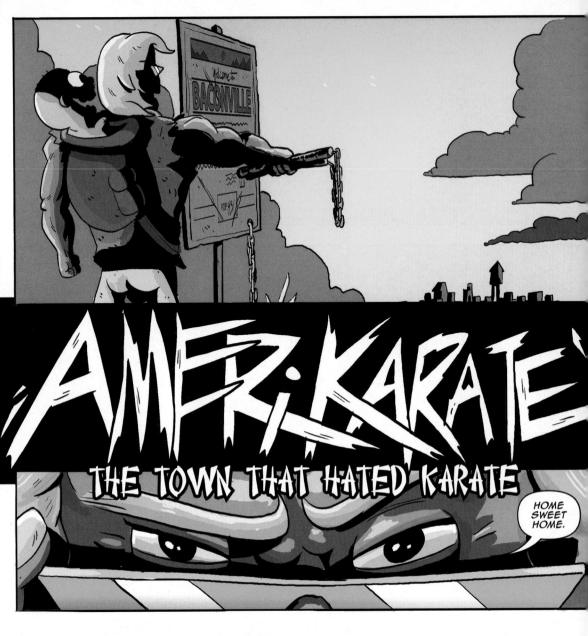

Welcome to
BACONVILLE
POP. 45
AMERIKARATE
THE TOWN THAT HATED KARATE
HOME SWEET HOME.
DROP!
KLUNK!!

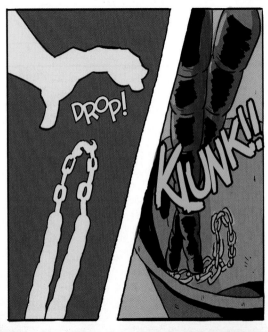

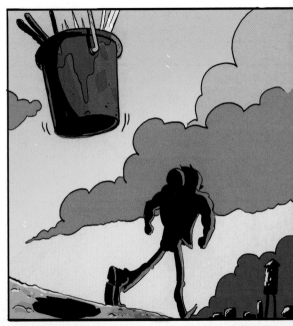

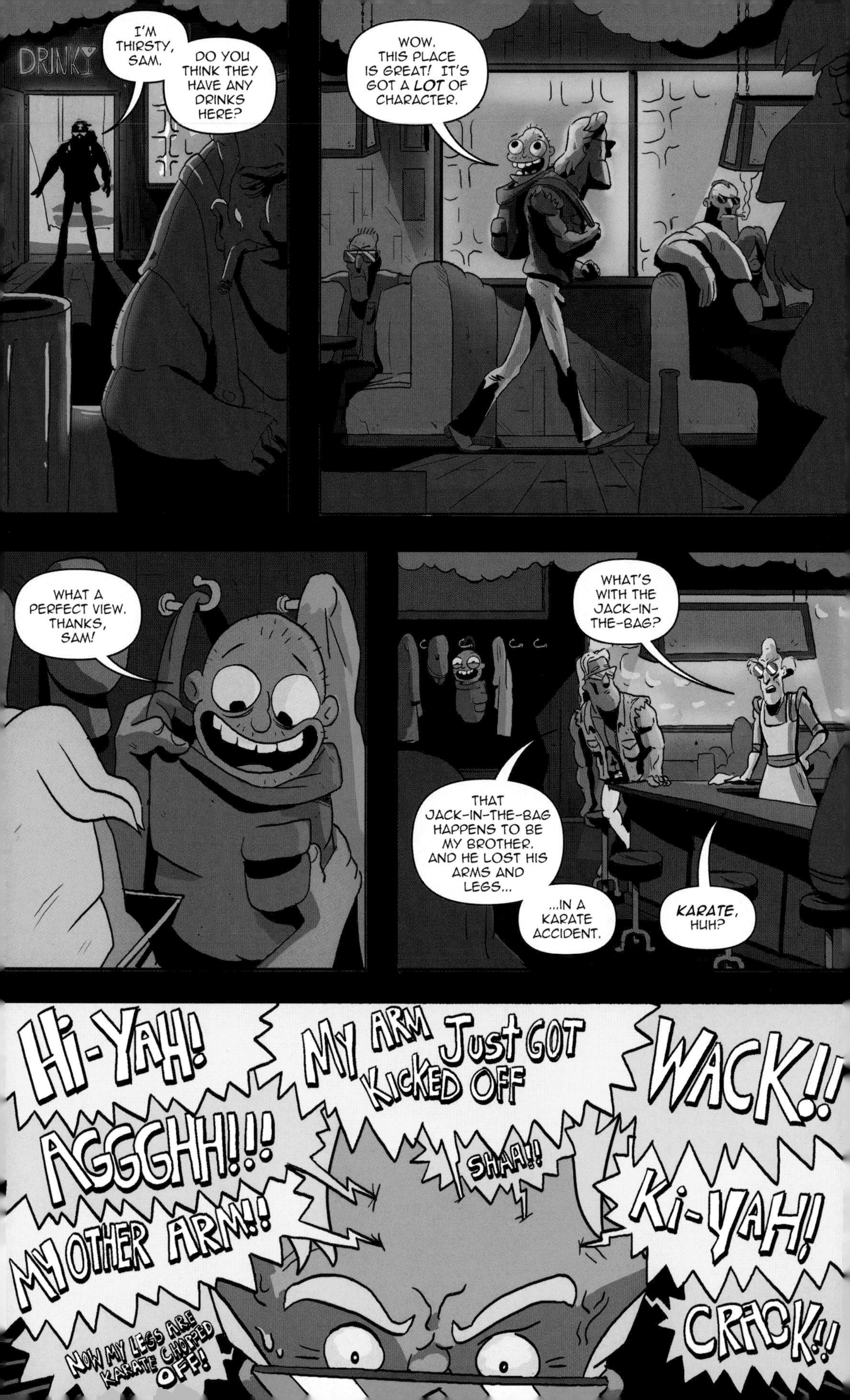
DRINKY
I'M THIRSTY, SAM.
DO YOU THINK THEY HAVE ANY DRINKS HERE?
WOW. THIS PLACE IS GREAT! IT'S GOT A *LOT* OF CHARACTER.
WHAT A PERFECT VIEW. THANKS, SAM!
WHAT'S WITH THE JACK-IN-THE-BAG?
THAT JACK-IN-THE-BAG HAPPENS TO BE MY BROTHER. AND HE LOST HIS ARMS AND LEGS...
...IN A KARATE ACCIDENT.
KARATE, HUH?
HI-YAH!
MY ARM JUST GOT KICKED OFF
WACK!!
AGGGH!!!
SHAA!!
MY OTHER ARM!!
KI-YAH!
NOW MY LEGS ARE KARATE CHOPPED OFF!
CRACK!!

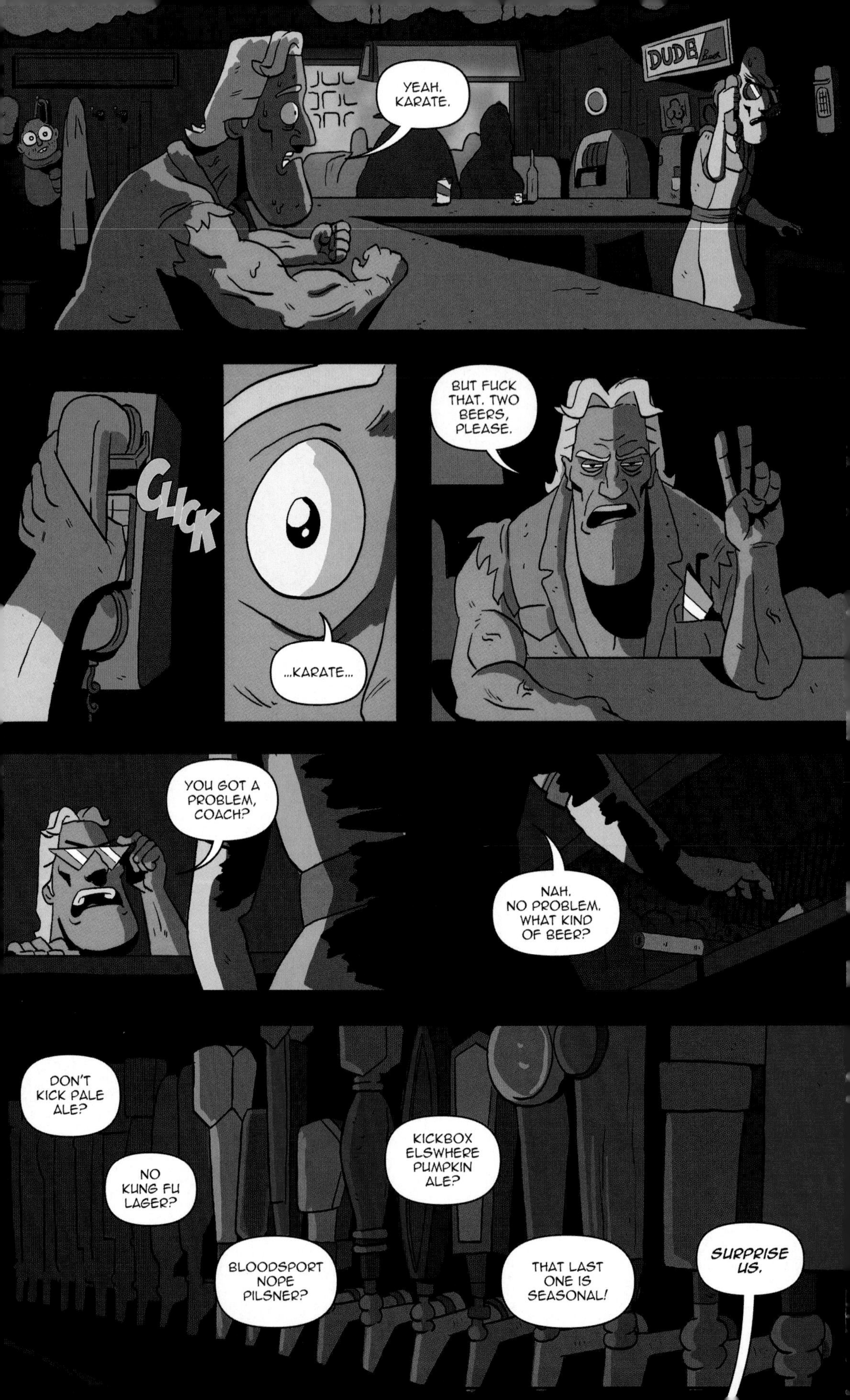
YEAH. KARATE.
CLICK
...KARATE...
BUT FUCK THAT. TWO BEERS, PLEASE.
YOU GOT A PROBLEM, COACH?
NAH. NO PROBLEM. WHAT KIND OF BEER?
DON'T KICK PALE ALE?
NO KUNG FU LAGER?
KICKBOX ELSWHERE PUMPKIN ALE?
BLOODSPORT NOPE PILSNER?
THAT LAST ONE IS SEASONAL!
SURPRISE US.

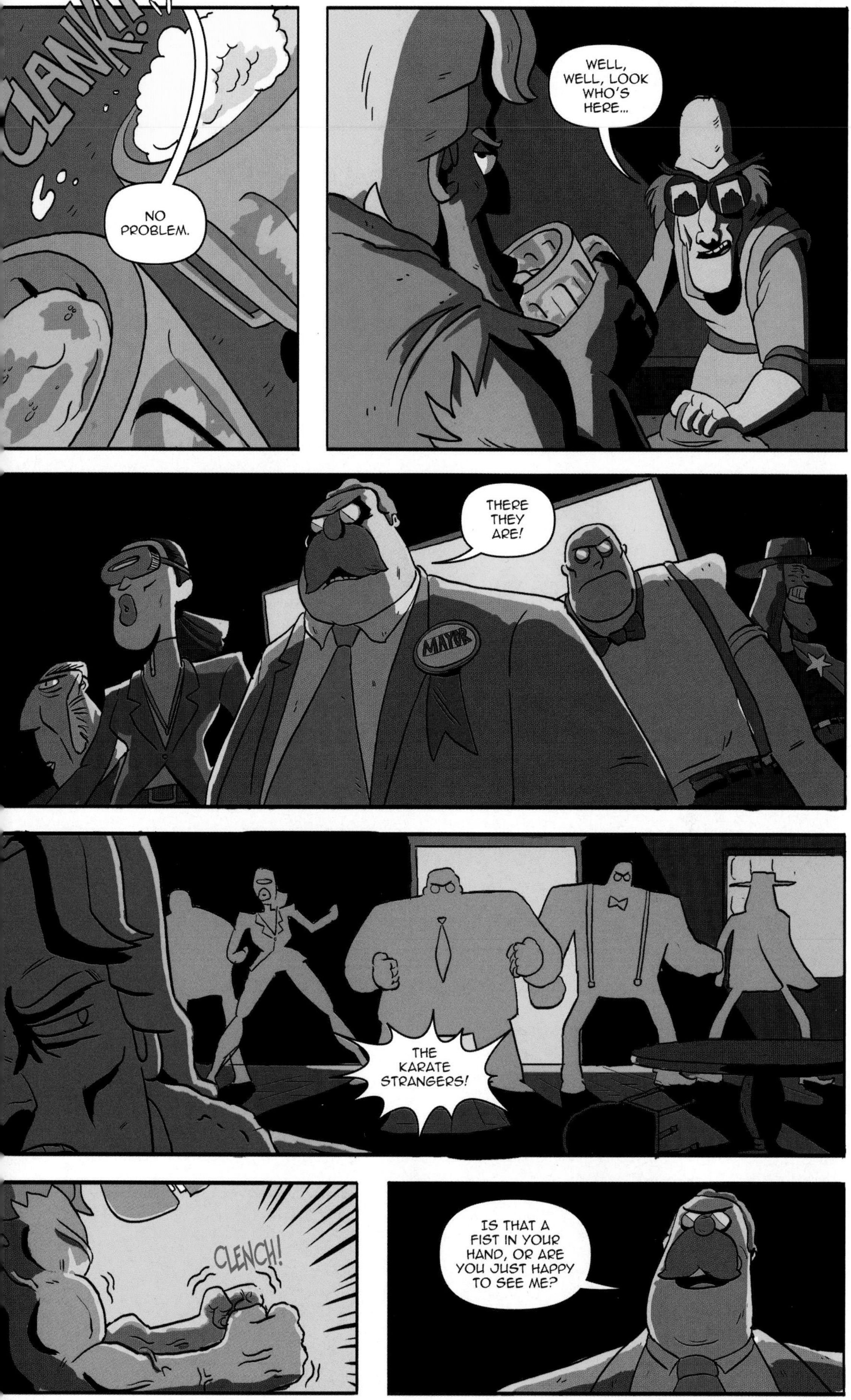
CLANK!!
NO PROBLEM.
WELL, WELL, LOOK WHO'S HERE...
THERE THEY ARE!
MAYOR
THE KARATE STRANGERS!
CLENCH!
IS THAT A FIST IN YOUR HAND, OR ARE YOU JUST HAPPY TO SEE ME?

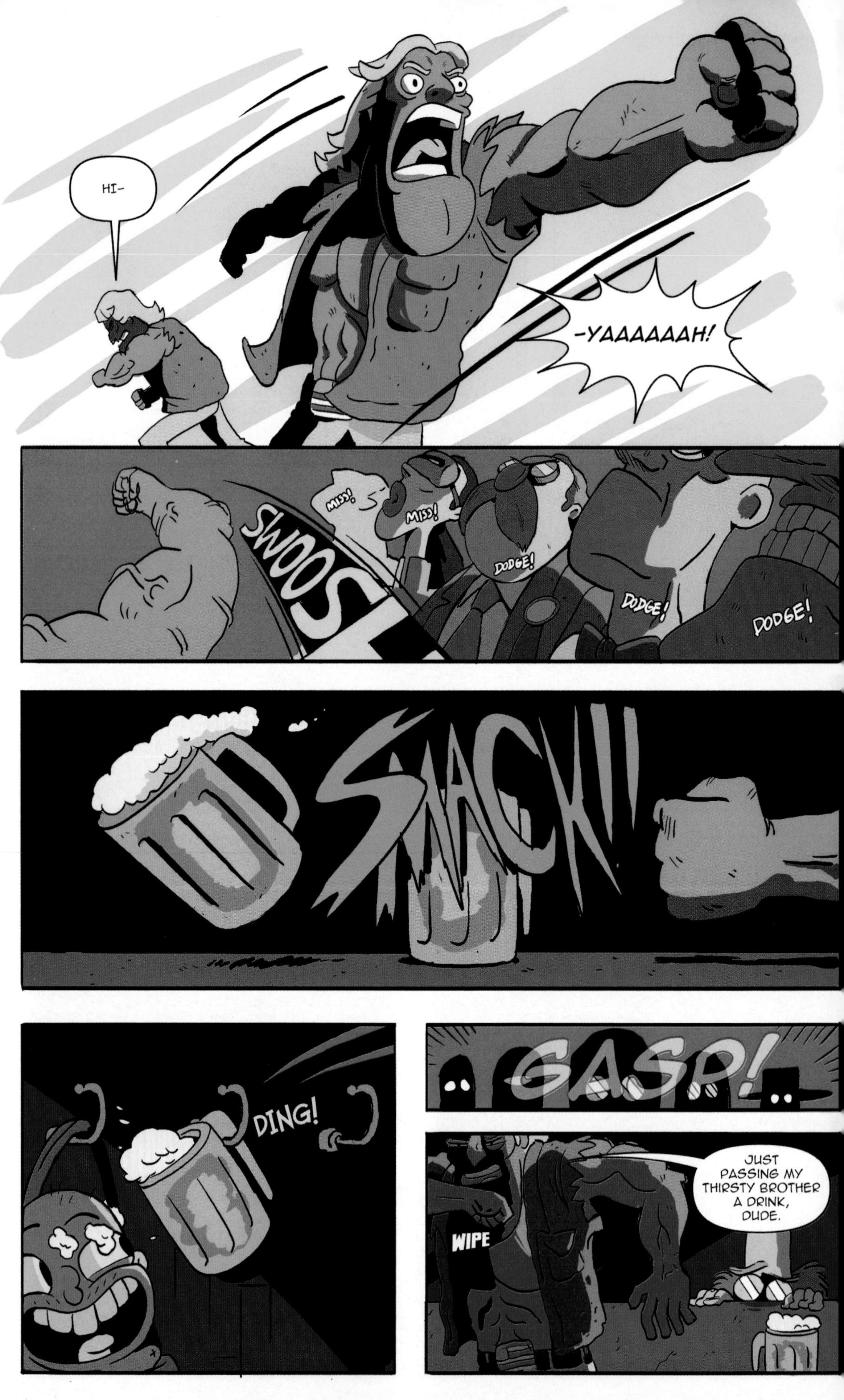

HI-
-YAAAAAAH!
SWOOSH
MISS!
MISS!
DODGE!
DODGE!
DODGE!
SMACK!!!
DING!
GASP!
WIPE
JUST PASSING MY THIRSTY BROTHER A DRINK, DUDE.

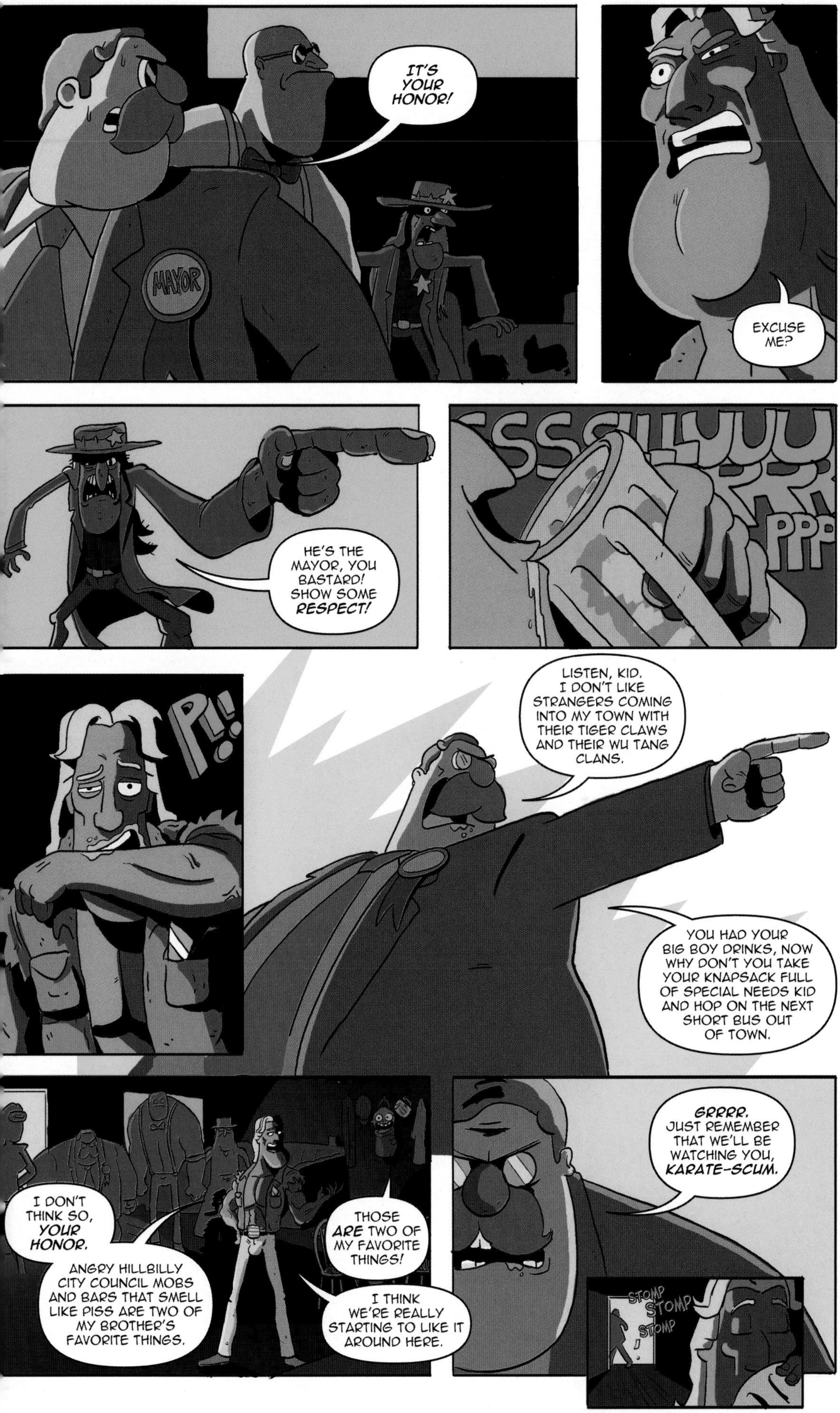
IT'S YOUR HONOR!
EXCUSE ME?
HE'S THE MAYOR, YOU BASTARD! SHOW SOME RESPECT!
LISTEN, KID. I DON'T LIKE STRANGERS COMING INTO MY TOWN WITH THEIR TIGER CLAWS AND THEIR WU TANG CLANS.
YOU HAD YOUR BIG BOY DRINKS, NOW WHY DON'T YOU TAKE YOUR KNAPSACK FULL OF SPECIAL NEEDS KID AND HOP ON THE NEXT SHORT BUS OUT OF TOWN.
I DON'T THINK SO, YOUR HONOR.
ANGRY HILLBILLY CITY COUNCIL MOBS AND BARS THAT SMELL LIKE PISS ARE TWO OF MY BROTHER'S FAVORITE THINGS.
THOSE ARE TWO OF MY FAVORITE THINGS!
I THINK WE'RE REALLY STARTING TO LIKE IT AROUND HERE.
GRRRR. JUST REMEMBER THAT WE'LL BE WATCHING YOU, KARATE-SCUM.
STOMP STOMP STOMP

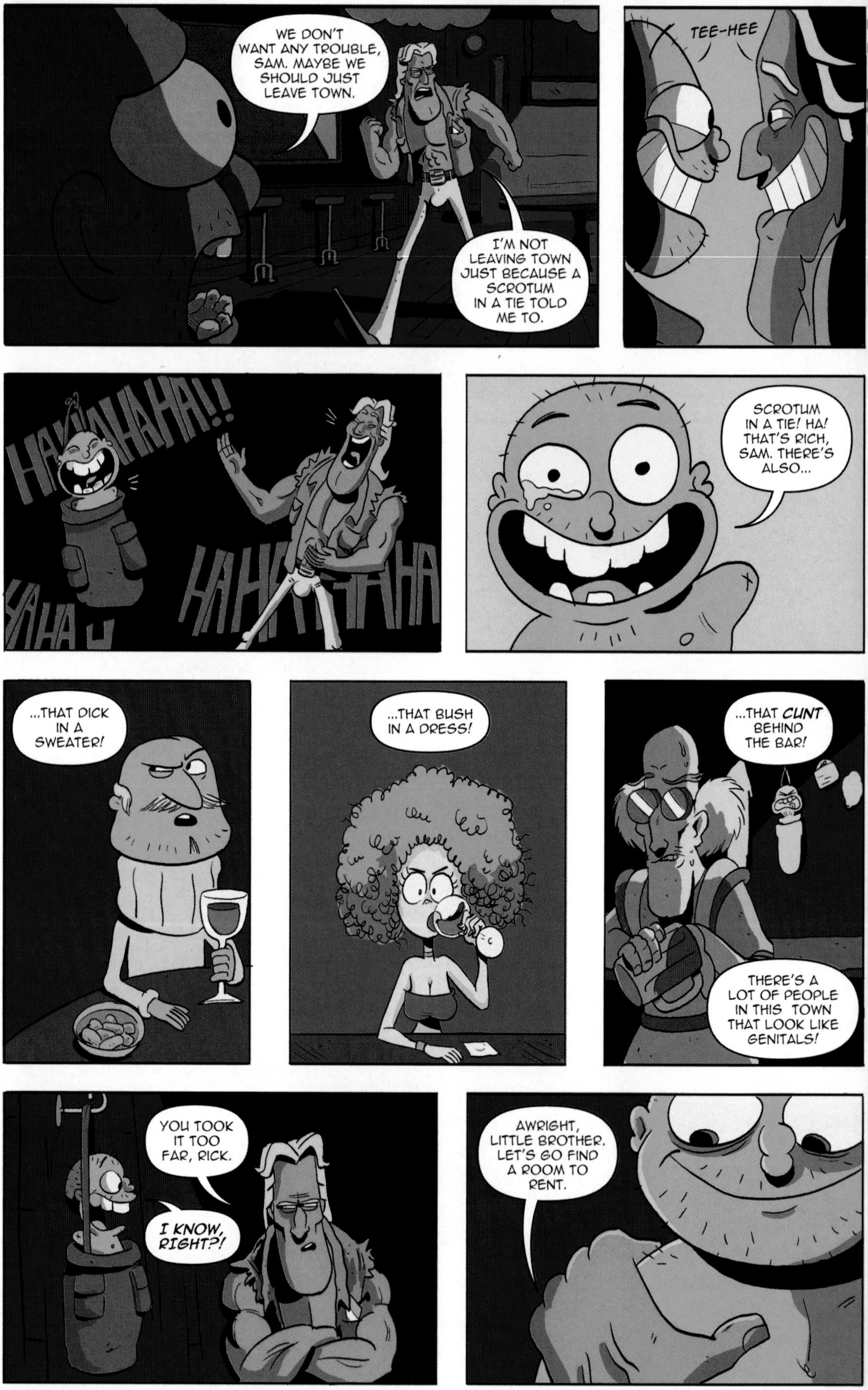
WE DON'T WANT ANY TROUBLE, SAM. MAYBE WE SHOULD JUST LEAVE TOWN.
I'M NOT LEAVING TOWN JUST BECAUSE A SCROTUM IN A TIE TOLD ME TO.
TEE-HEE
HAHAHAHA!!
HAHAHAHA
SCROTUM IN A TIE! HA! THAT'S RICH, SAM. THERE'S ALSO...
...THAT DICK IN A SWEATER!
...THAT BUSH IN A DRESS!
...THAT CUNT BEHIND THE BAR!
THERE'S A LOT OF PEOPLE IN THIS TOWN THAT LOOK LIKE GENITALS!
YOU TOOK IT TOO FAR, RICK.
I KNOW, RIGHT?!
AWRIGHT, LITTLE BROTHER. LET'S GO FIND A ROOM TO RENT.

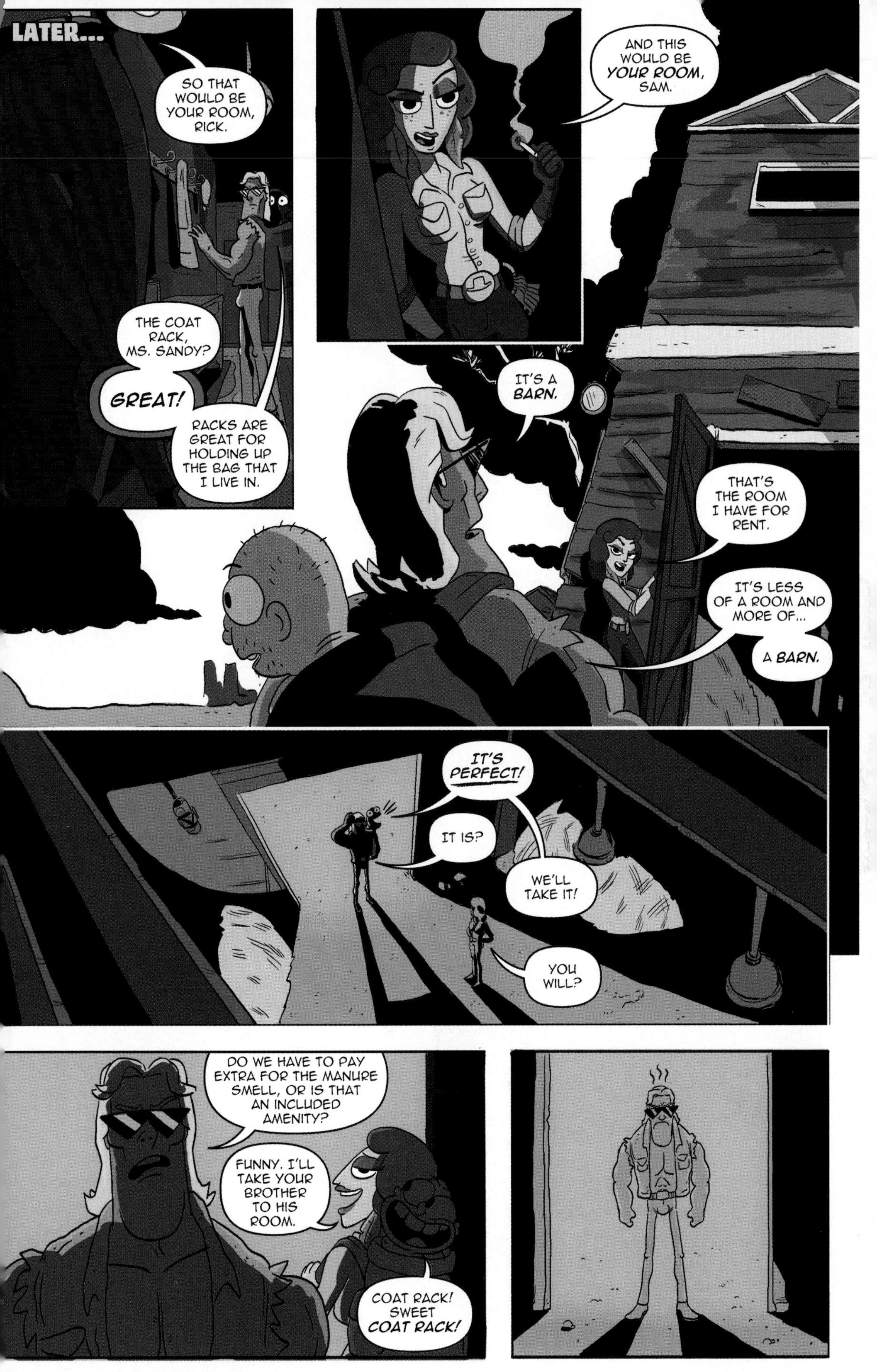
LATER...
SO THAT WOULD BE YOUR ROOM, RICK.
AND THIS WOULD BE YOUR ROOM, SAM.
THE COAT RACK, MS. SANDY?
GREAT!
RACKS ARE GREAT FOR HOLDING UP THE BAG THAT I LIVE IN.
IT'S A BARN.
THAT'S THE ROOM I HAVE FOR RENT.
IT'S LESS OF A ROOM AND MORE OF...
A BARN.
IT'S PERFECT!
IT IS?
WE'LL TAKE IT!
YOU WILL?
DO WE HAVE TO PAY EXTRA FOR THE MANURE SMELL, OR IS THAT AN INCLUDED AMENITY?
FUNNY. I'LL TAKE YOUR BROTHER TO HIS ROOM.
COAT RACK! SWEET COAT RACK!

CLICK

flick

FFFERRRR

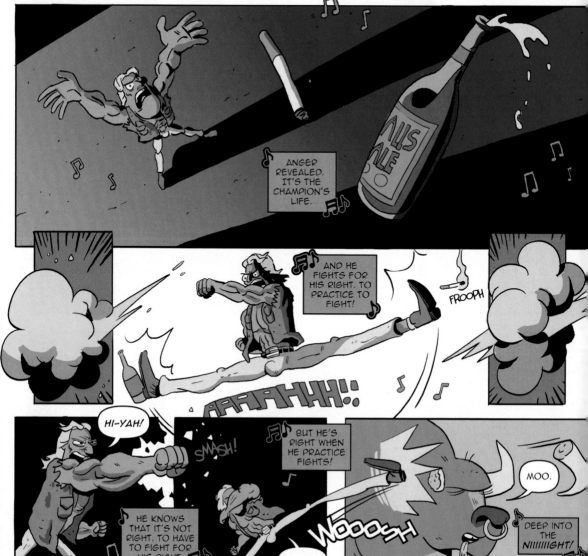

ANGER REVEALED. IT'S THE CHAMPION'S LIFE.

AND HE FIGHTS FOR HIS RIGHT. TO PRACTICE TO FIGHT!

FROOPH

AAAAHHH!!

HI-YAH!

SMASH!

BUT HE'S RIGHT WHEN HE PRACTICE FIGHTS!

HE KNOWS THAT IT'S NOT RIGHT. TO HAVE TO FIGHT FOR HIS RIGHT.

WOOOSH

KI-YAH!

MOO.

DEEP INTO THE NIIIIIIGHT!

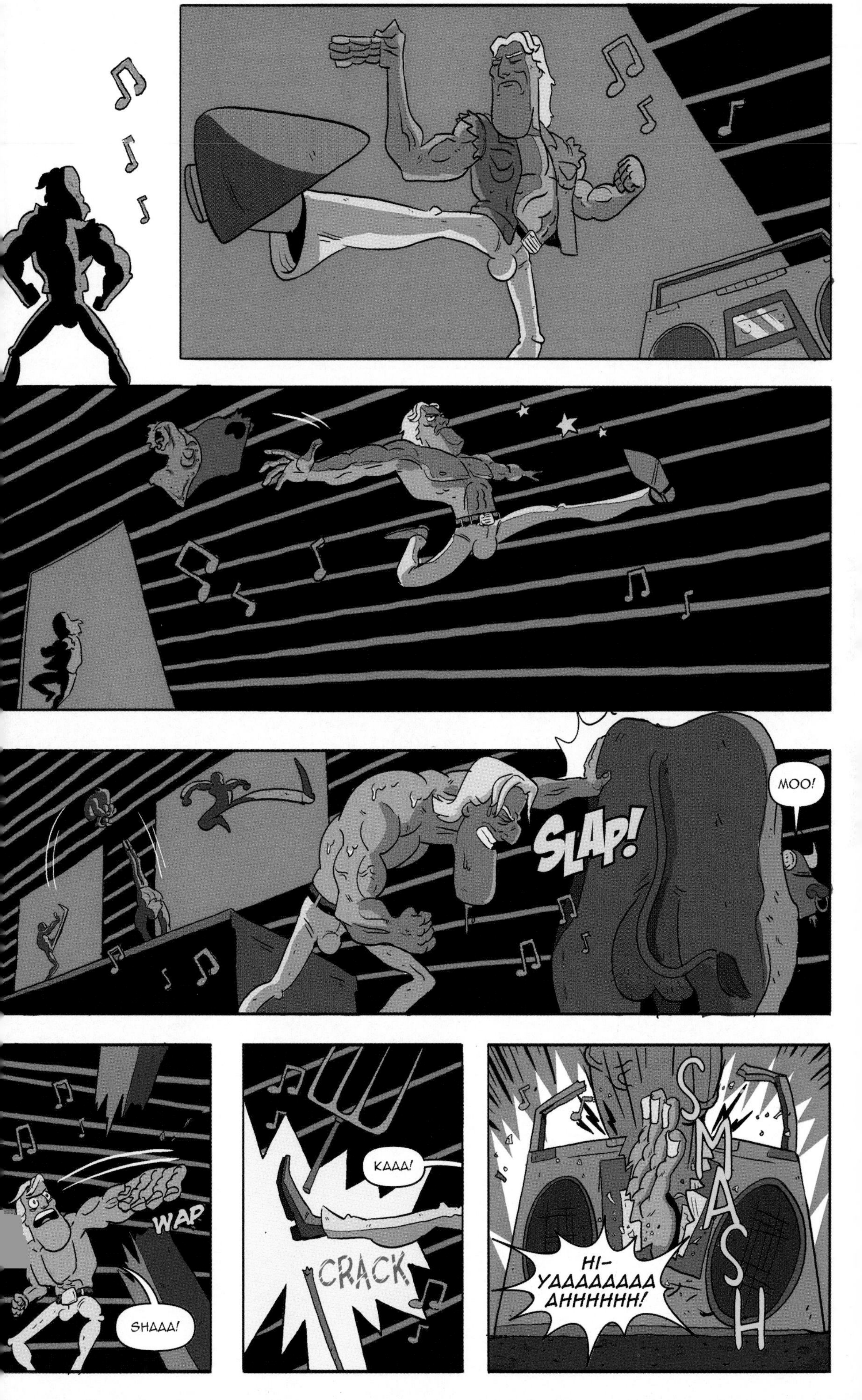
MOO!
SLAP!
WAP
SHAAA!
KAAA!
CRACK
SMASH
HI-
YAAAAAAAA
AHHHHHH!

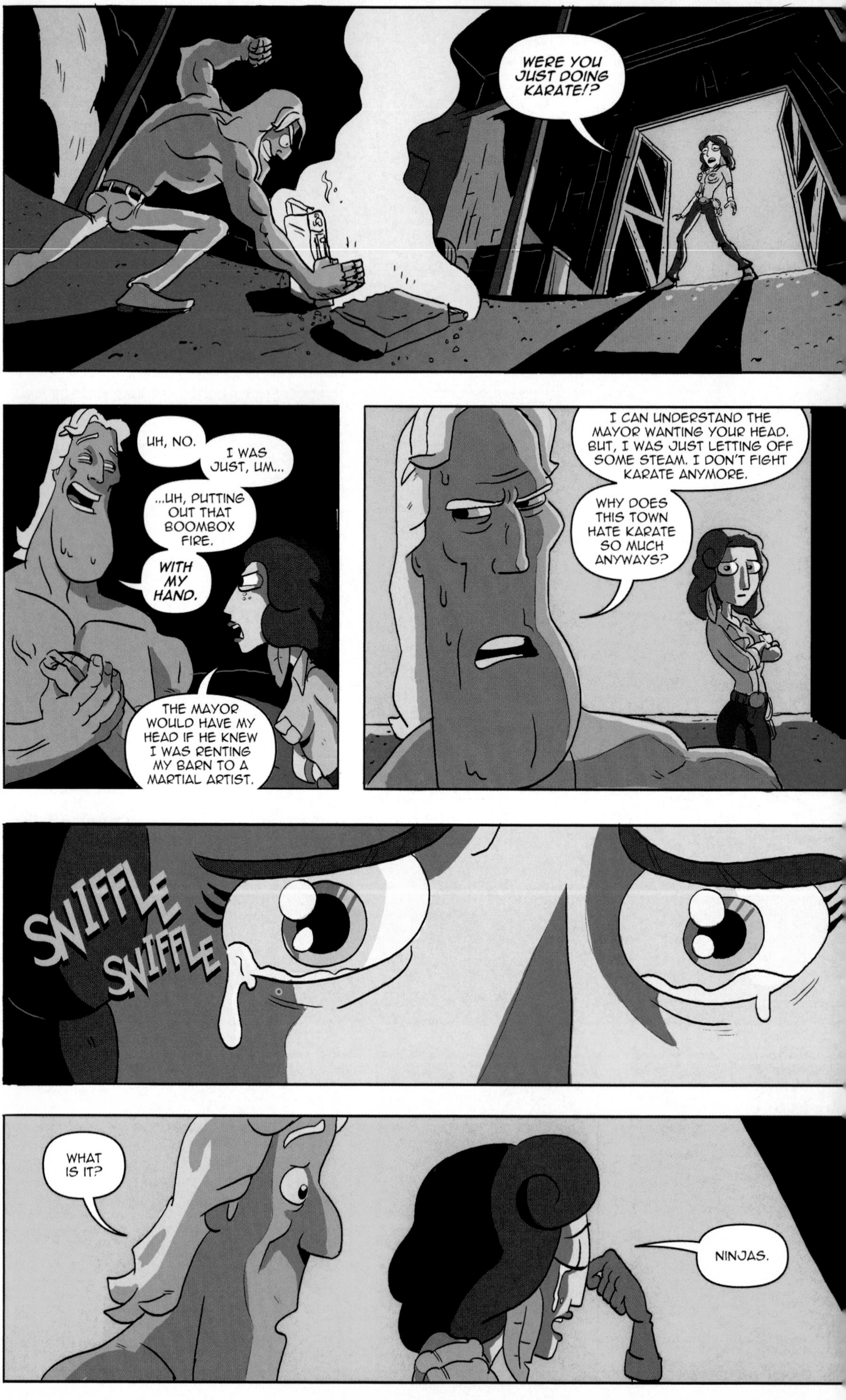
WERE YOU JUST DOING KARATE!?
UH, NO.
I WAS JUST, UM...
...UH, PUTTING OUT THAT BOOMBOX FIRE.
WITH MY HAND.
THE MAYOR WOULD HAVE MY HEAD IF HE KNEW I WAS RENTING MY BARN TO A MARTIAL ARTIST.
I CAN UNDERSTAND THE MAYOR WANTING YOUR HEAD. BUT, I WAS JUST LETTING OFF SOME STEAM. I DON'T FIGHT KARATE ANYMORE.
WHY DOES THIS TOWN HATE KARATE SO MUCH ANYWAYS?
SNIFFLE
SNIFFLE
WHAT IS IT?
NINJAS.

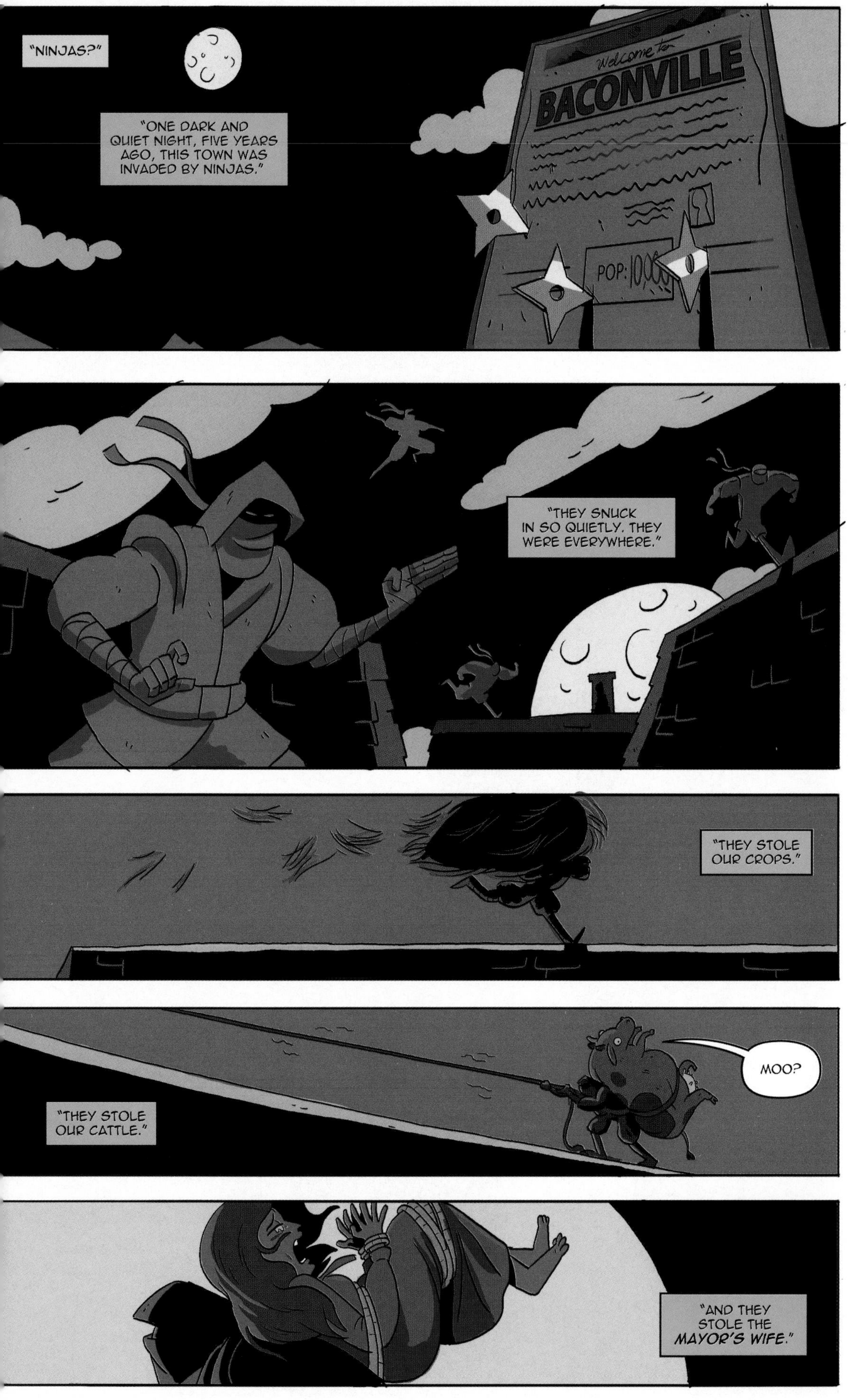

"NINJAS?"
"ONE DARK AND QUIET NIGHT, FIVE YEARS AGO, THIS TOWN WAS INVADED BY NINJAS."
Welcome to
BACONVILLE
POP:
"THEY SNUCK IN SO QUIETLY. THEY WERE EVERYWHERE."
"THEY STOLE OUR CROPS."
"THEY STOLE OUR CATTLE."
MOO?
"AND THEY STOLE THE *MAYOR'S WIFE*."

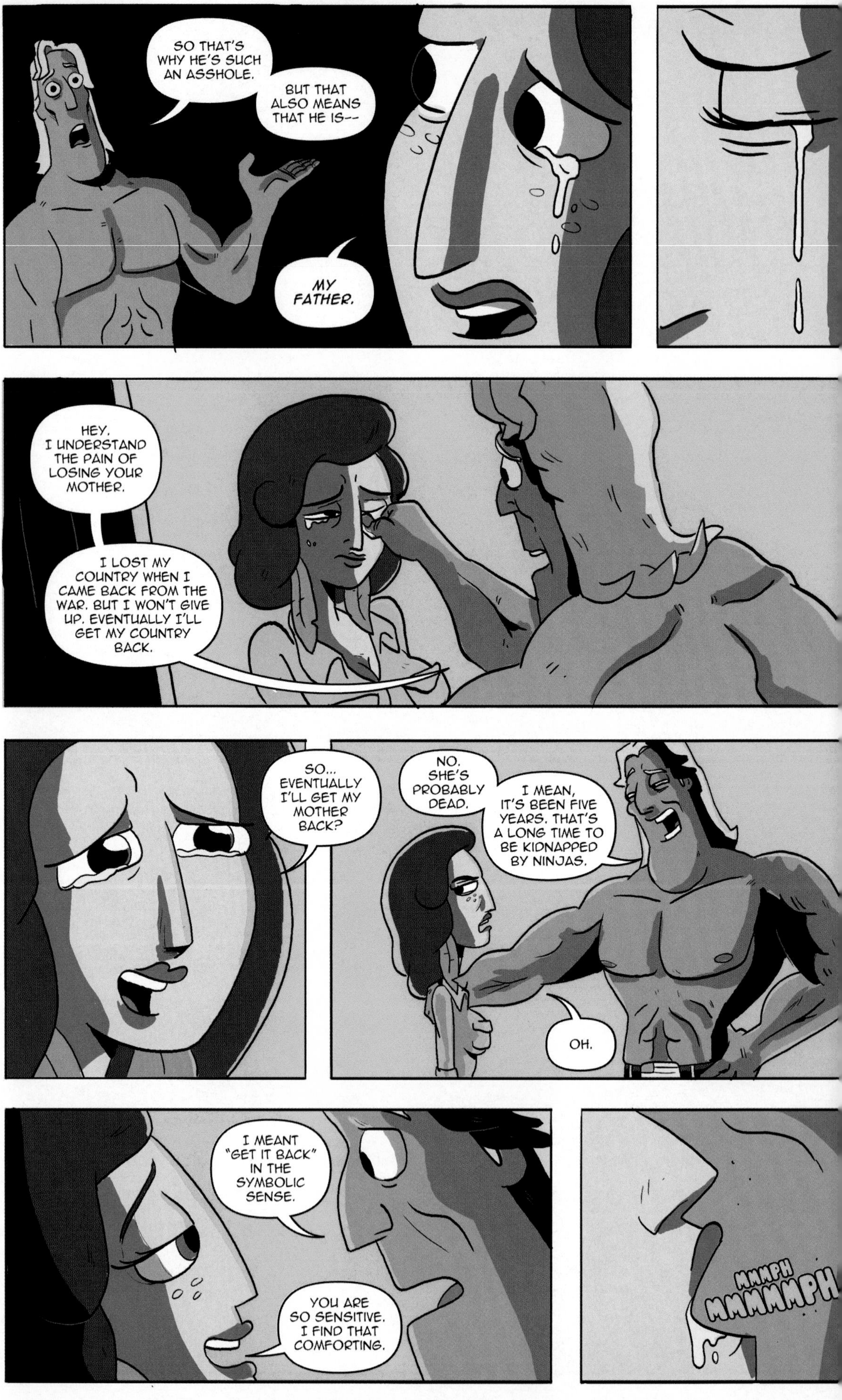
SO THAT'S WHY HE'S SUCH AN ASSHOLE.
BUT THAT ALSO MEANS THAT HE IS--
MY FATHER.
HEY. I UNDERSTAND THE PAIN OF LOSING YOUR MOTHER.
I LOST MY COUNTRY WHEN I CAME BACK FROM THE WAR. BUT I WON'T GIVE UP. EVENTUALLY I'LL GET MY COUNTRY BACK.
SO... EVENTUALLY I'LL GET MY MOTHER BACK?
NO. SHE'S PROBABLY DEAD.
I MEAN, IT'S BEEN FIVE YEARS. THAT'S A LONG TIME TO BE KIDNAPPED BY NINJAS.
OH.
I MEANT "GET IT BACK" IN THE SYMBOLIC SENSE.
YOU ARE SO SENSITIVE. I FIND THAT COMFORTING.
MMMPH
MMMMMPH

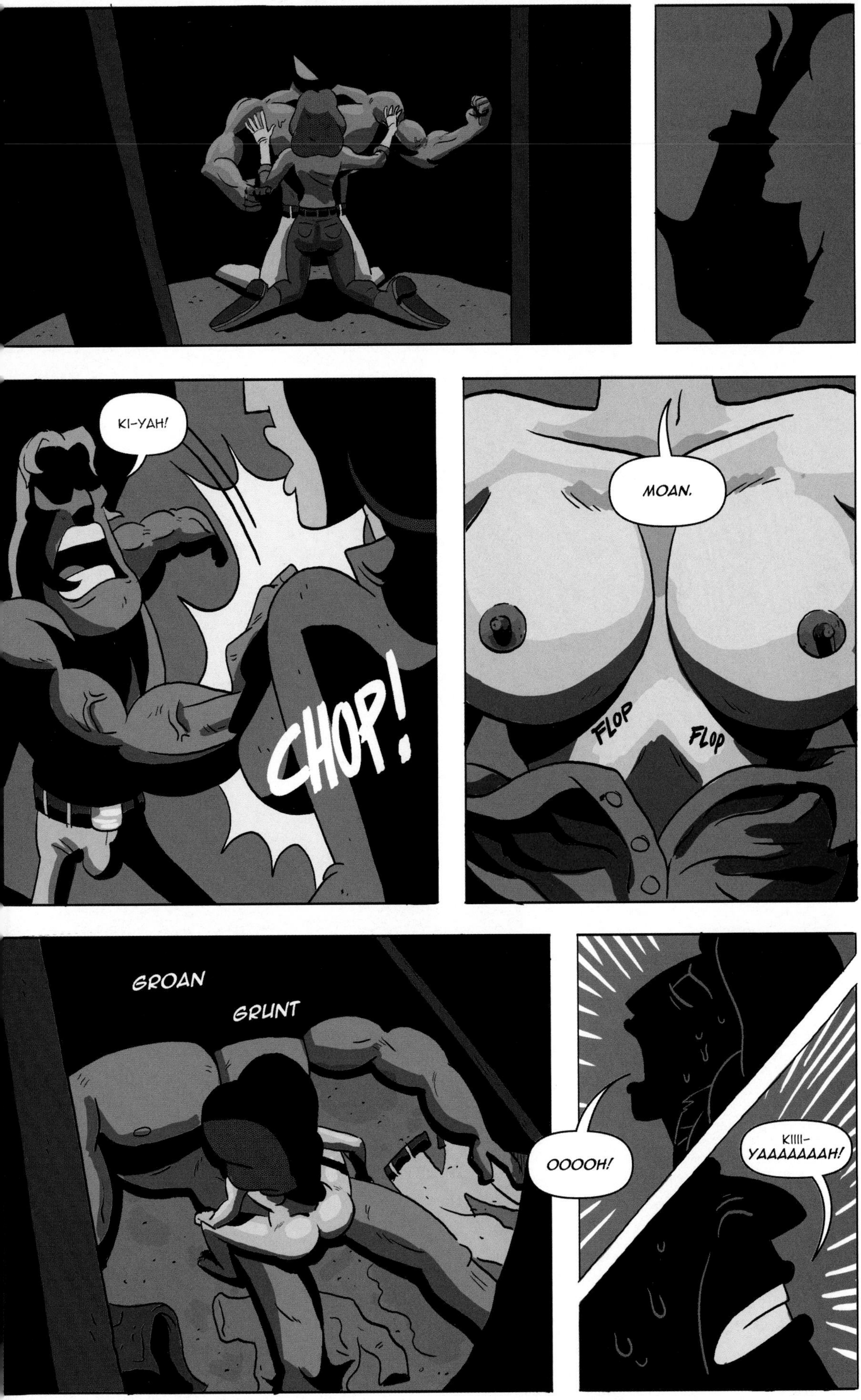
KI-YAH!
CHOP!
MOAN.
FLOP
FLOP
GROAN
GRUNT
OOOOH!
KIIII-
YAAAAAAAH!

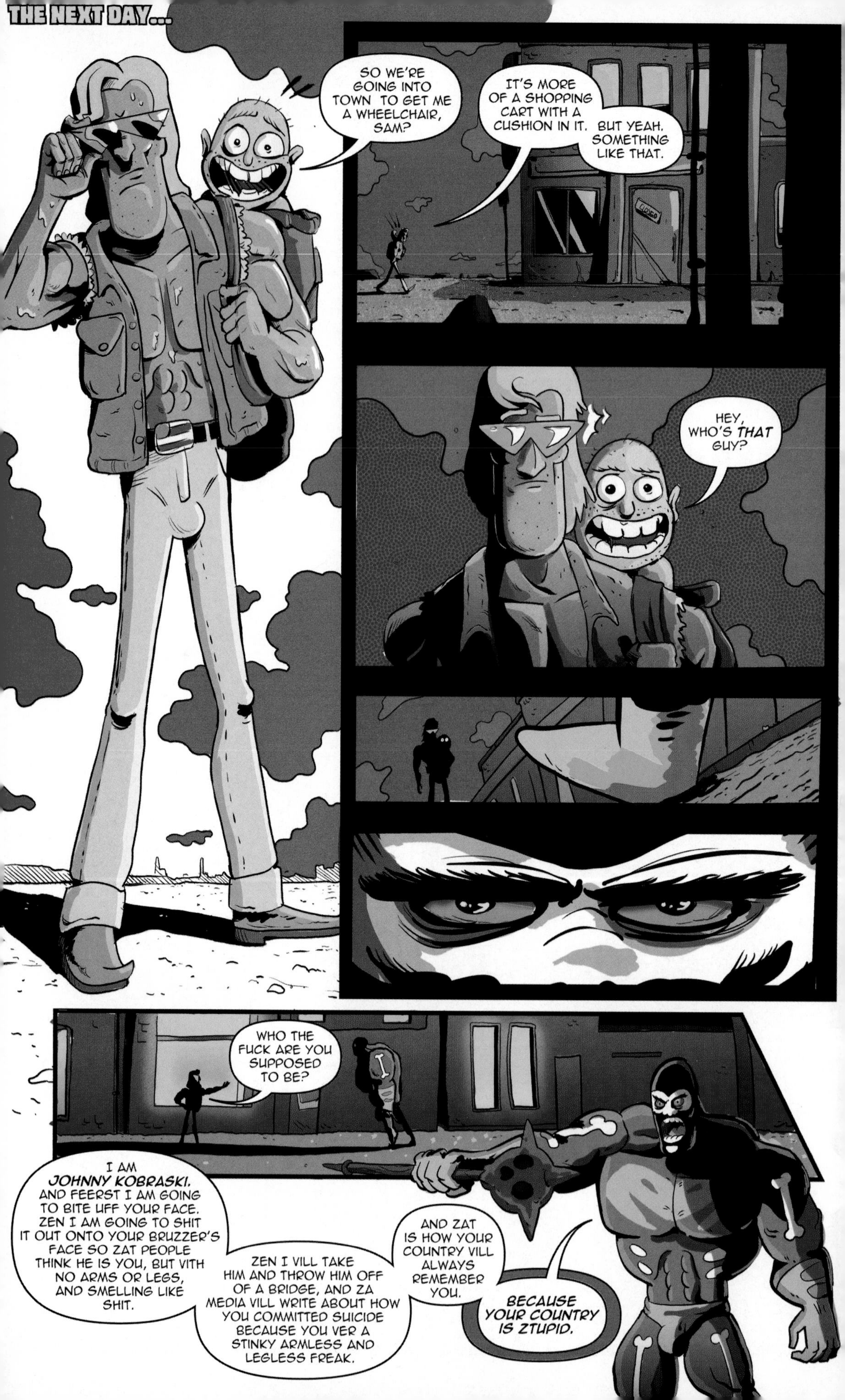
THE NEXT DAY...
SO WE'RE GOING INTO TOWN TO GET ME A WHEELCHAIR, SAM?
IT'S MORE OF A SHOPPING CART WITH A CUSHION IN IT.
BUT YEAH. SOMETHING LIKE THAT.
CLOSED
HEY, WHO'S *THAT* GUY?
WHO THE FUCK ARE YOU SUPPOSED TO BE?
I AM *JOHNNY KOBRASKI.* AND FEERST I AM GOING TO BITE UFF YOUR FACE. ZEN I AM GOING TO SHIT IT OUT ONTO YOUR BRUZZER'S FACE SO ZAT PEOPLE THINK HE IS YOU, BUT VITH NO ARMS OR LEGS, AND SMELLING LIKE SHIT.
ZEN I VILL TAKE HIM AND THROW HIM OFF OF A BRIDGE, AND ZA MEDIA VILL WRITE ABOUT HOW YOU COMMITTED SUICIDE BECAUSE YOU VER A STINKY ARMLESS AND LEGLESS FREAK.
AND ZAT IS HOW YOUR COUNTRY VILL ALWAYS REMEMBER YOU.
BECAUSE YOUR COUNTRY IS ZTUPID.

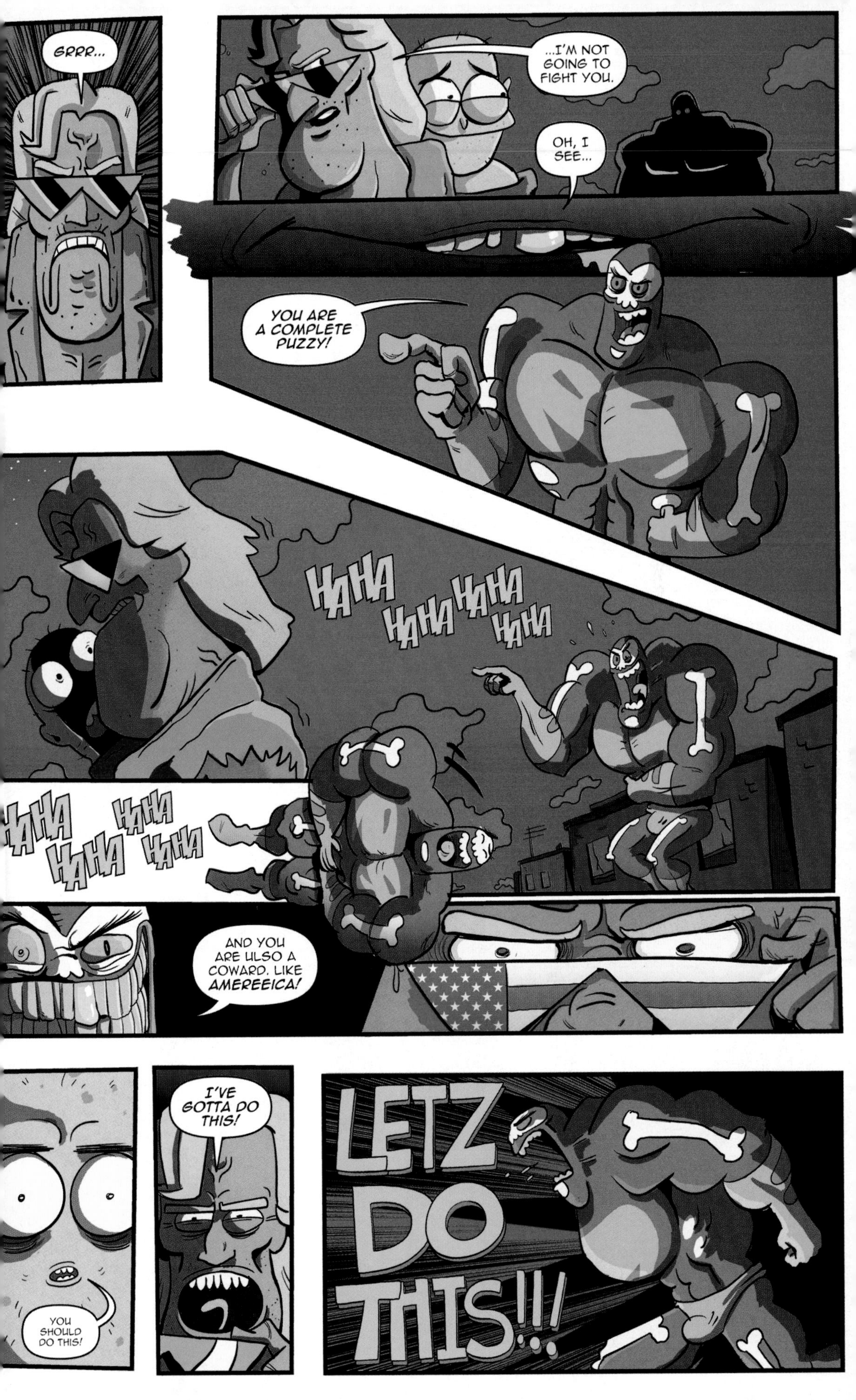
GRRR...
...I'M NOT GOING TO FIGHT YOU.
OH, I SEE...
YOU ARE A COMPLETE PUZZY!
HAHA HAHA HAHA HAHA
HAHA HAHA HAHA HAHA
AND YOU ARE ULSO A COWARD. LIKE AMEREEICA!
YOU SHOULD DO THIS!
I'VE GOTTA DO THIS!
LETZ DO THIS!!!

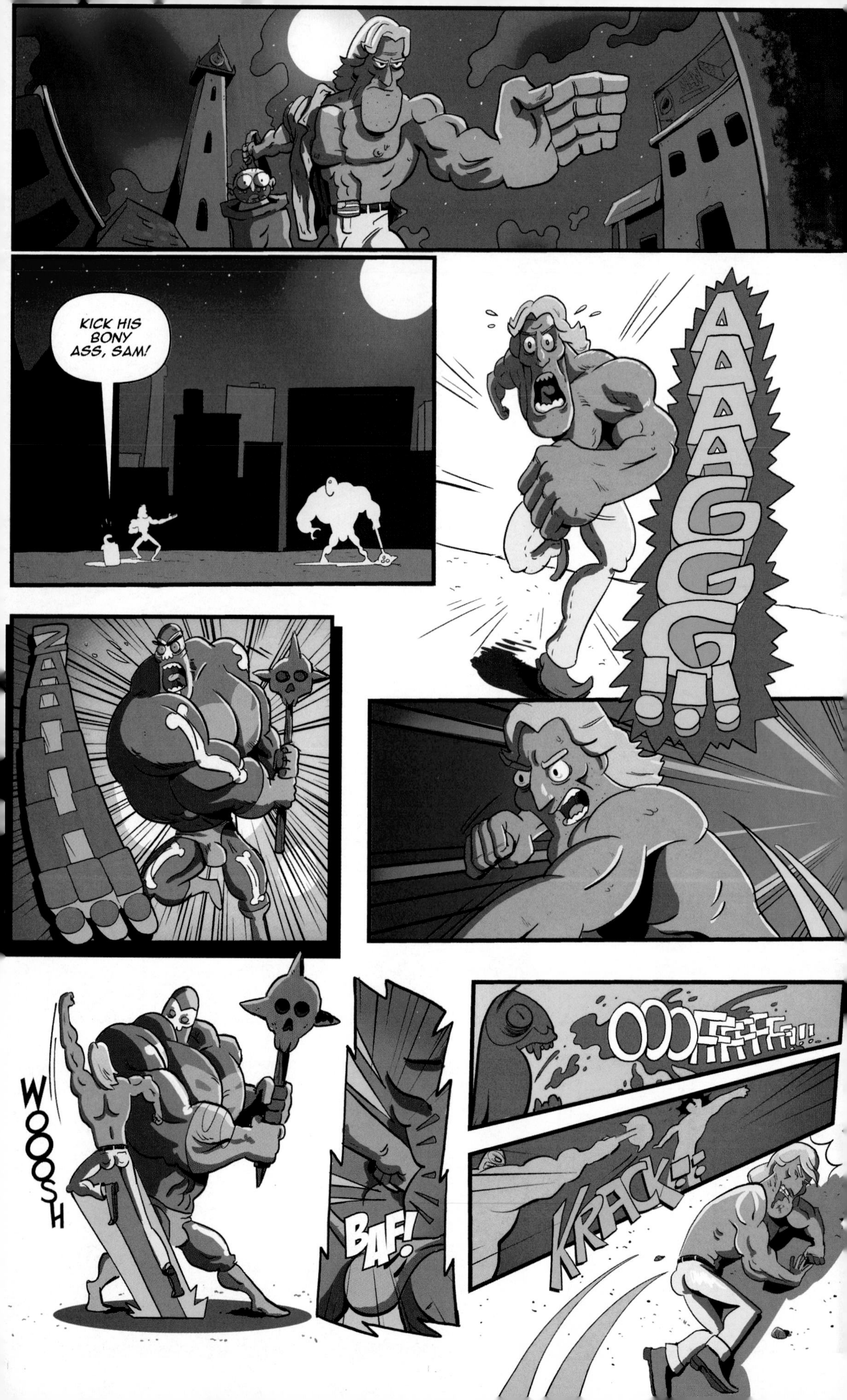
KICK HIS BONY ASS, SAM!
AAAAAGGG!!!
ZAAAAAA
WOOOSH
BAF!
OOOFFFFFF!!!
KRACK!!!

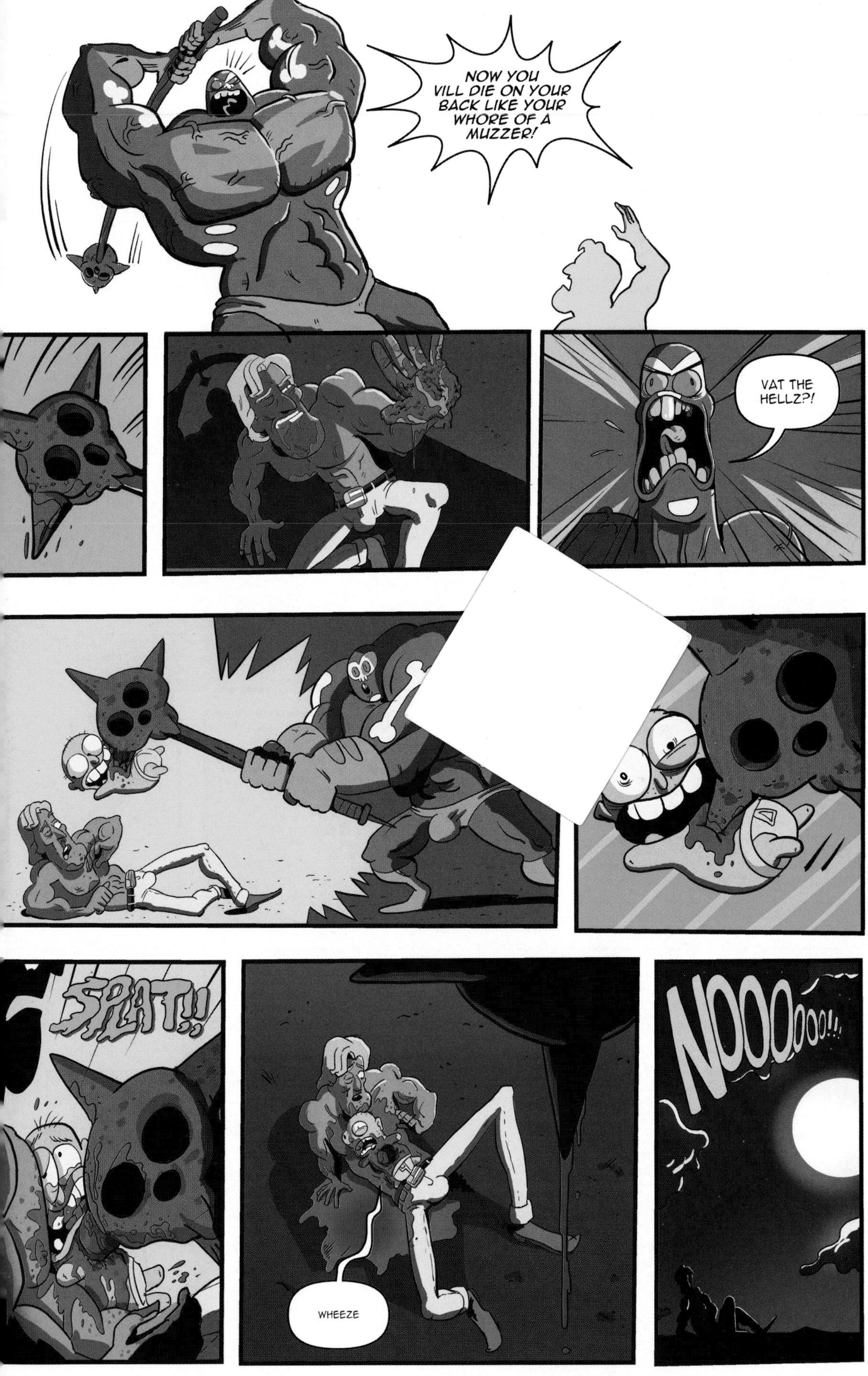
NOW YOU VILL DIE ON YOUR BACK LIKE YOUR WHORE OF A MUZZER!
VAT THE HELLZ?!
SPLAT!!
WHEEZE
NOOOOOO!!!

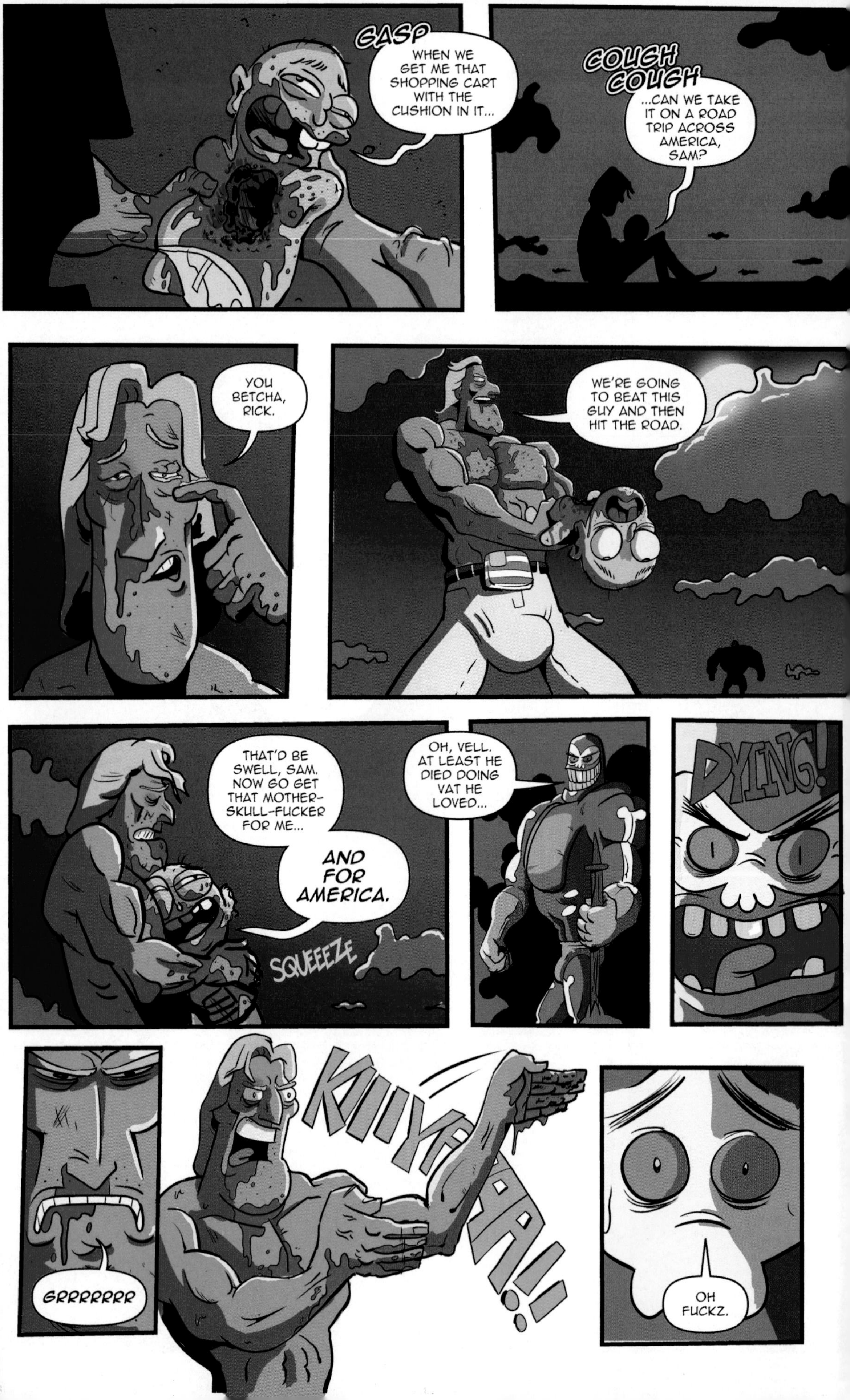
GASP
WHEN WE GET ME THAT SHOPPING CART WITH THE CUSHION IN IT...
COUGH COUGH
...CAN WE TAKE IT ON A ROAD TRIP ACROSS AMERICA, SAM?
YOU BETCHA, RICK.
WE'RE GOING TO BEAT THIS GUY AND THEN HIT THE ROAD.
THAT'D BE SWELL, SAM. NOW GO GET THAT MOTHER-SKULL-FUCKER FOR ME...
AND FOR AMERICA.
SQUEEEZE
OH, VELL. AT LEAST HE DIED DOING VAT HE LOVED...
DYING!
GRRRRRRR
OH FUCKZ.

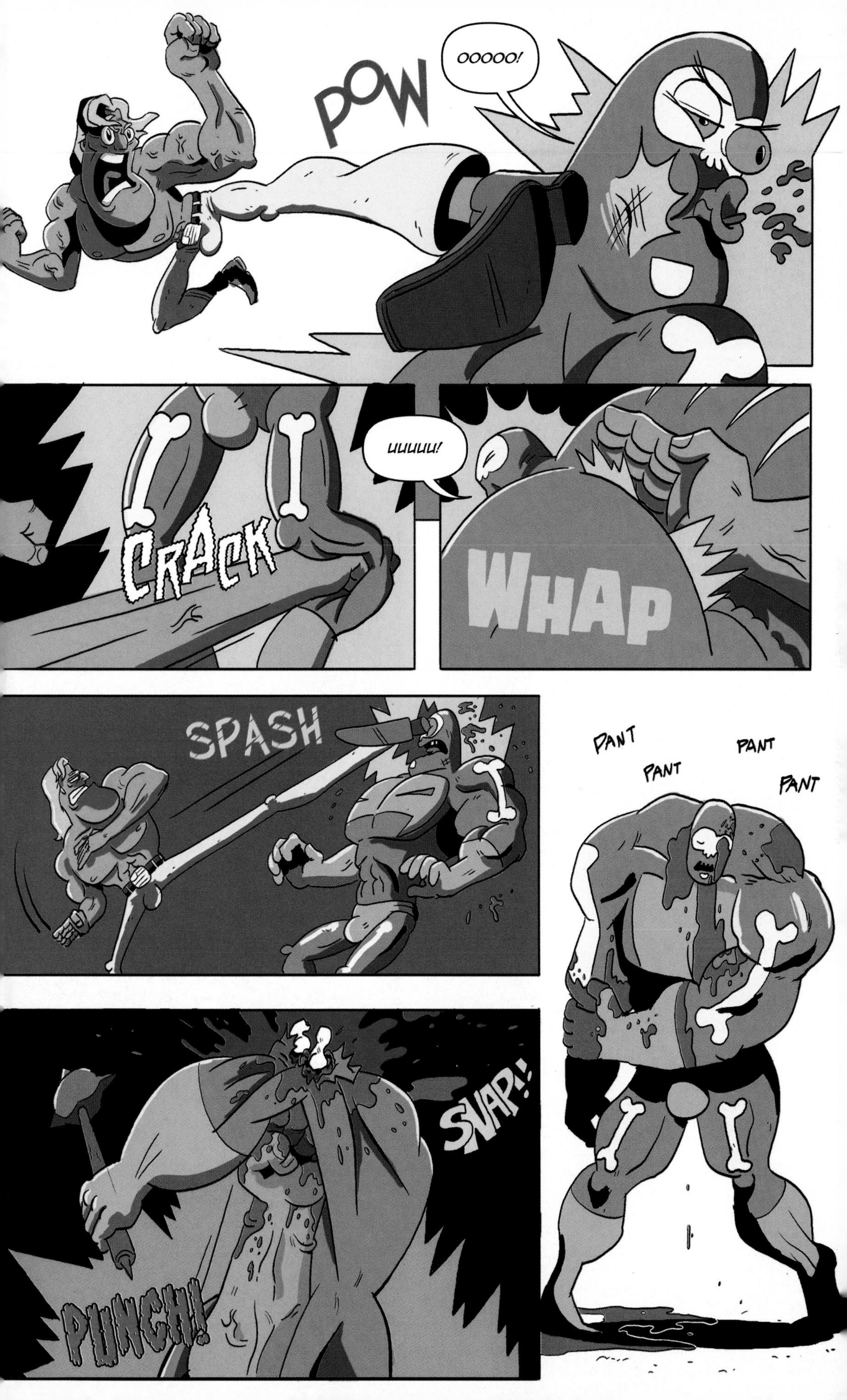
POW
OOOOO!
CRACK
UUUUU!
WHAP
SPASH
PANT
PANT
PANT
PANT
SNAP!
PUNCH!

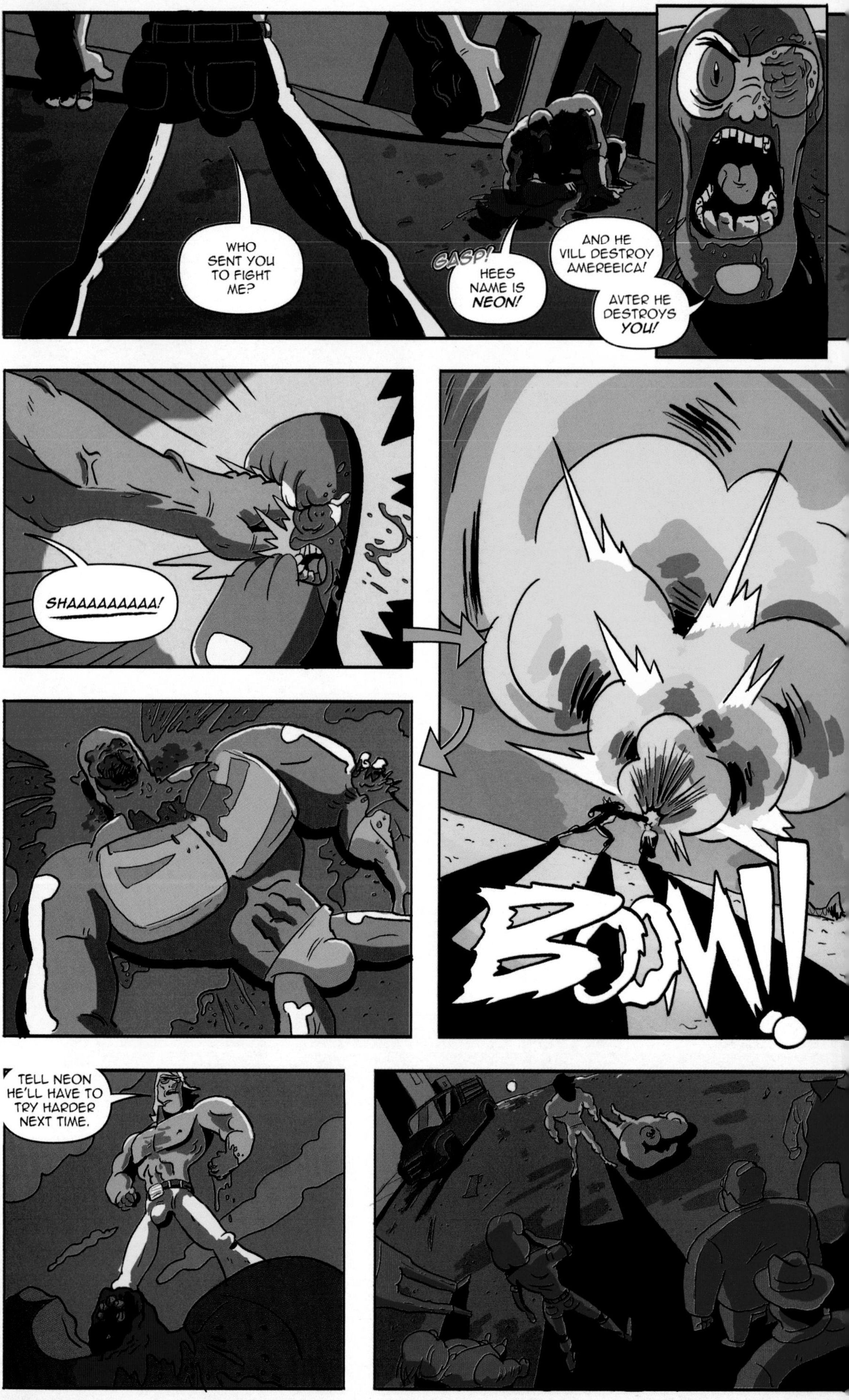
WHO SENT YOU TO FIGHT ME?
GASP!
HEES NAME IS NEON!
AND HE VILL DESTROY AMEREEICA!
AVTER HE DESTROYS YOU!
SHAAAAAAAAAA!
BOW!!
TELL NEON HE'LL HAVE TO TRY HARDER NEXT TIME.

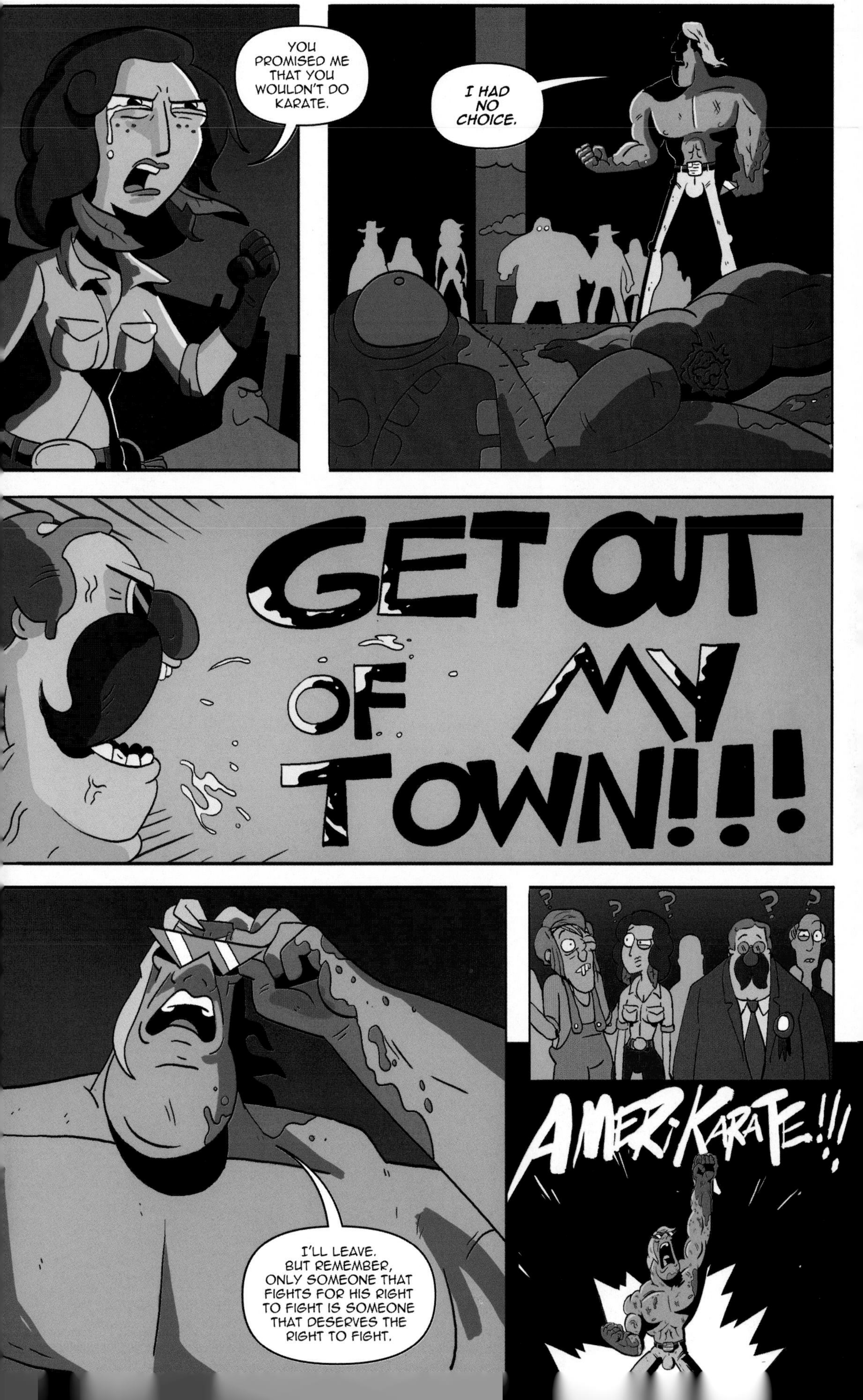
YOU PROMISED ME THAT YOU WOULDN'T DO KARATE.
I HAD NO CHOICE.
GET OUT OF MY TOWN!!!
?
I'LL LEAVE. BUT REMEMBER, ONLY SOMEONE THAT FIGHTS FOR HIS RIGHT TO FIGHT IS SOMEONE THAT DESERVES THE RIGHT TO FIGHT.
AMERI-KARATE!!!

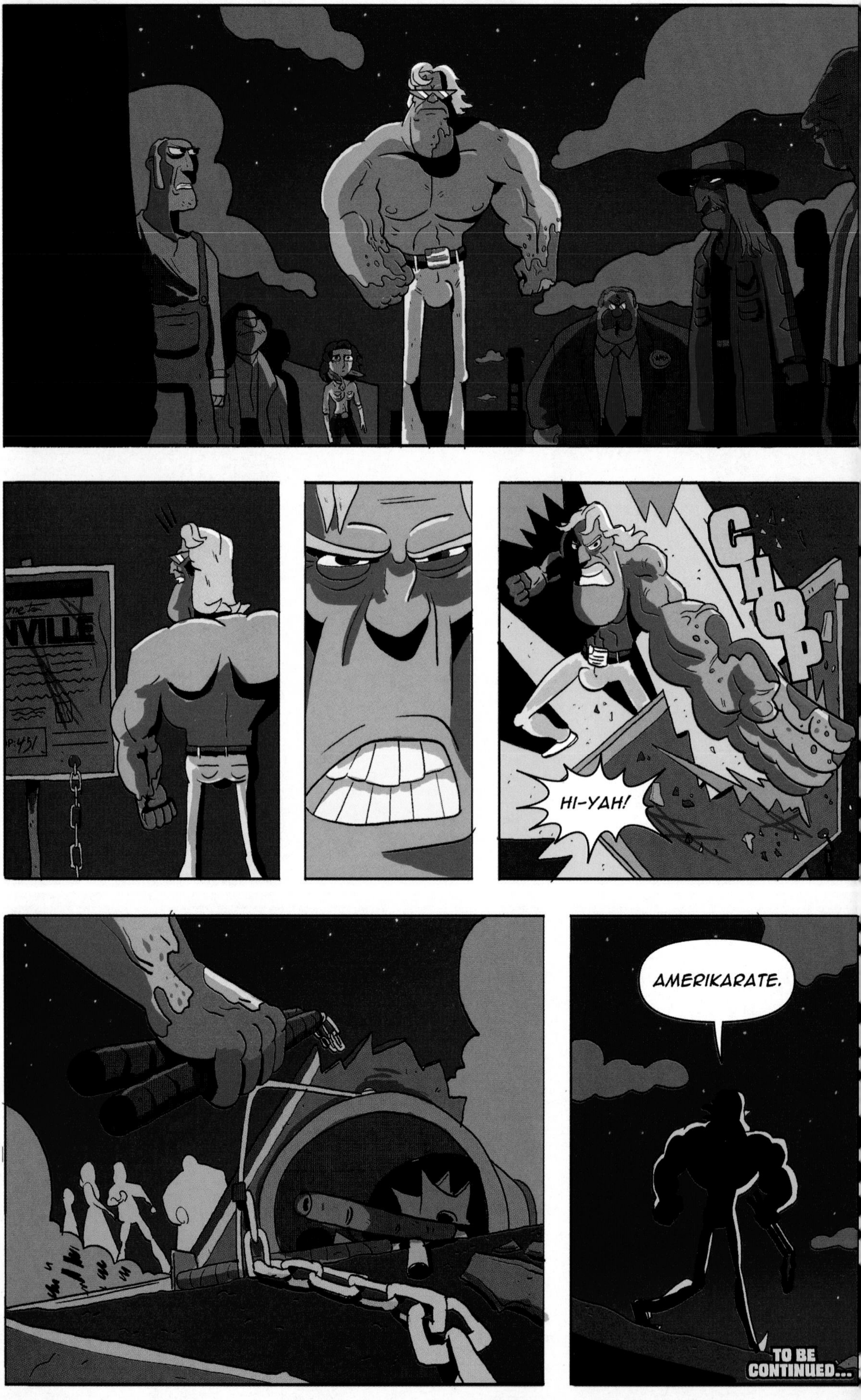
CHOP
HI-YAH!
AMERIKARATE.
TO BE CONTINUED...

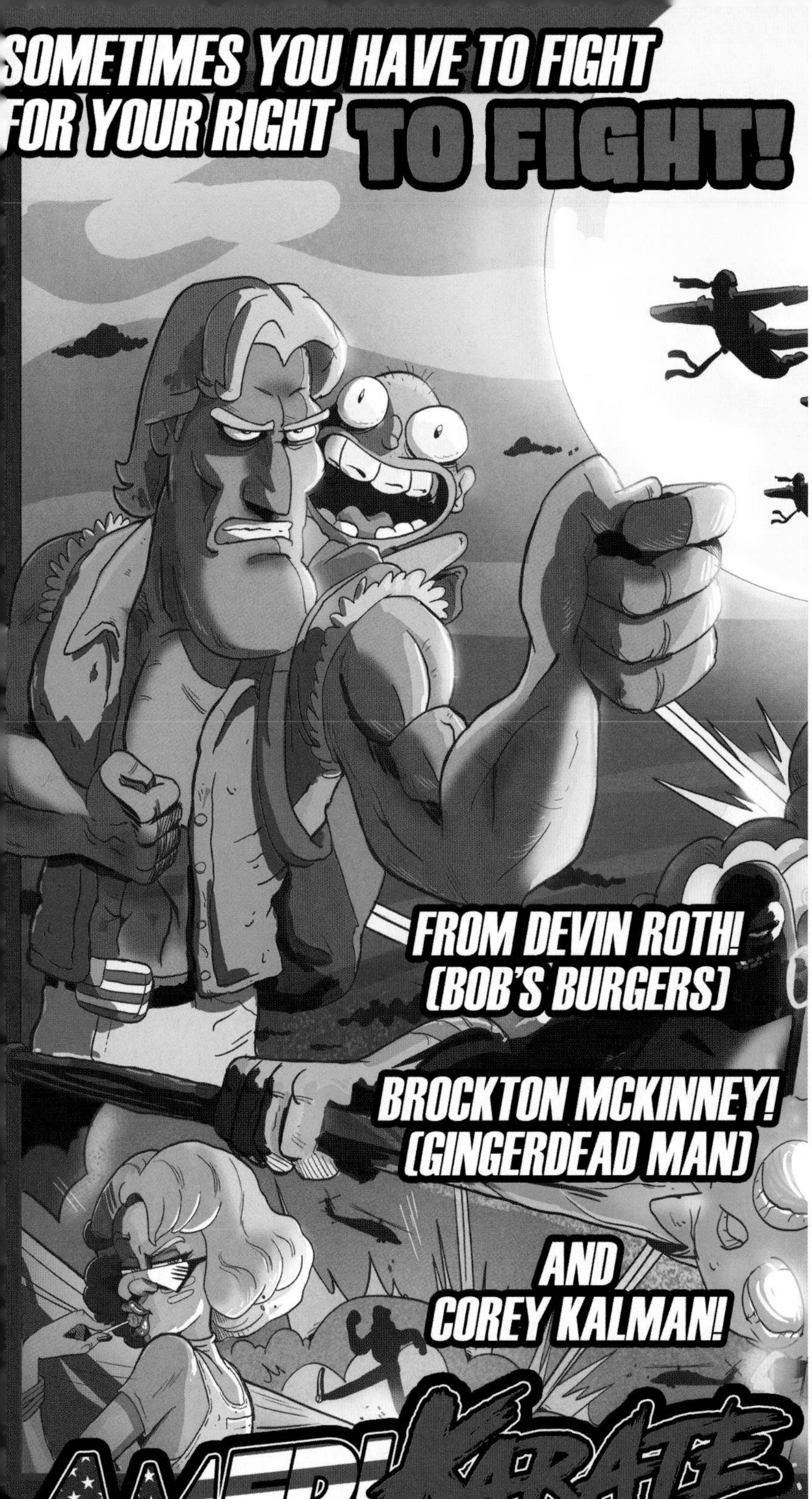
SOMETIMES YOU HAVE TO FIGHT
FOR YOUR RIGHT TO FIGHT!
FROM DEVIN ROTH!
(BOB'S BURGERS)
BROCKTON MCKINNEY!
(GINGERDEAD MAN)
AND
COREY KALMAN!
AMERIKARATE
#1
ON SALE NOW!

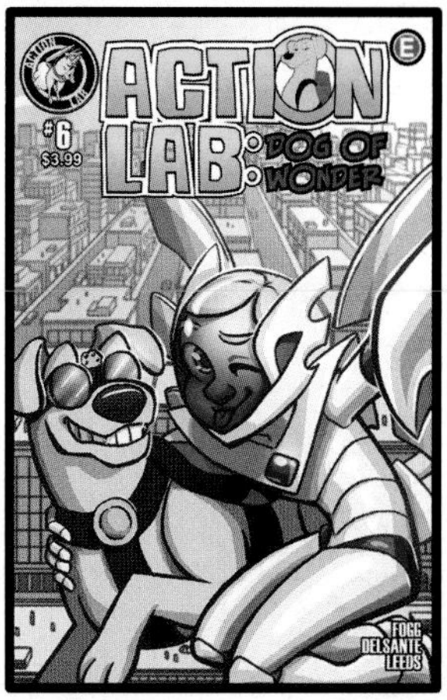
ACTION LAB
DOG OF WONDER
#6
$3.99
FOGG
DELSANTE
LEEDS

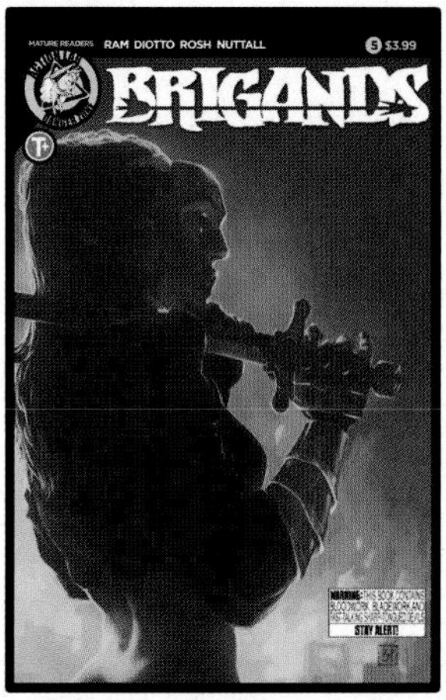
MATURE READERS RAM DIOTTO ROSH NUTTALL
5 $3.99
BRIGANDS
STAY ALERT!

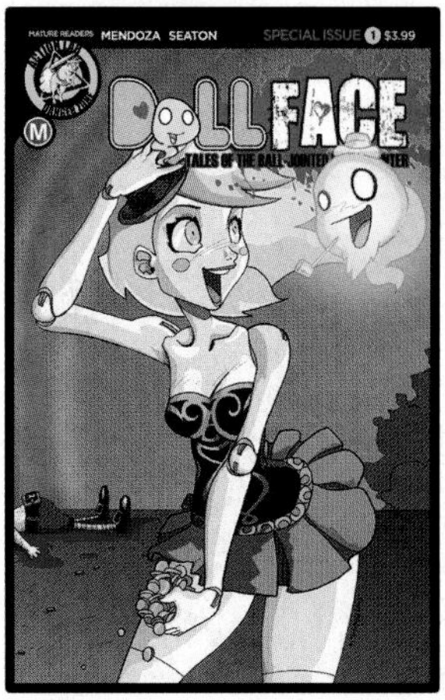
MATURE READERS MENDOZA SEATON
SPECIAL ISSUE 1 $3.99
DOLLFACE

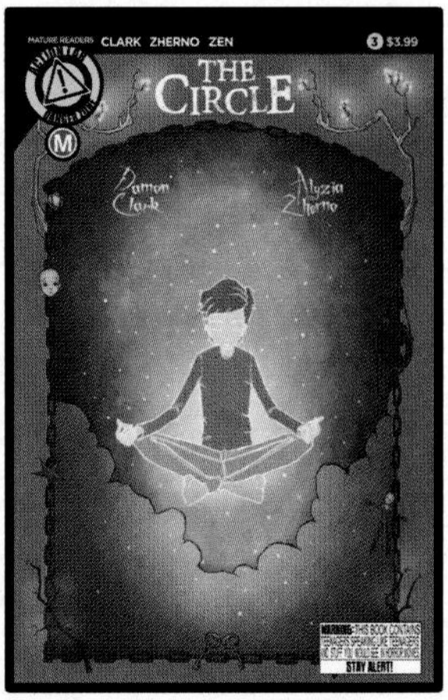
MATURE READERS CLARK ZHERNO ZEN
3 $3.99
THE CIRCLE
STAY ALERT!

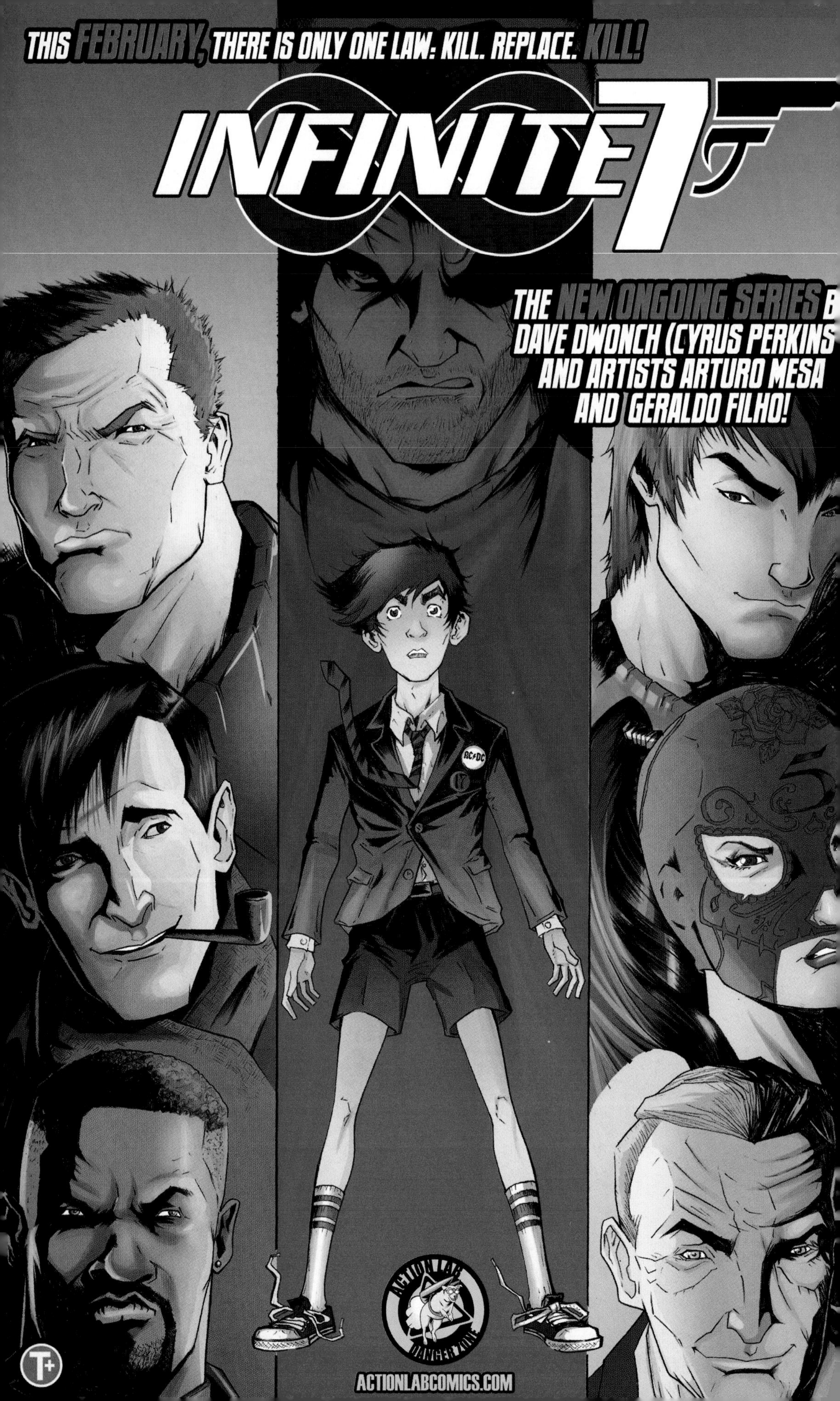
THIS FEBRUARY, THERE IS ONLY ONE LAW: KILL. REPLACE. KILL!
INFINITE 7
THE NEW ONGOING SERIES B
DAVE DWONCH (CYRUS PERKINS
AND ARTISTS ARTURO MESA
AND GERALDO FILHO!
AC/DC
ACTION LAB
DANGER ZONE
T+
ACTIONLABCOMICS.COM

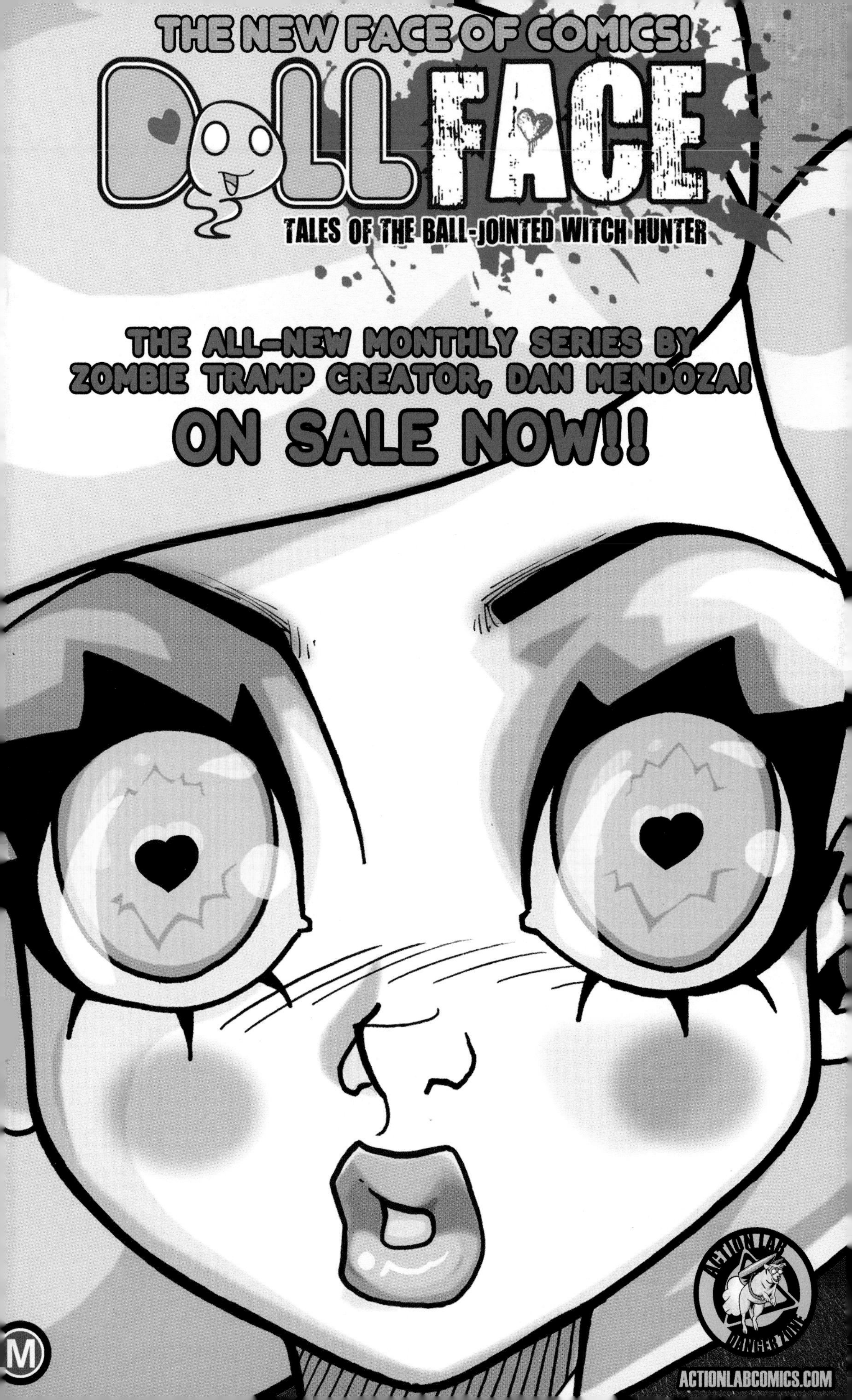
THE NEW FACE OF COMICS!
DOLL FACE
TALES OF THE BALL-JOINTED WITCH HUNTER
THE ALL-NEW MONTHLY SERIES BY
ZOMBIE TRAMP CREATOR, DAN MENDOZA!
ON SALE NOW!!
M
ACTION LAB
DANGER ZONE
ACTIONLABCOMICS.COM

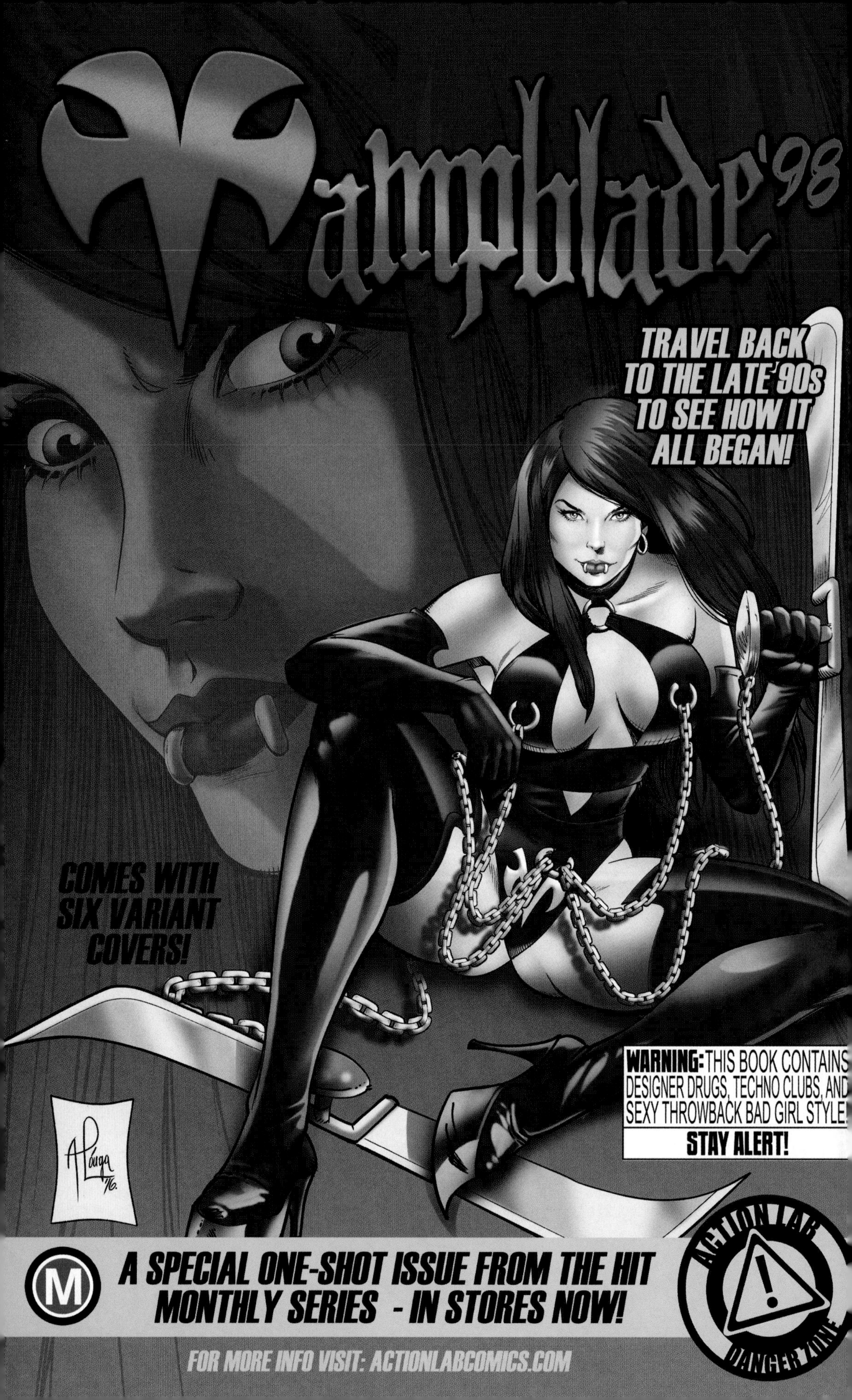
Vampblade '98
TRAVEL BACK TO THE LATE '90s TO SEE HOW IT ALL BEGAN!
COMES WITH SIX VARIANT COVERS!
WARNING: THIS BOOK CONTAINS DESIGNER DRUGS, TECHNO CLUBS, AND SEXY THROWBACK BAD GIRL STYLE!
STAY ALERT!
M
A SPECIAL ONE-SHOT ISSUE FROM THE HIT MONTHLY SERIES - IN STORES NOW!
ACTION LAB DANGER ZONE
FOR MORE INFO VISIT: ACTIONLABCOMICS.COM

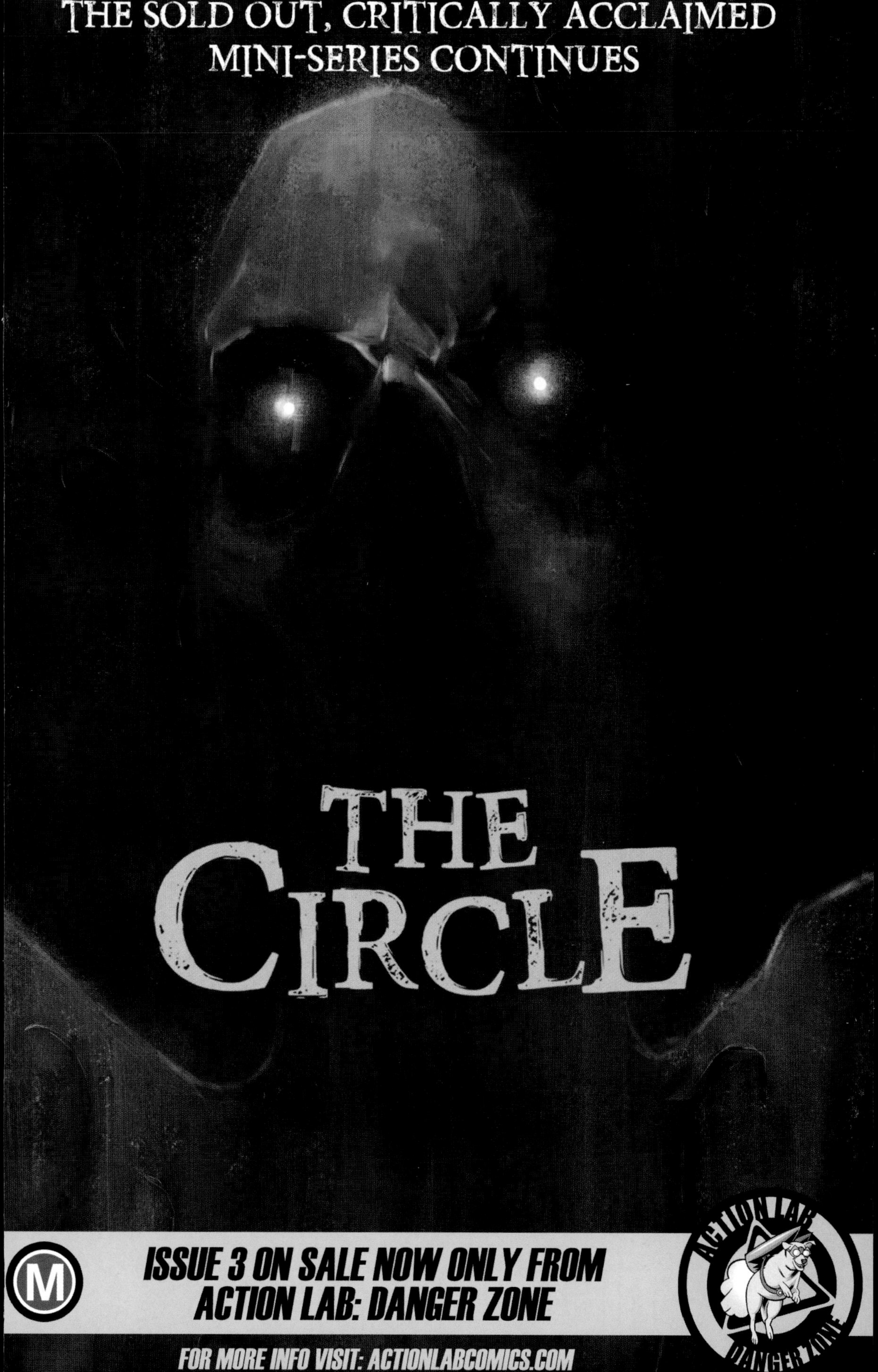
THE SOLD OUT, CRITICALLY ACCLAIMED
MINI-SERIES CONTINUES
THE CIRCLE
M
ISSUE 3 ON SALE NOW ONLY FROM
ACTION LAB: DANGER ZONE
ACTION LAB
DANGER ZONE
FOR MORE INFO VISIT: ACTIONLABCOMICS.COM

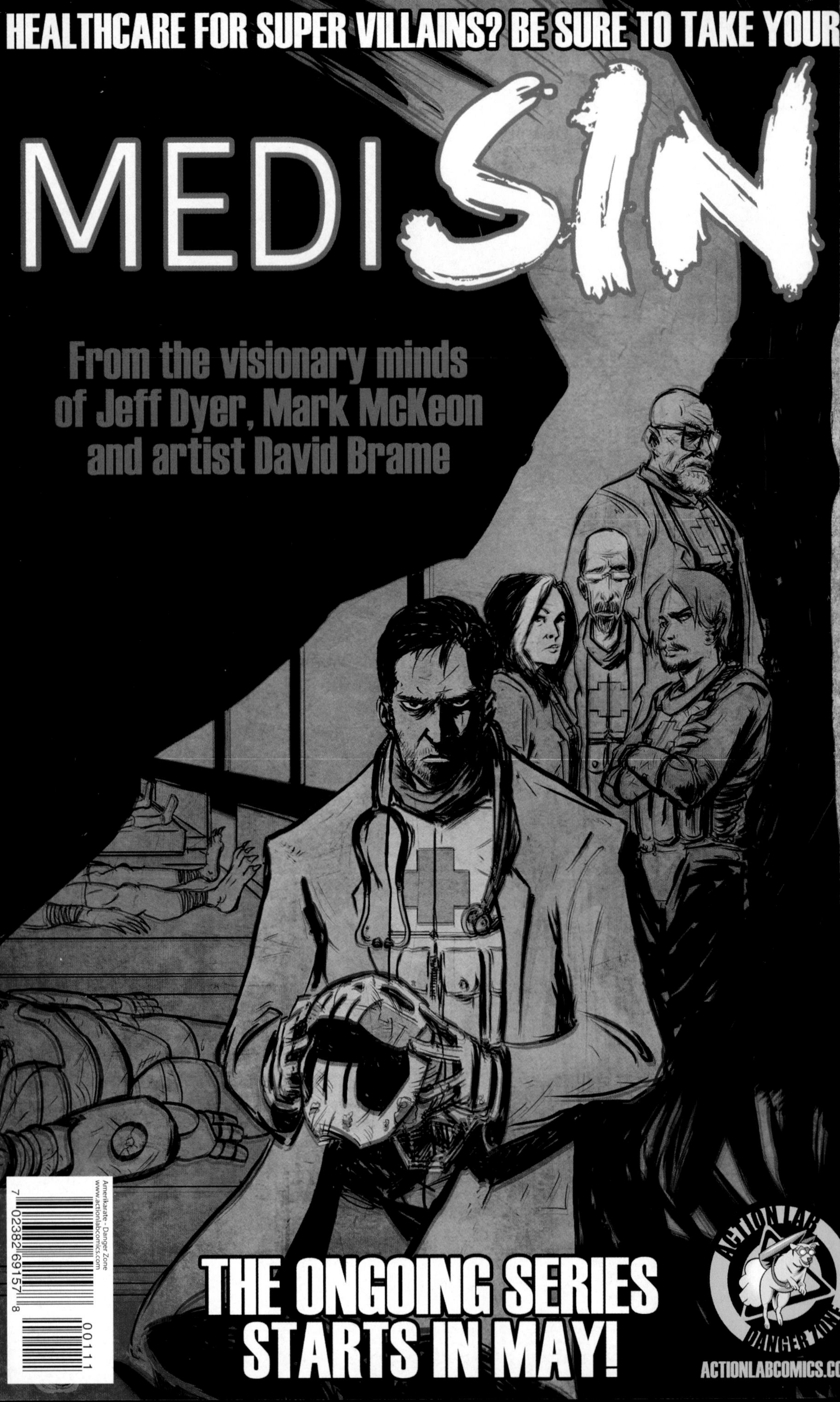
HEALTHCARE FOR SUPER VILLAINS? BE SURE TO TAKE YOUR
MEDISIN
From the visionary minds of Jeff Dyer, Mark McKeon and artist David Brame
THE ONGOING SERIES STARTS IN MAY!
ACTION LAB DANGER ZONE
ACTIONLABCOMICS.CO
Amerikarate - Danger Zone
www.actionlabcomics.com

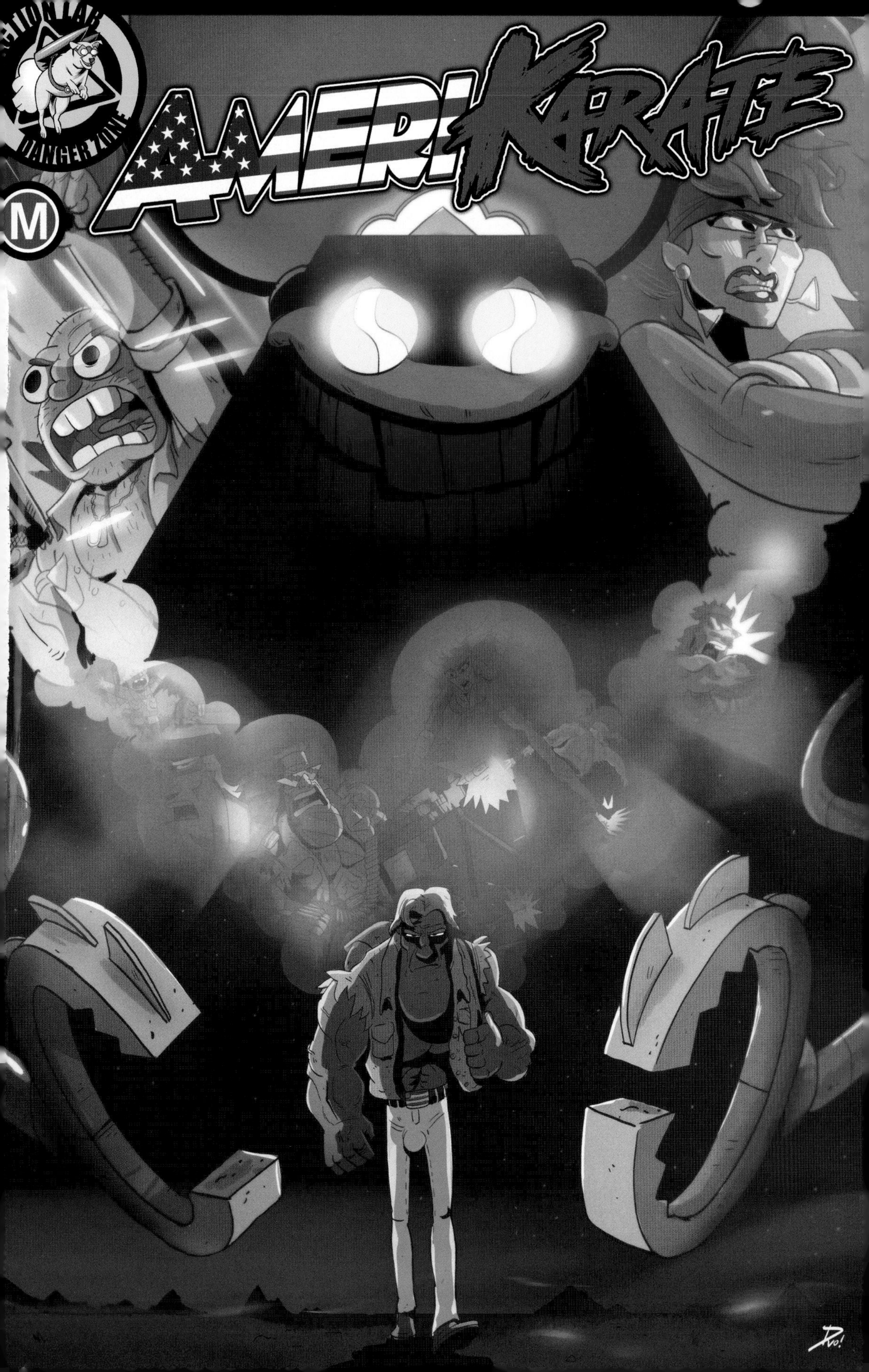
CTION LAB
DANGER ZONE
M
AMERIKARATE

ACTION LAB: DANGER ZONE PRESENTS

These colors don't run.
They fight.

AMERIKARATE

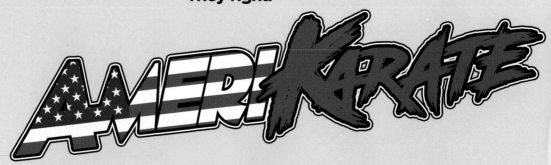

WRITTEN BY
COREY KALMAN & BROCKTON McKINNEY

ILLUSTRATED BY
DEVIN ROTH

LETTERS BY
DAVE DWONCH

MATURE READERS MCKINNEY KALMAN ROTH
2 $3.99
AMERIKARATE
Kalman and McKinney REGULAR
Devin Roth

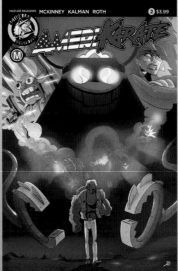

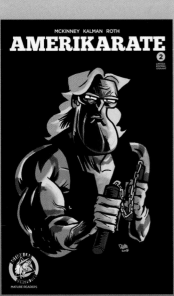

MCKINNEY KALMAN ROTH
AMERIKARATE
2
LIMITED EDITION VARIANT
MATURE READERS
Daniel Arruda Massa ARTIST VARIANT
"Karate Commando"
Limited to 1500

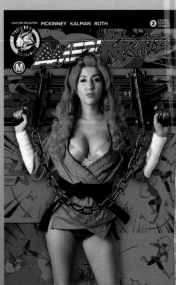

MATURE READERS MCKINNEY KALMAN ROTH
2 LIMITED EDITION VARIANT
AMERIKARATE
April O'Neil PHOTO VARIANT
Limited to 1500

JASON MARTIN - PUBLISHER
DAVE DWONCH - PRESIDENT OF MARKETING
SHAWN GABBORIN - EDITOR IN CHIEF
NICOLE D'ANDRIA - MARKETING DIRECTOR/EDITOR
JIM DIETZ - SOCIAL MEDIA MANAGER
SCOTT BRADLEY - CFO
BRYAN SEATON - CEO

AMERIKARATE #2 April 2017.

Published by Action Lab Comics.

Printed in Canada.
First printing.

ACTIONLABCOMICS.COM

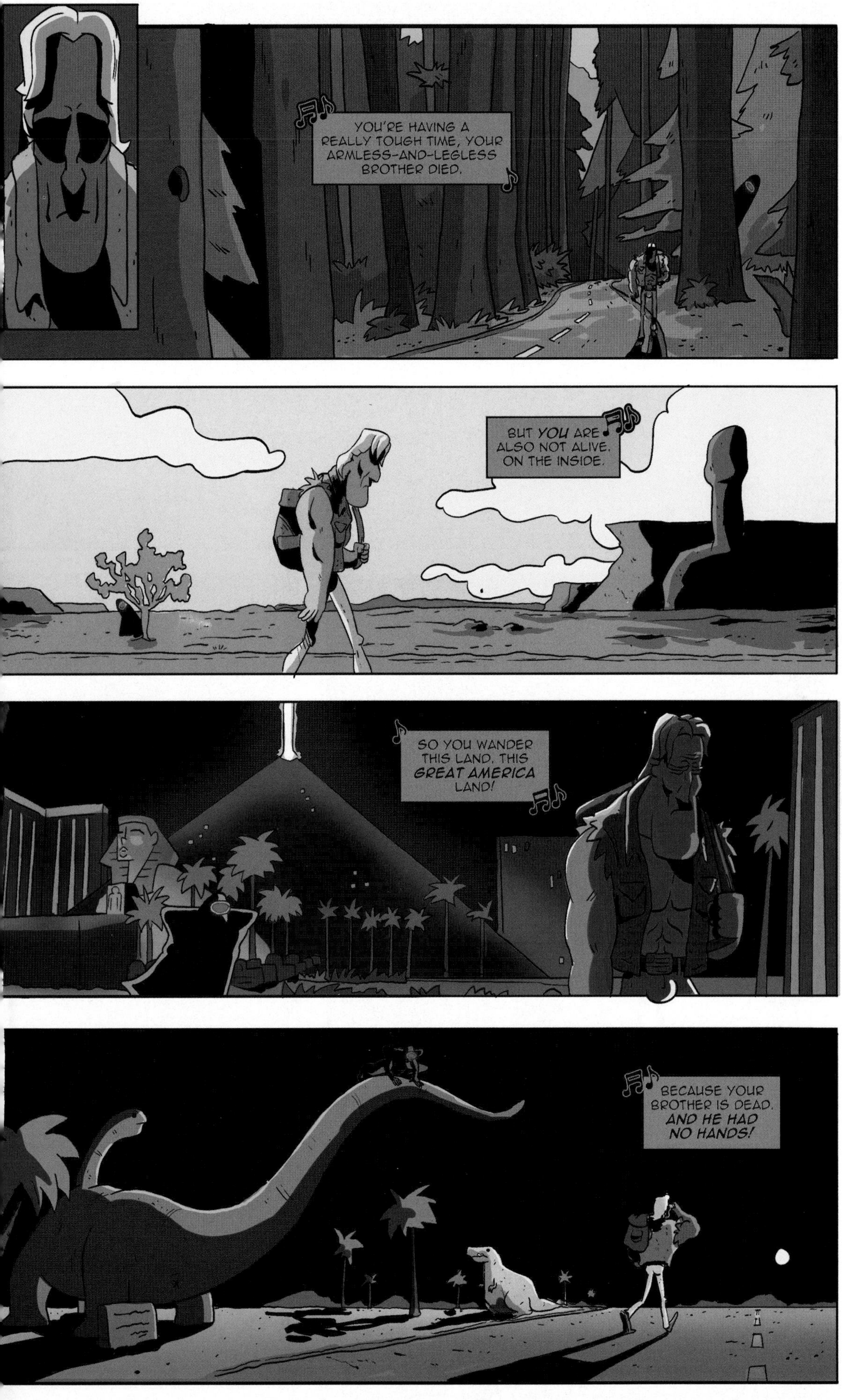
YOU'RE HAVING A REALLY TOUGH TIME, YOUR ARMLESS-AND-LEGLESS BROTHER DIED.
BUT *YOU* ARE ALSO NOT ALIVE. ON THE INSIDE.
SO YOU WANDER THIS LAND. THIS *GREAT AMERICA* LAND!
BECAUSE YOUR BROTHER IS DEAD. *AND HE HAD NO HANDS!*

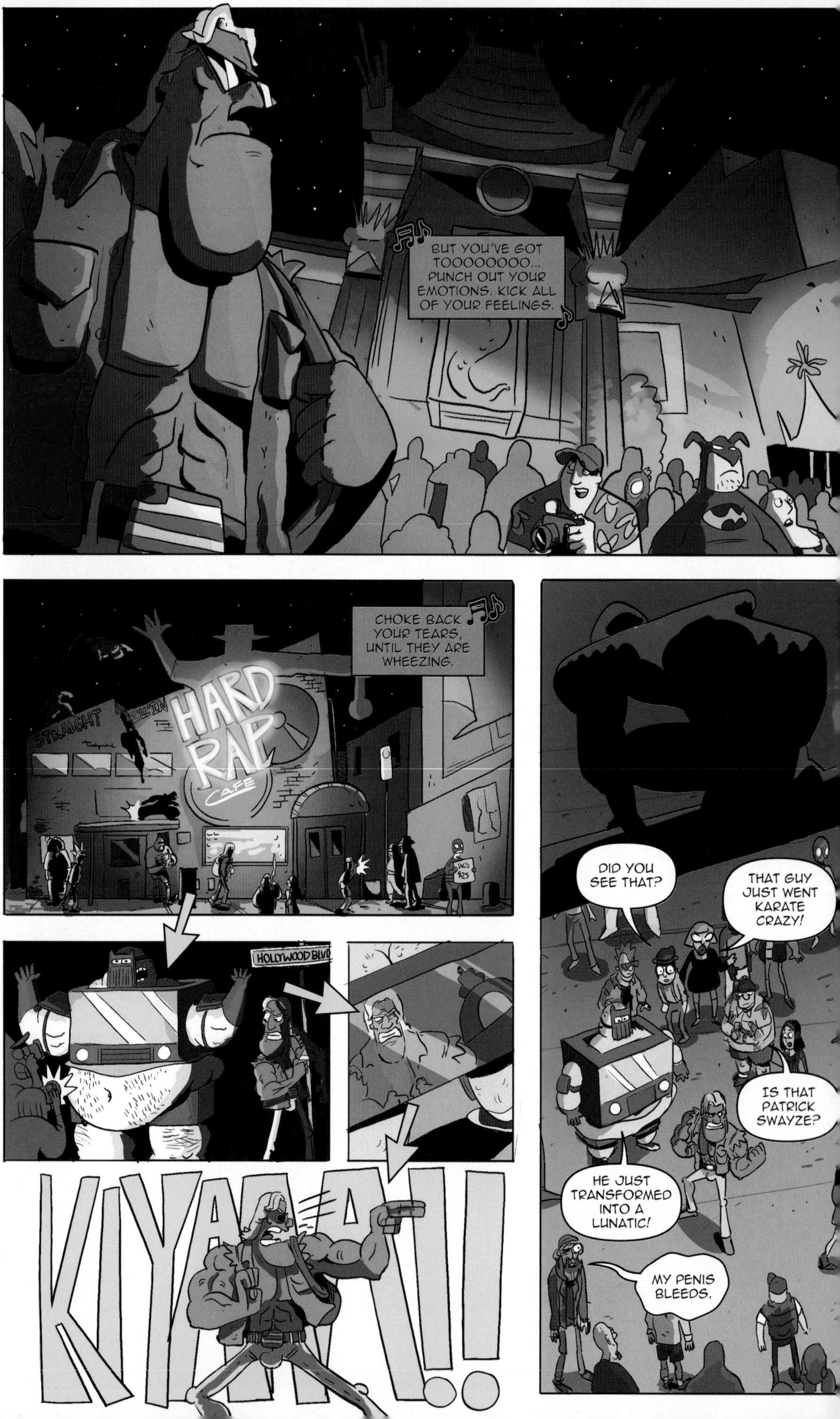
BUT YOU'VE GOT TOOOOOOOO... PUNCH OUT YOUR EMOTIONS. KICK ALL OF YOUR FEELINGS.
CHOKE BACK YOUR TEARS, UNTIL THEY ARE WHEEZING.
HARD RAP CAFE
STRAIGHT
HOLLYWOOD BLVD
KIYAAAH!!
DID YOU SEE THAT?
THAT GUY JUST WENT KARATE CRAZY!
IS THAT PATRICK SWAYZE?
HE JUST TRANSFORMED INTO A LUNATIC!
MY PENIS BLEEDS.

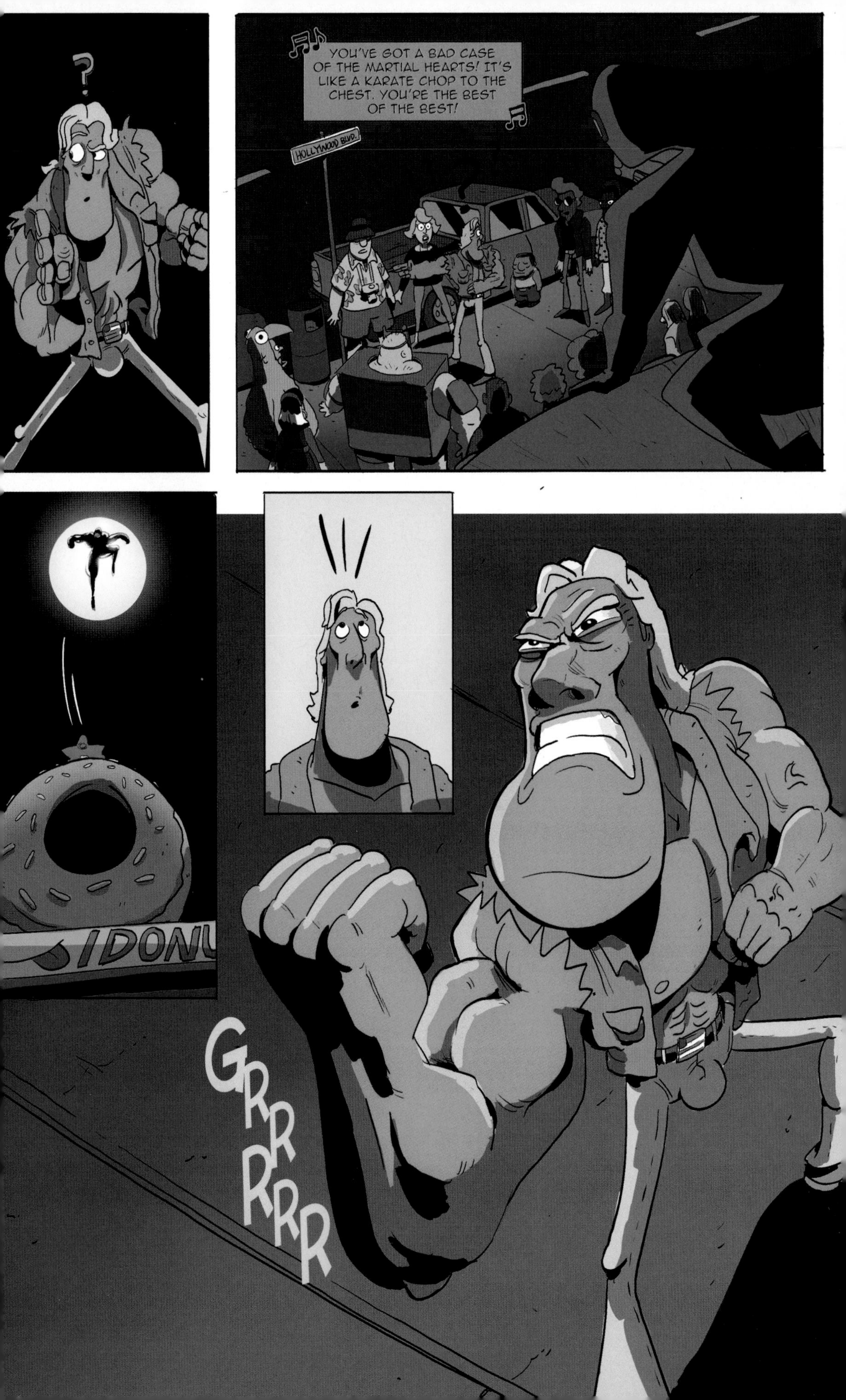
?
YOU'VE GOT A BAD CASE OF THE MARTIAL HEARTS! IT'S LIKE A KARATE CHOP TO THE CHEST. YOU'RE THE BEST OF THE BEST!
HOLLYWOOD BLVD.
IDONU
GRRRRRR

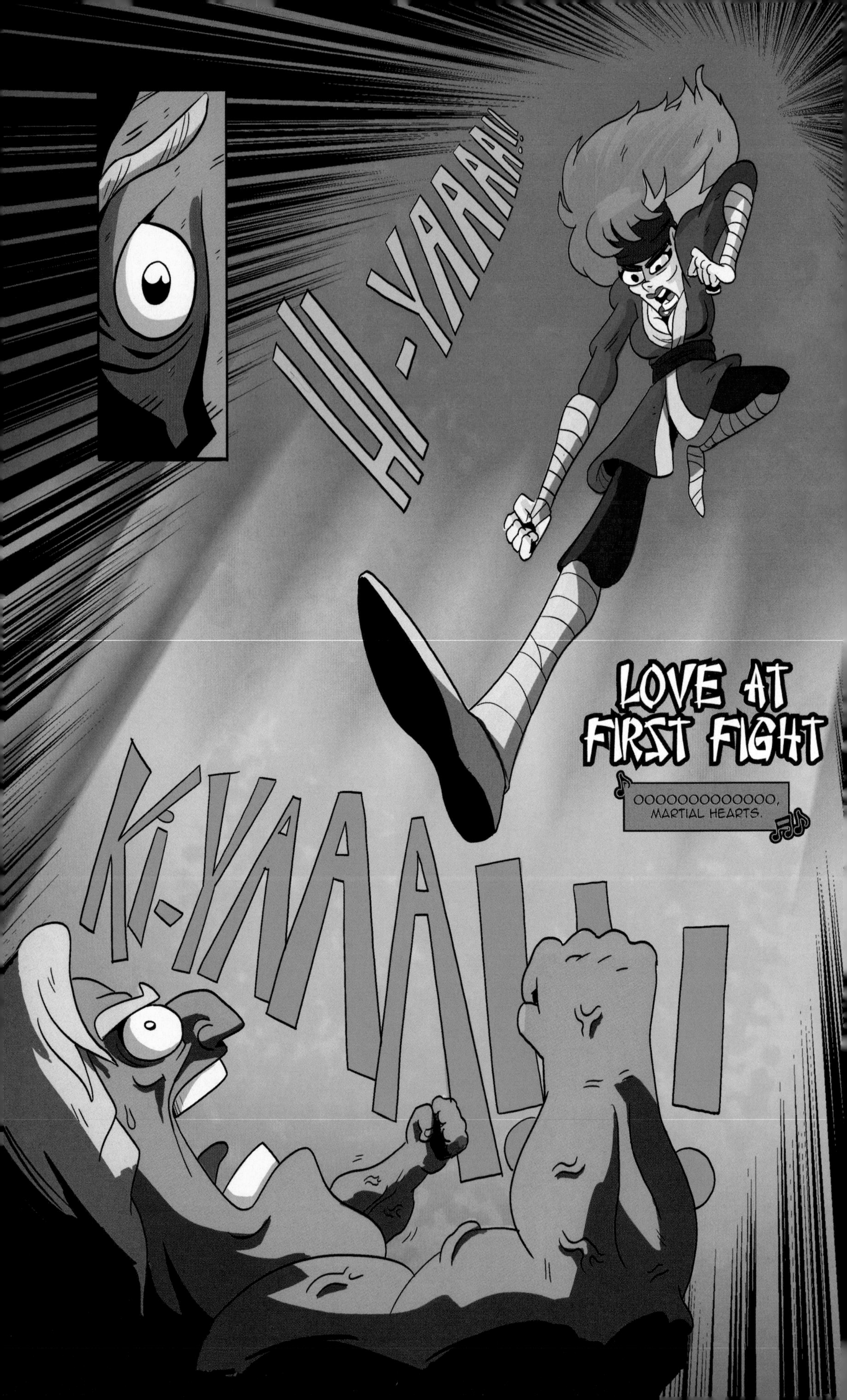
HII-YAAAH!
LOVE AT FIRST FIGHT
OOOOOOOOOOOOOO, MARTIAL HEARTS.
KI-YAAAAH!

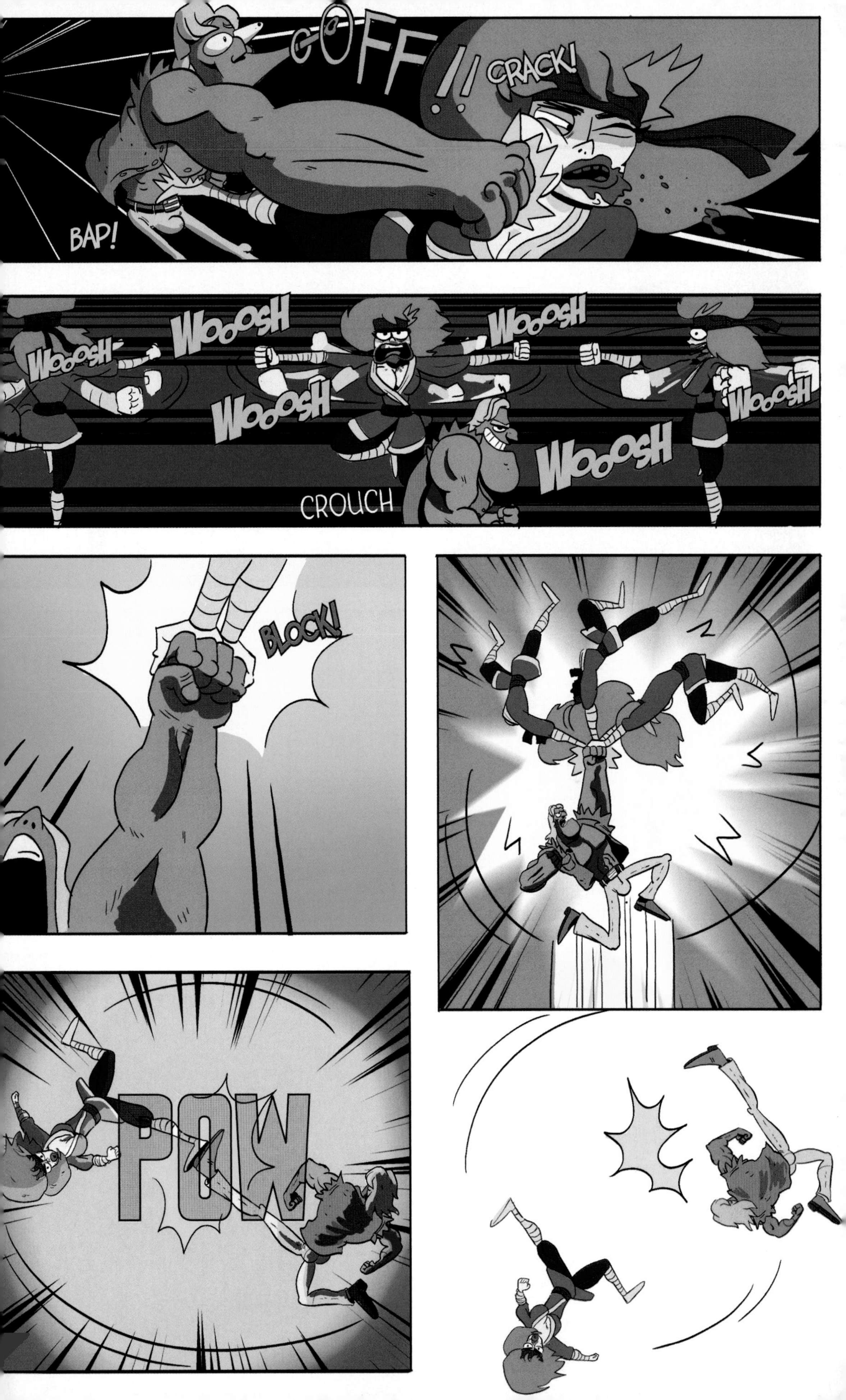
COFF
!!
CRACK!
BAP!
WOOOSH
WOOOSH
WOOOSH
WOOOSH
WOOOSH
WOOOSH
CROUCH
BLOCK!
POW

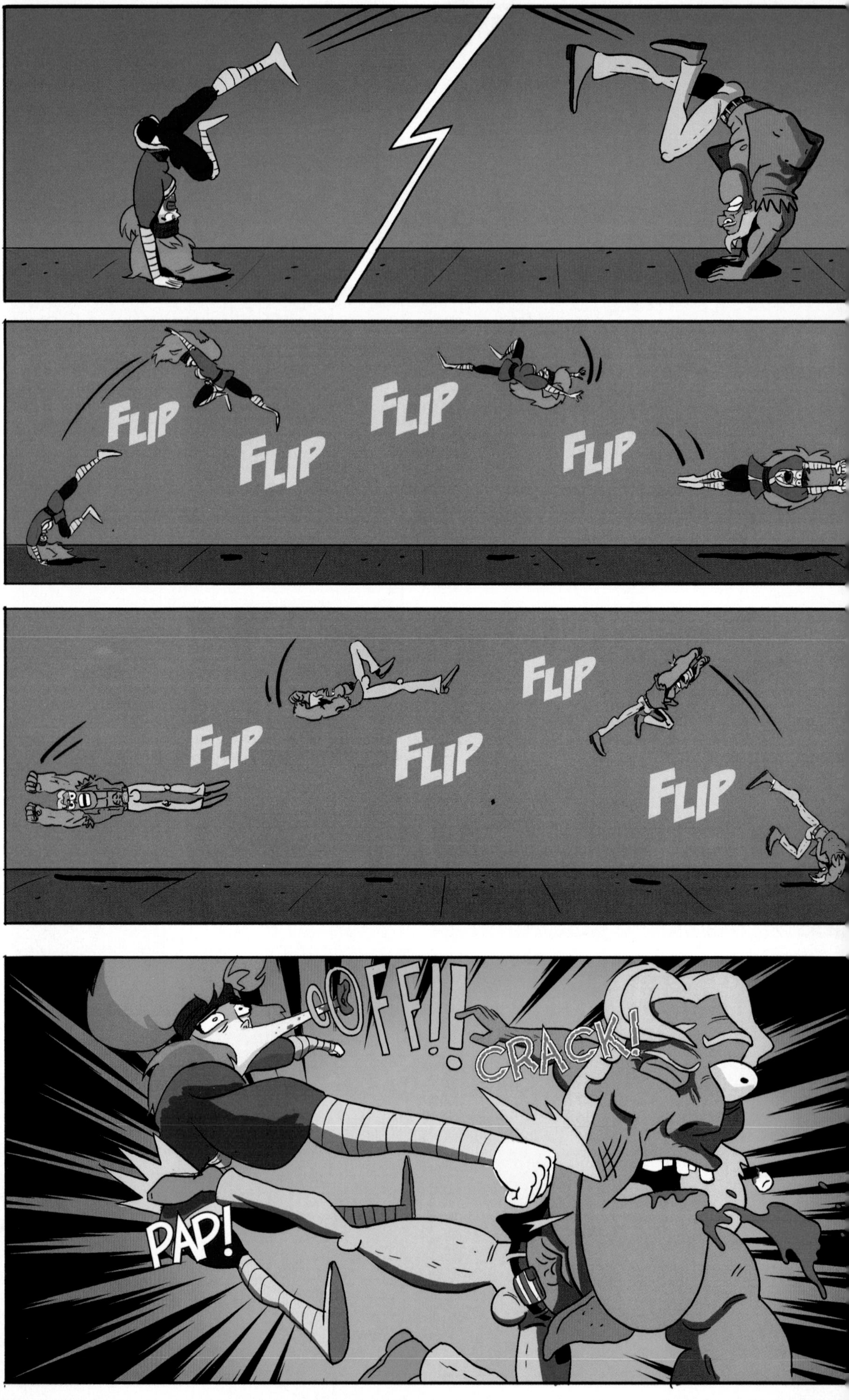
FLIP
FLIP
FLIP
FLIP
FLIP
FLIP
FLIP
FLIP
GOFF!!
CRACK!
PAP!

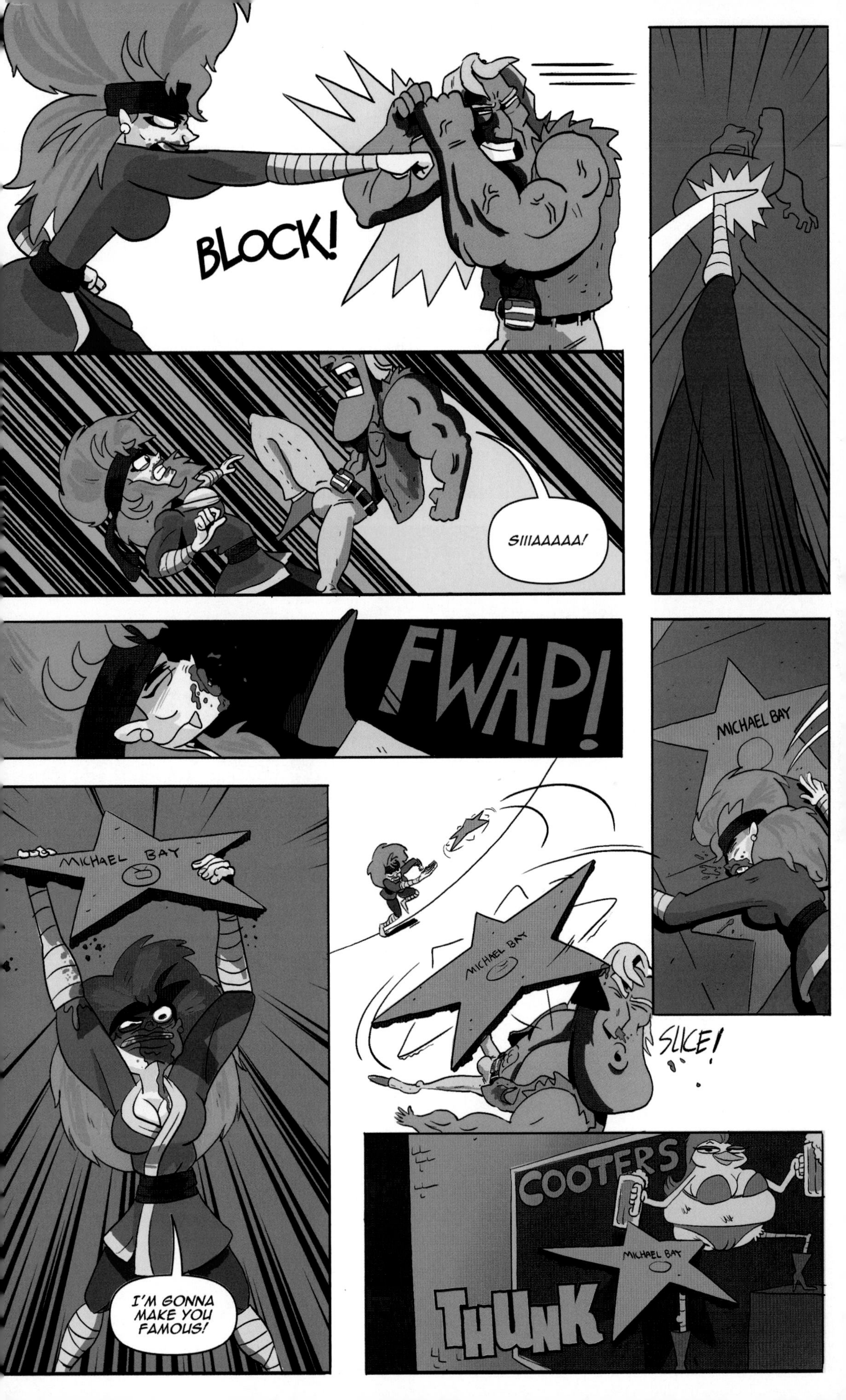
BLOCK!
SIIIAAAAAA!
FWAP!
MICHAEL BAY
MICHAEL BAY
I'M GONNA MAKE YOU FAMOUS!
MICHAEL BAY
SLICE!
COOTERS
MICHAEL BAY
THUNK

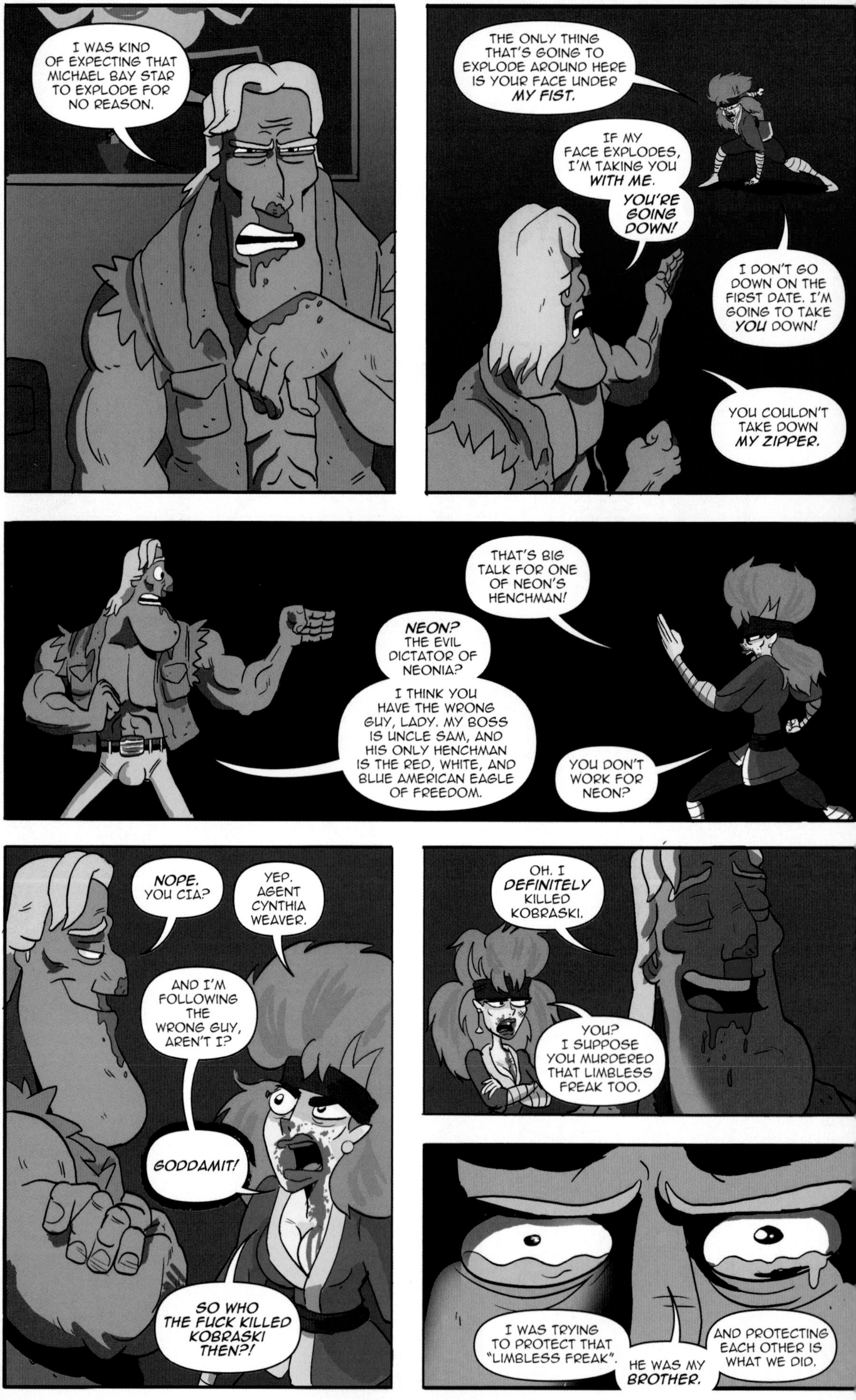
I WAS KIND OF EXPECTING THAT MICHAEL BAY STAR TO EXPLODE FOR NO REASON.
THE ONLY THING THAT'S GOING TO EXPLODE AROUND HERE IS YOUR FACE UNDER MY FIST.
IF MY FACE EXPLODES, I'M TAKING YOU WITH ME.
YOU'RE GOING DOWN!
I DON'T GO DOWN ON THE FIRST DATE. I'M GOING TO TAKE YOU DOWN!
YOU COULDN'T TAKE DOWN MY ZIPPER.
THAT'S BIG TALK FOR ONE OF NEON'S HENCHMAN!
NEON? THE EVIL DICTATOR OF NEONIA?
I THINK YOU HAVE THE WRONG GUY, LADY. MY BOSS IS UNCLE SAM, AND HIS ONLY HENCHMAN IS THE RED, WHITE, AND BLUE AMERICAN EAGLE OF FREEDOM.
YOU DON'T WORK FOR NEON?
NOPE. YOU CIA?
YEP. AGENT CYNTHIA WEAVER.
AND I'M FOLLOWING THE WRONG GUY, AREN'T I?
GODDAMIT!
SO WHO THE FUCK KILLED KOBRASKI THEN?!
OH. I DEFINITELY KILLED KOBRASKI.
YOU? I SUPPOSE YOU MURDERED THAT LIMBLESS FREAK TOO.
I WAS TRYING TO PROTECT THAT "LIMBLESS FREAK".
HE WAS MY BROTHER.
AND PROTECTING EACH OTHER IS WHAT WE DID.

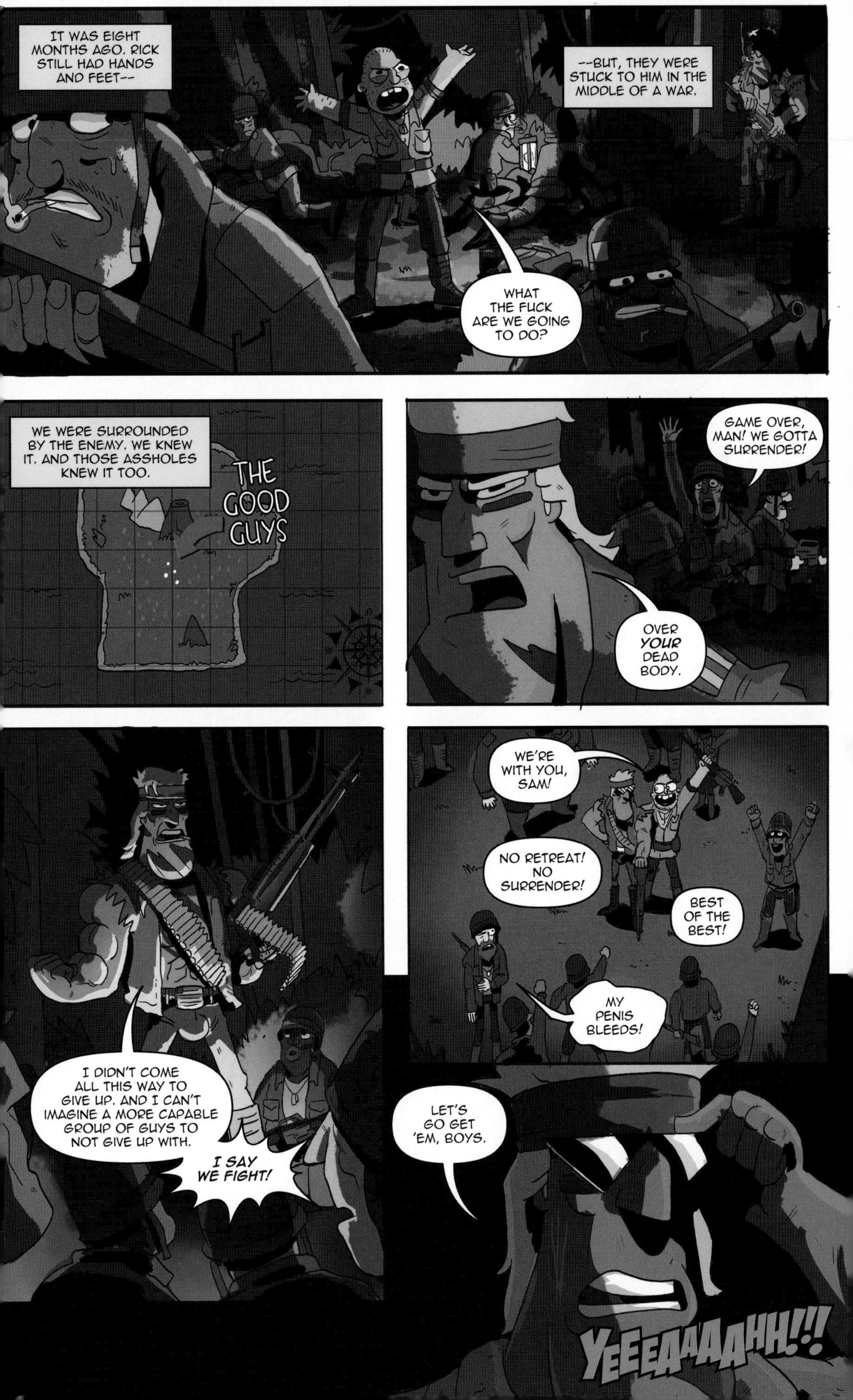
IT WAS EIGHT MONTHS AGO. RICK STILL HAD HANDS AND FEET--
--BUT, THEY WERE STUCK TO HIM IN THE MIDDLE OF A WAR.
WHAT THE FUCK ARE WE GOING TO DO?
WE WERE SURROUNDED BY THE ENEMY. WE KNEW IT. AND THOSE ASSHOLES KNEW IT TOO.
THE GOOD GUYS
GAME OVER, MAN! WE GOTTA SURRENDER!
OVER YOUR DEAD BODY.
I DIDN'T COME ALL THIS WAY TO GIVE UP. AND I CAN'T IMAGINE A MORE CAPABLE GROUP OF GUYS TO NOT GIVE UP WITH.
I SAY WE FIGHT!
WE'RE WITH YOU, SAM!
NO RETREAT! NO SURRENDER!
BEST OF THE BEST!
MY PENIS BLEEDS!
LET'S GO GET 'EM, BOYS.
YEEEAAAAHH!!!

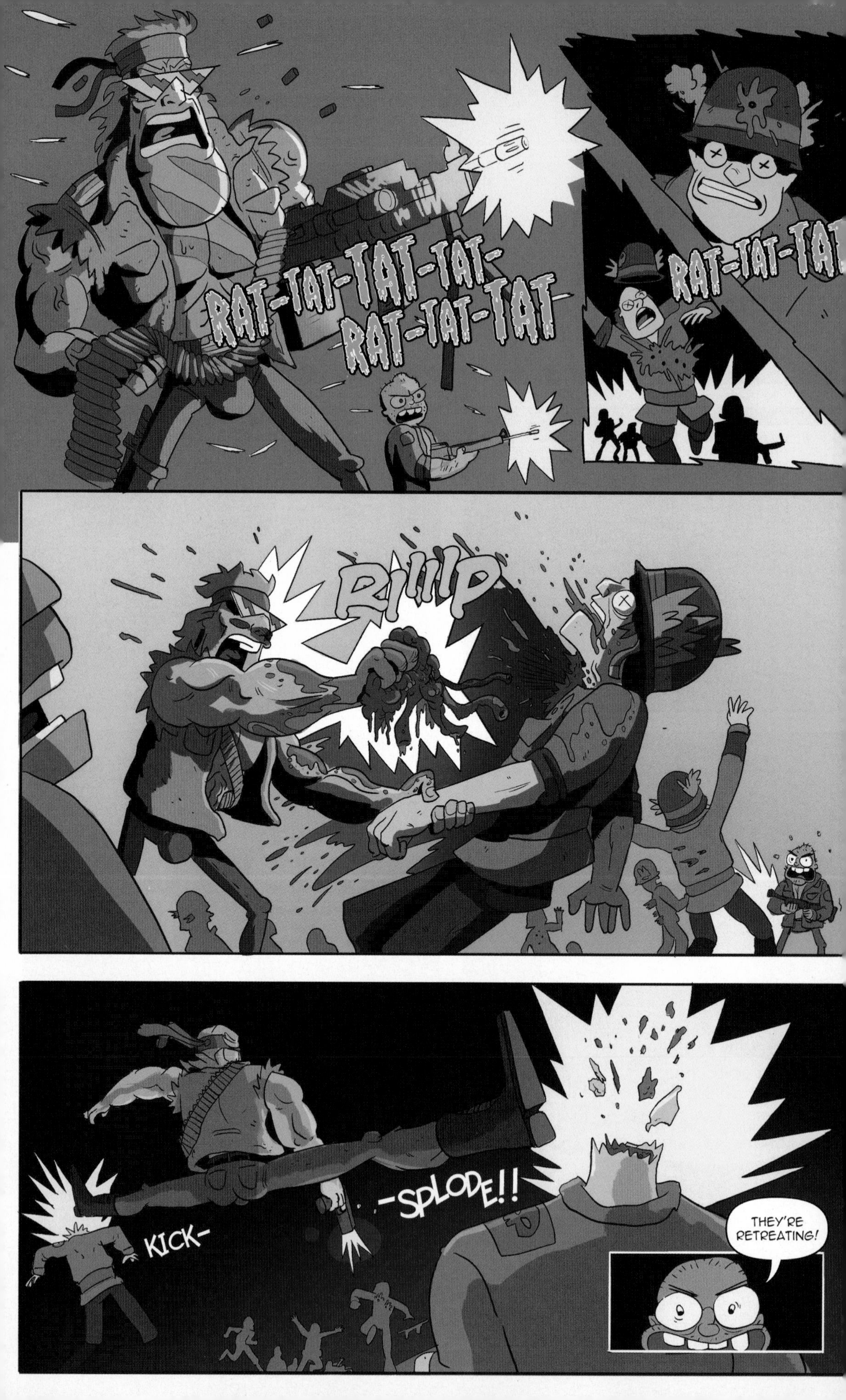
RAT-TAT-TAT-TAT-
RAT-TAT-TAT
RAT-TAT-TAT
RIIIIP
KICK-
-SPLODE!!
THEY'RE RETREATING!

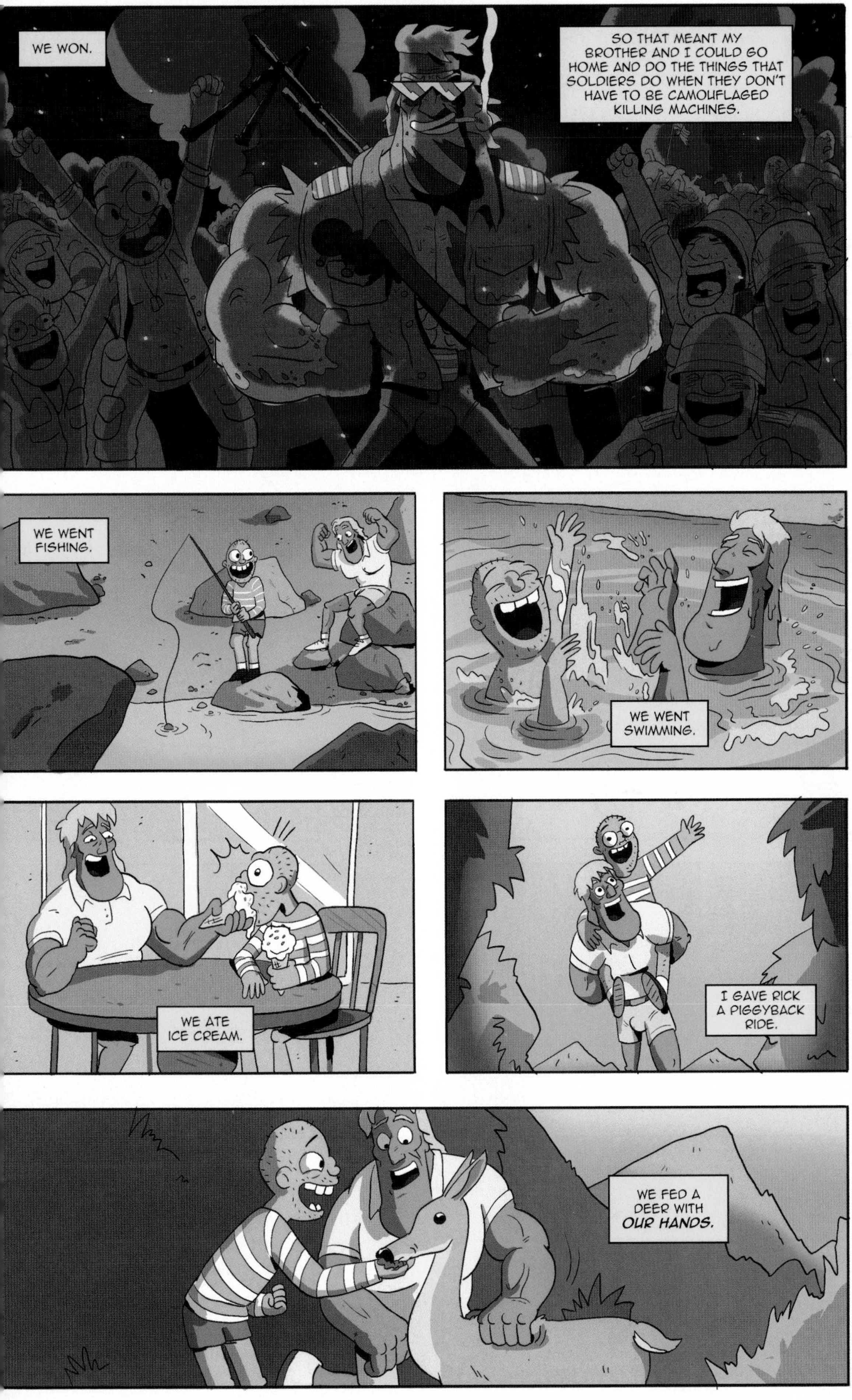
WE WON.
SO THAT MEANT MY BROTHER AND I COULD GO HOME AND DO THE THINGS THAT SOLDIERS DO WHEN THEY DON'T HAVE TO BE CAMOUFLAGED KILLING MACHINES.
WE WENT FISHING.
WE WENT SWIMMING.
WE ATE ICE CREAM.
I GAVE RICK A PIGGYBACK RIDE.
WE FED A DEER WITH *OUR HANDS.*

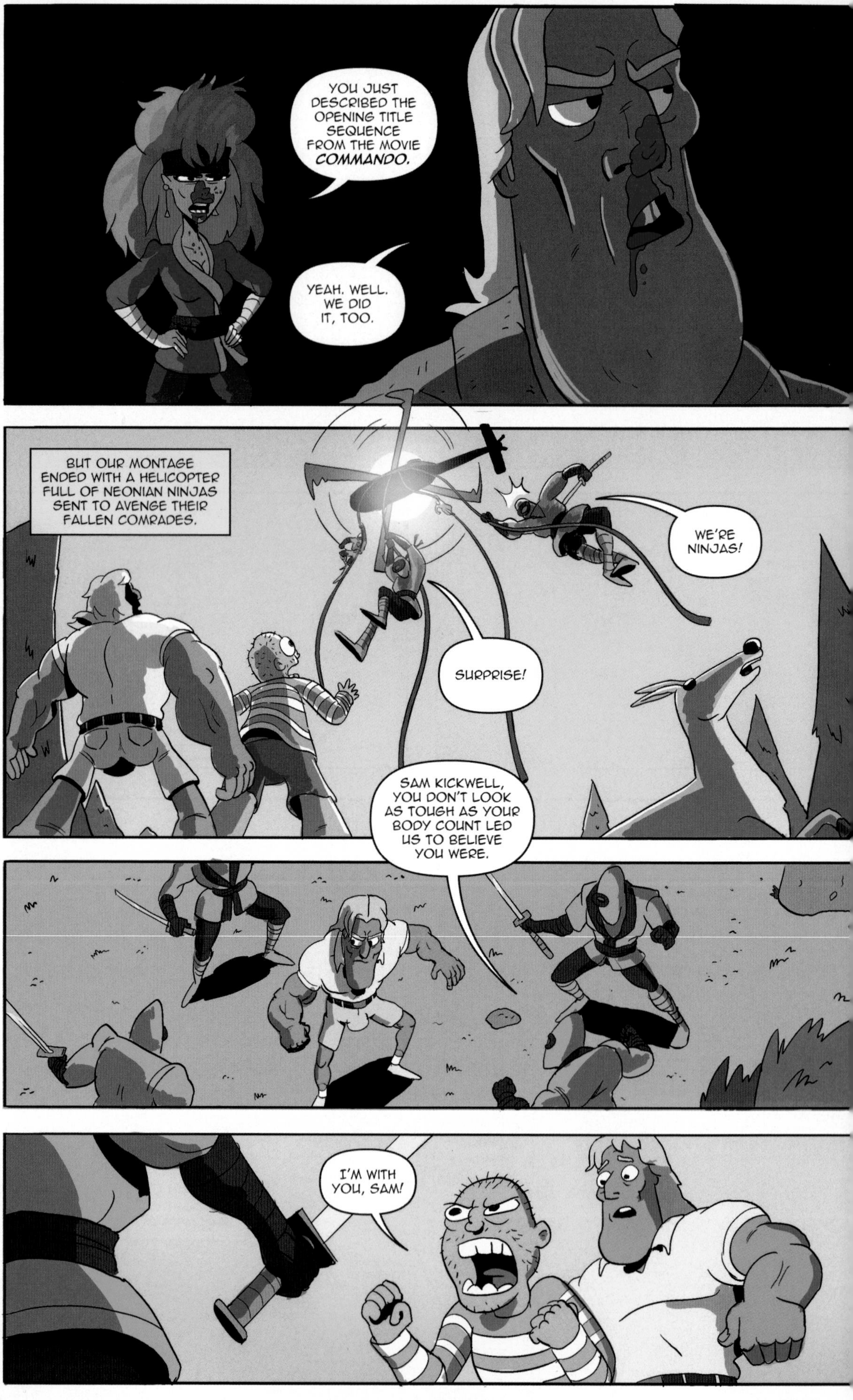
YOU JUST DESCRIBED THE OPENING TITLE SEQUENCE FROM THE MOVIE *COMMANDO.*
YEAH. WELL. WE DID IT, TOO.
BUT OUR MONTAGE ENDED WITH A HELICOPTER FULL OF NEONIAN NINJAS SENT TO AVENGE THEIR FALLEN COMRADES.
WE'RE NINJAS!
SURPRISE!
SAM KICKWELL, YOU DON'T LOOK AS TOUGH AS YOUR BODY COUNT LED US TO BELIEVE YOU WERE.
I'M WITH YOU, SAM!

HI-YAH!
MY ARM JUST GOT KICKED OFF! AGGGHHH!
CRACK
KEE-YAH!
MY OTHER ARM!
SLICE
SHAAA!
WOOOSH
GAAA!
NOW MY LEGS! KARATE-CHOPPED OFF!
WOOOSH
HOW AM I GONNA ENJOY FISHING AND SWIMMING AND EATING ICE CREAM AND FEEDING THAT DEER OUT OF MY HANDS NOW?
YOU TOOK MY BROTHER'S PASTIMES AWAY!
WAPP!!
POKE!!

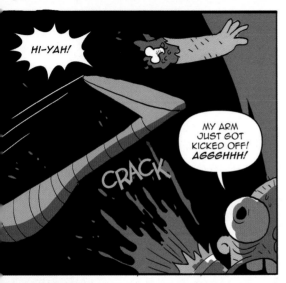

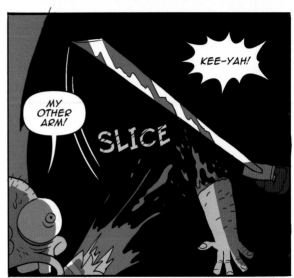

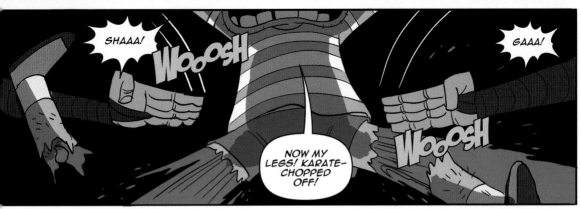

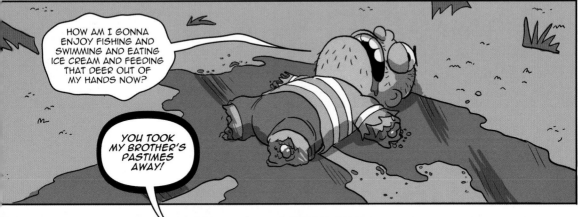

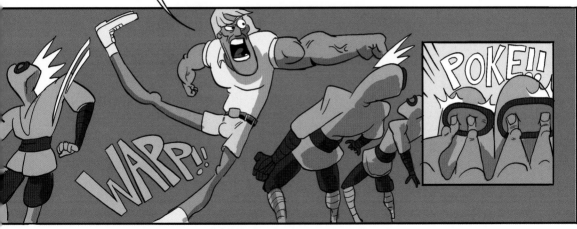

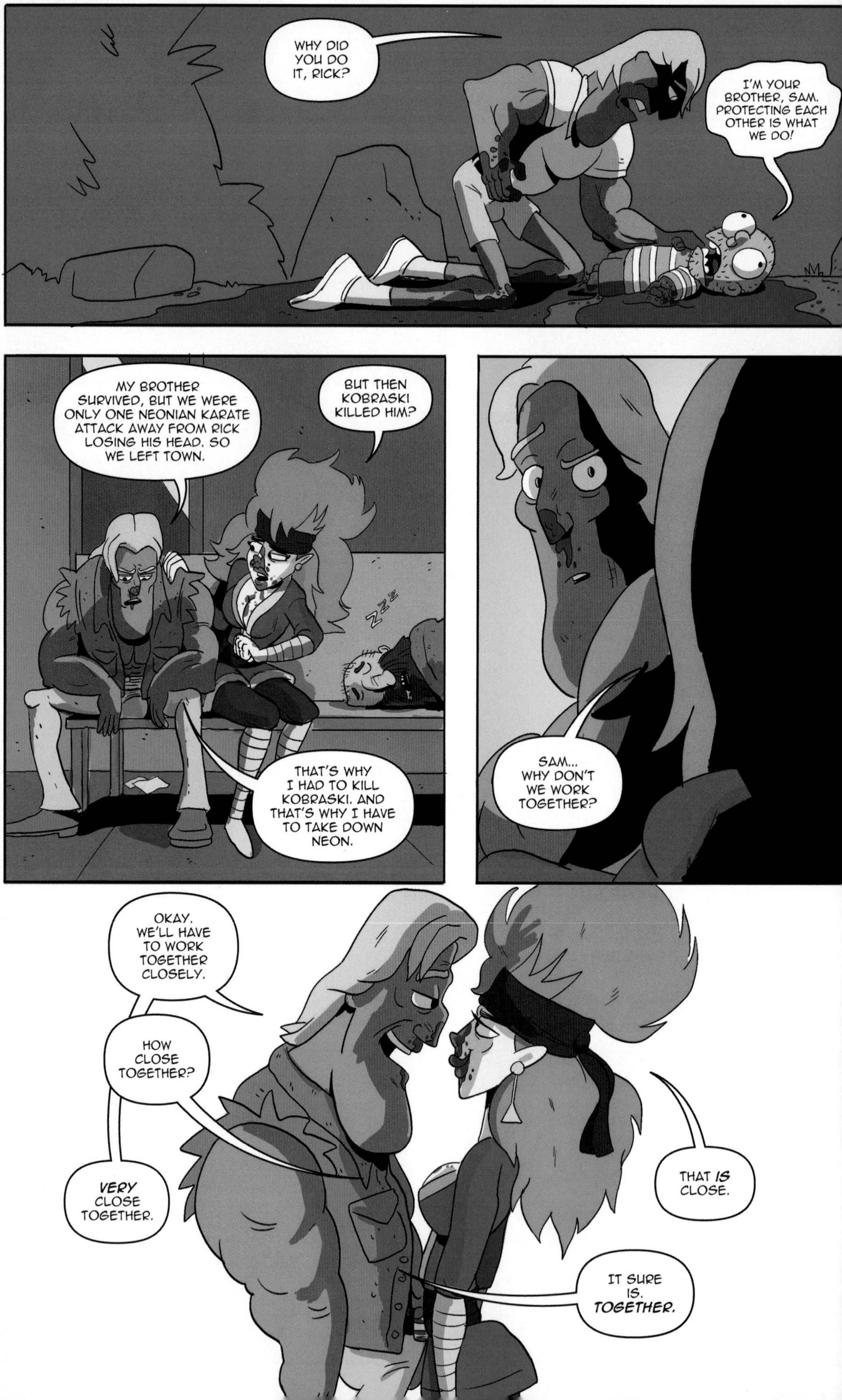
WHY DID YOU DO IT, RICK?
I'M YOUR BROTHER, SAM. PROTECTING EACH OTHER IS WHAT WE DO!
MY BROTHER SURVIVED, BUT WE WERE ONLY ONE NEONIAN KARATE ATTACK AWAY FROM RICK LOSING HIS HEAD. SO WE LEFT TOWN.
BUT THEN KOBRASKI KILLED HIM?
ZZZ
THAT'S WHY I HAD TO KILL KOBRASKI. AND THAT'S WHY I HAVE TO TAKE DOWN NEON.
SAM... WHY DON'T WE WORK TOGETHER?
OKAY. WE'LL HAVE TO WORK TOGETHER CLOSELY.
HOW CLOSE TOGETHER?
VERY CLOSE TOGETHER.
THAT *IS* CLOSE.
IT SURE IS. *TOGETHER.*

COLOSSEUM MOTEL. ROMAN LUXURY, AT AN HOURLY RATE.

KI-YAHHHHHHHH!

MMMMMMMM.

MOAN

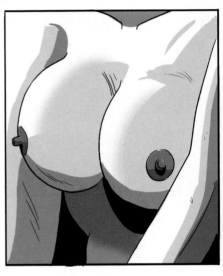

OH. FUCK.

UH HUH.

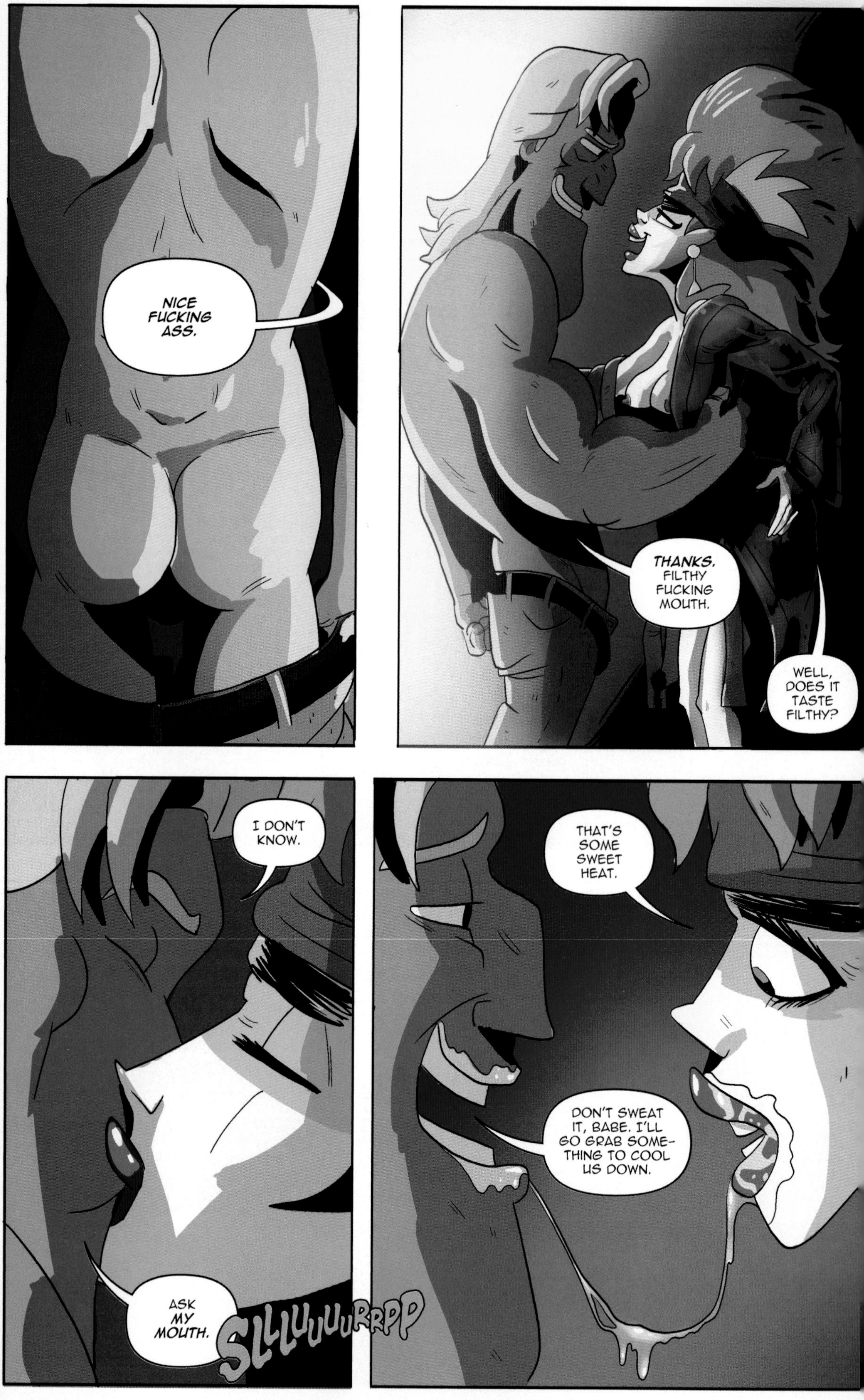
NICE FUCKING ASS.
THANKS. FILTHY FUCKING MOUTH.
WELL, DOES IT TASTE FILTHY?
I DON'T KNOW.
ASK MY MOUTH.
SLLLUUUURRPP
THAT'S SOME SWEET HEAT.
DON'T SWEAT IT, BABE. I'LL GO GRAB SOME-THING TO COOL US DOWN.

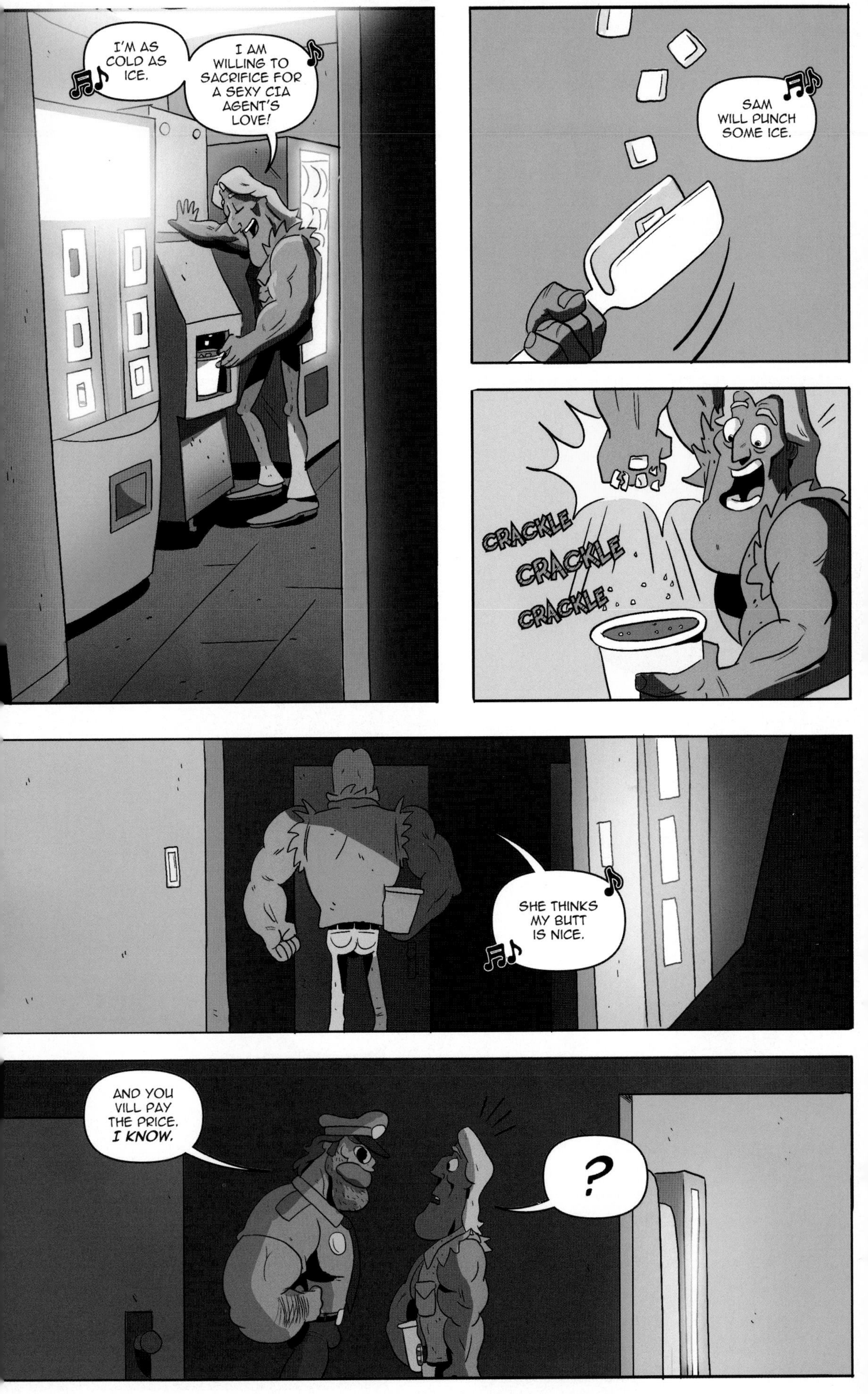
I'M AS COLD AS ICE.
I AM WILLING TO SACRIFICE FOR A SEXY CIA AGENT'S LOVE!
SAM WILL PUNCH SOME ICE.
CRACKLE
CRACKLE
CRACKLE
SHE THINKS MY BUTT IS NICE.
AND YOU VILL PAY THE PRICE. *I KNOW.*
?

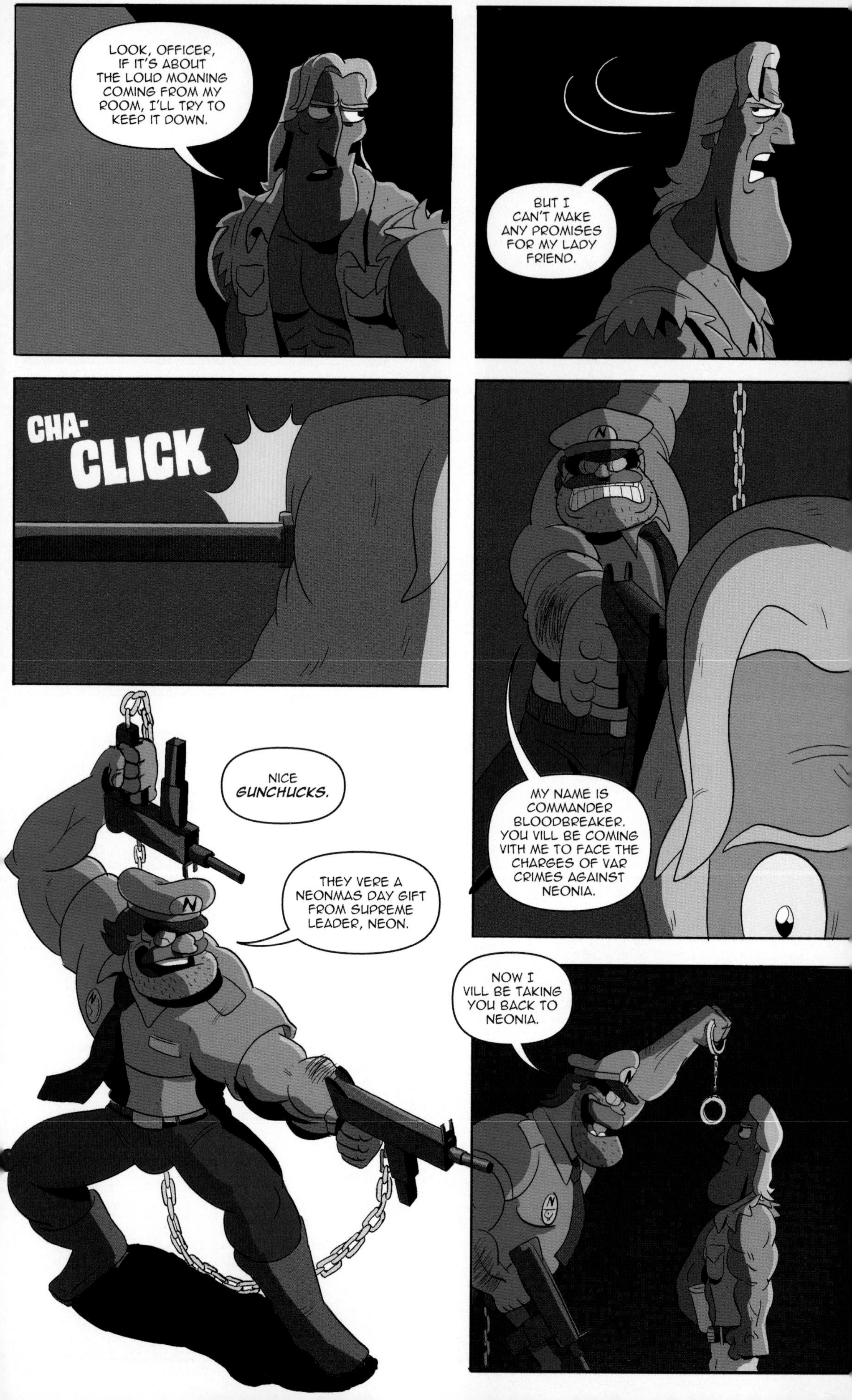

LOOK, OFFICER, IF IT'S ABOUT THE LOUD MOANING COMING FROM MY ROOM, I'LL TRY TO KEEP IT DOWN.
BUT I CAN'T MAKE ANY PROMISES FOR MY LADY FRIEND.
CHA-CLICK
MY NAME IS COMMANDER BLOODBREAKER. YOU VILL BE COMING VITH ME TO FACE THE CHARGES OF VAR CRIMES AGAINST NEONIA.
NICE GUNCHUCKS.
THEY VERE A NEONMAS DAY GIFT FROM SUPREME LEADER, NEON.
NOW I VILL BE TAKING YOU BACK TO NEONIA.

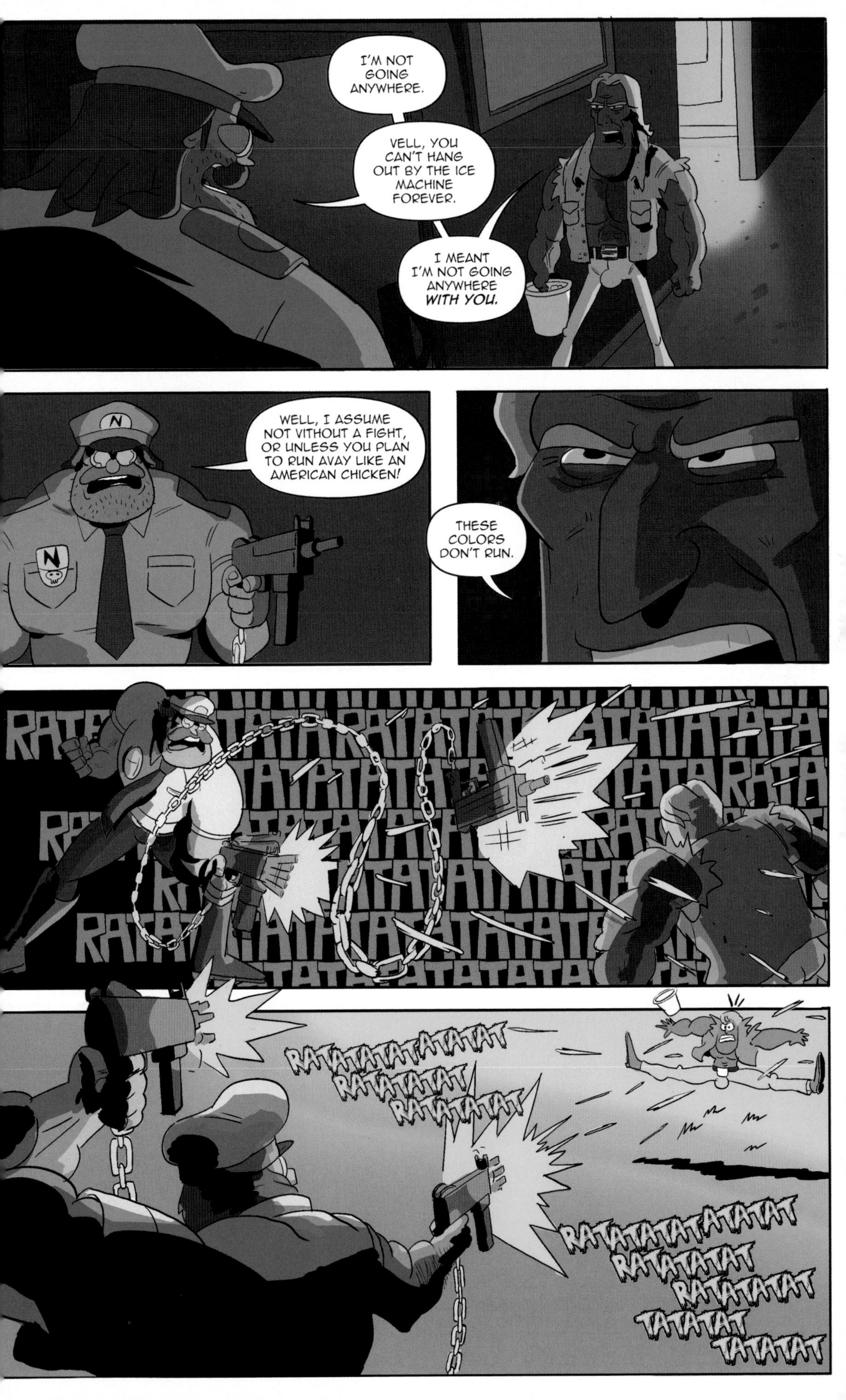

I'M NOT GOING ANYWHERE.
VELL, YOU CAN'T HANG OUT BY THE ICE MACHINE FOREVER.
I MEANT I'M NOT GOING ANYWHERE *WITH YOU.*
WELL, I ASSUME NOT VITHOUT A FIGHT, OR UNLESS YOU PLAN TO RUN AVAY LIKE AN AMERICAN CHICKEN!
THESE COLORS DON'T RUN.
RATATATATATATAT
RATATATAT
RATATATAT
RATATATATATATAT
RATATATAT
RATATATAT
TATATAT
TATATAT

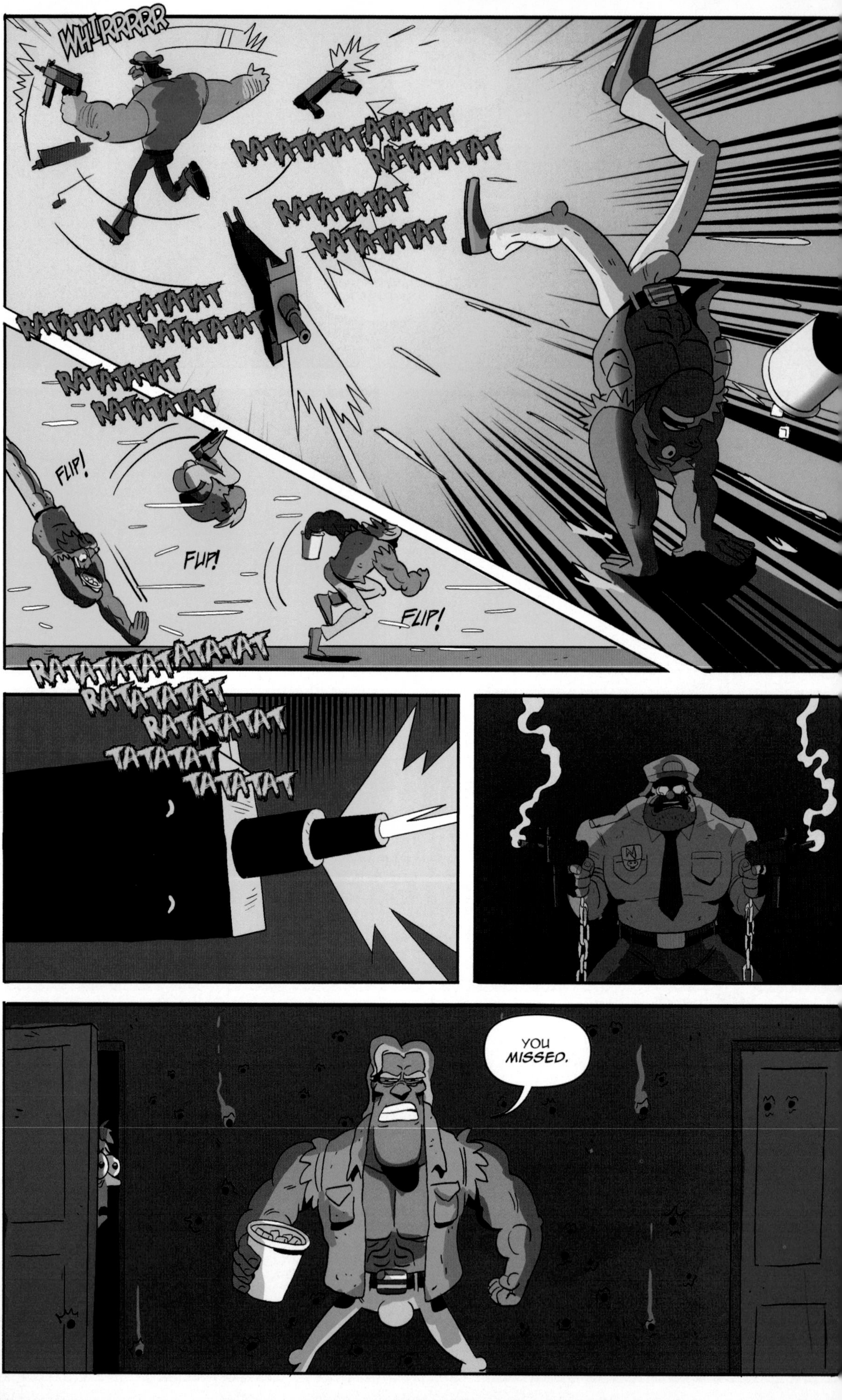
WHIRRRRR
RATATATATATATAT
RATATATAT
RATATATAT
RATATATAT
RATATATATATATAT
RATATATAT
RATATATAT
RATATATAT
FLIP!
FLIP!
FLIP!
RATATATATATATAT
RATATATAT
RATATATAT
TATATAT
TATATAT
YOU
MISSED.

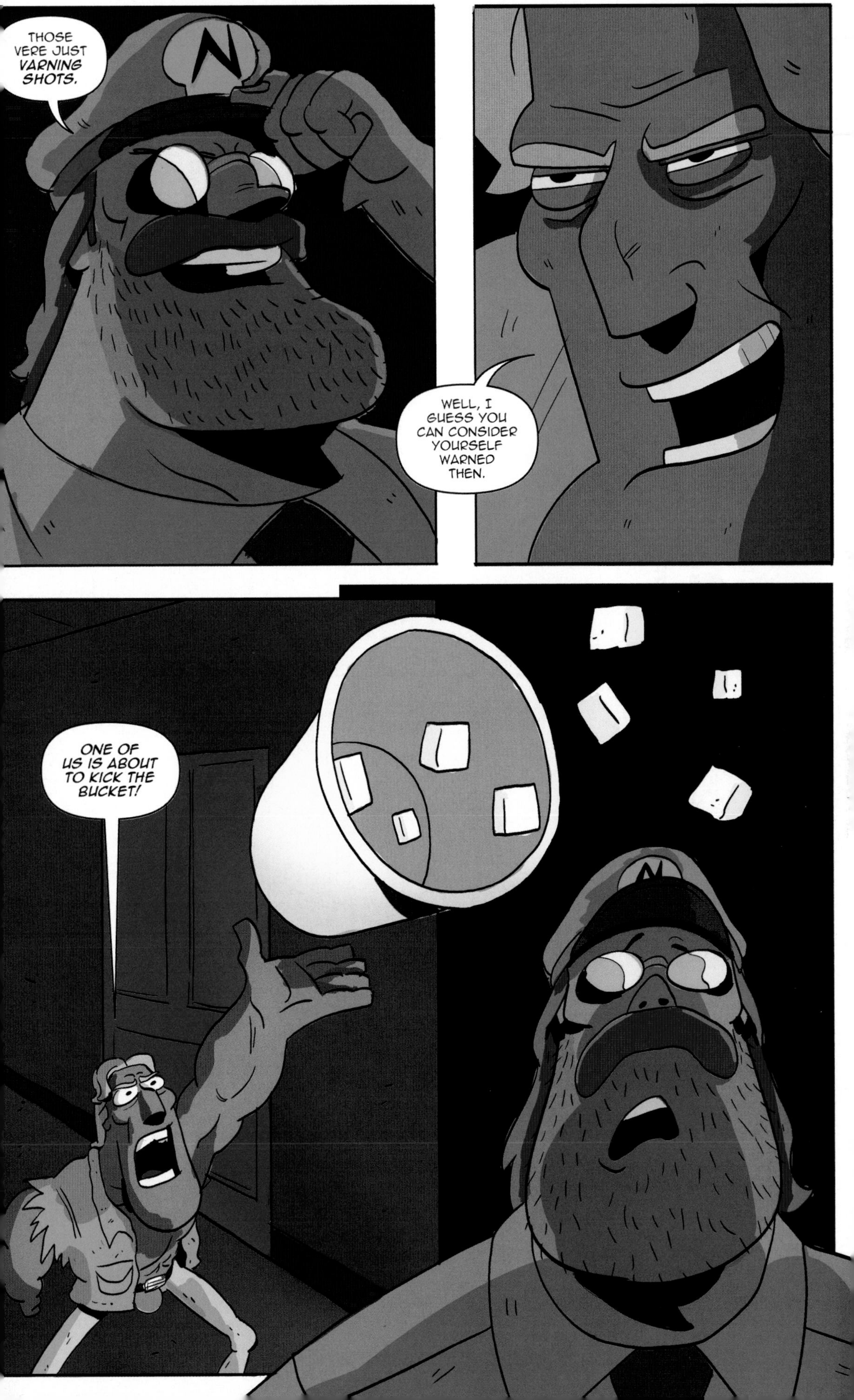
THOSE VERE JUST *VARNING SHOTS.*
WELL, I GUESS YOU CAN CONSIDER YOURSELF WARNED THEN.
ONE OF US IS ABOUT TO KICK THE BUCKET!

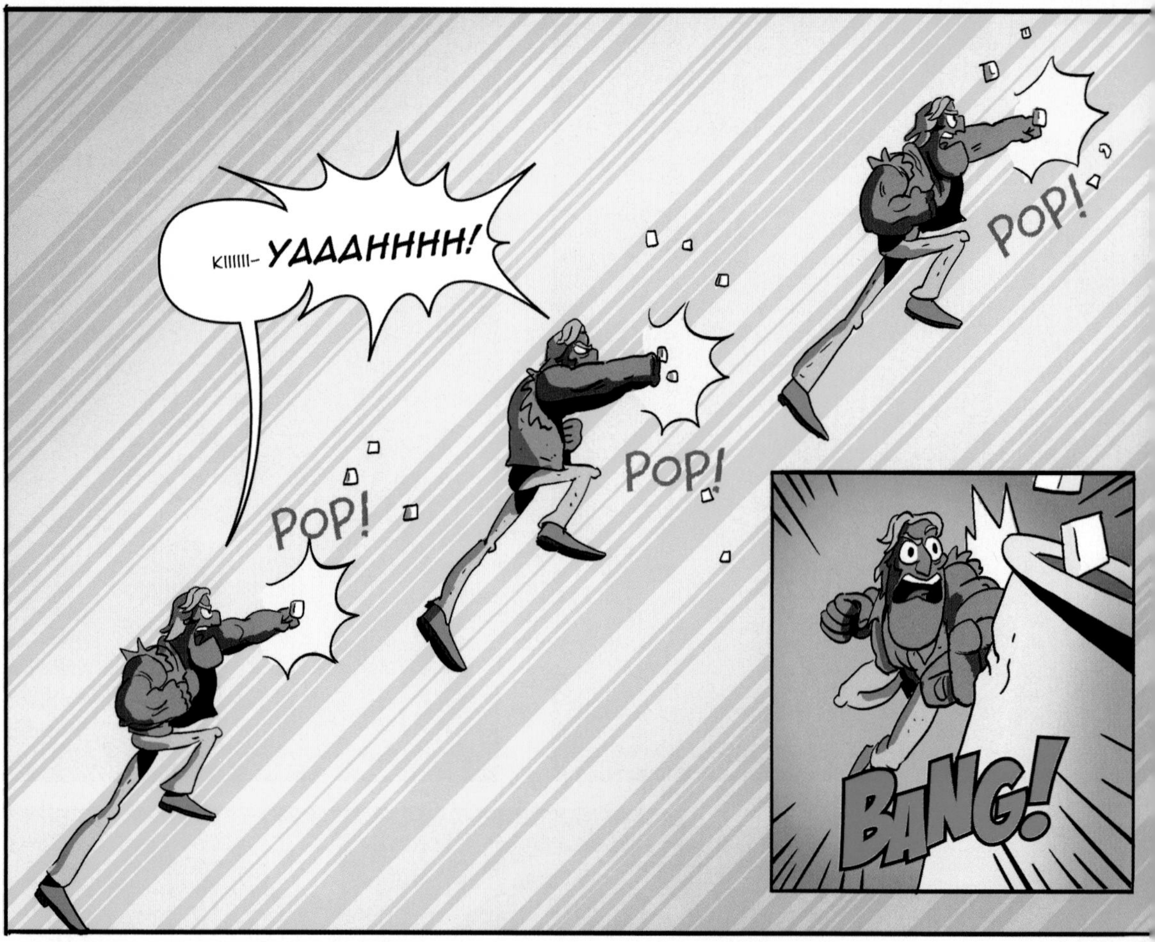
KIIIIII- YAAAHHHH!
POP!
POP!
POP!
BANG!

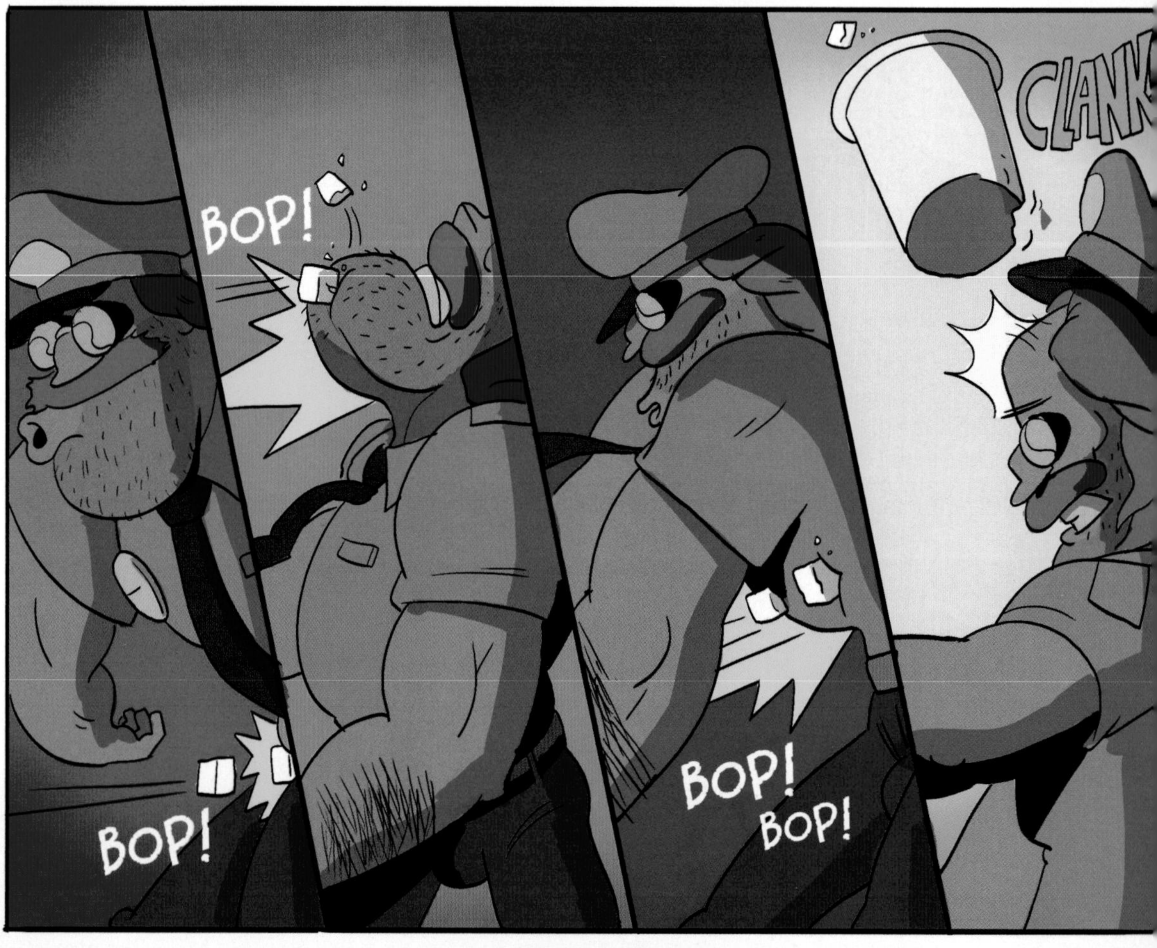
BOP!
BOP!
BOP!
BOP!
CLANK

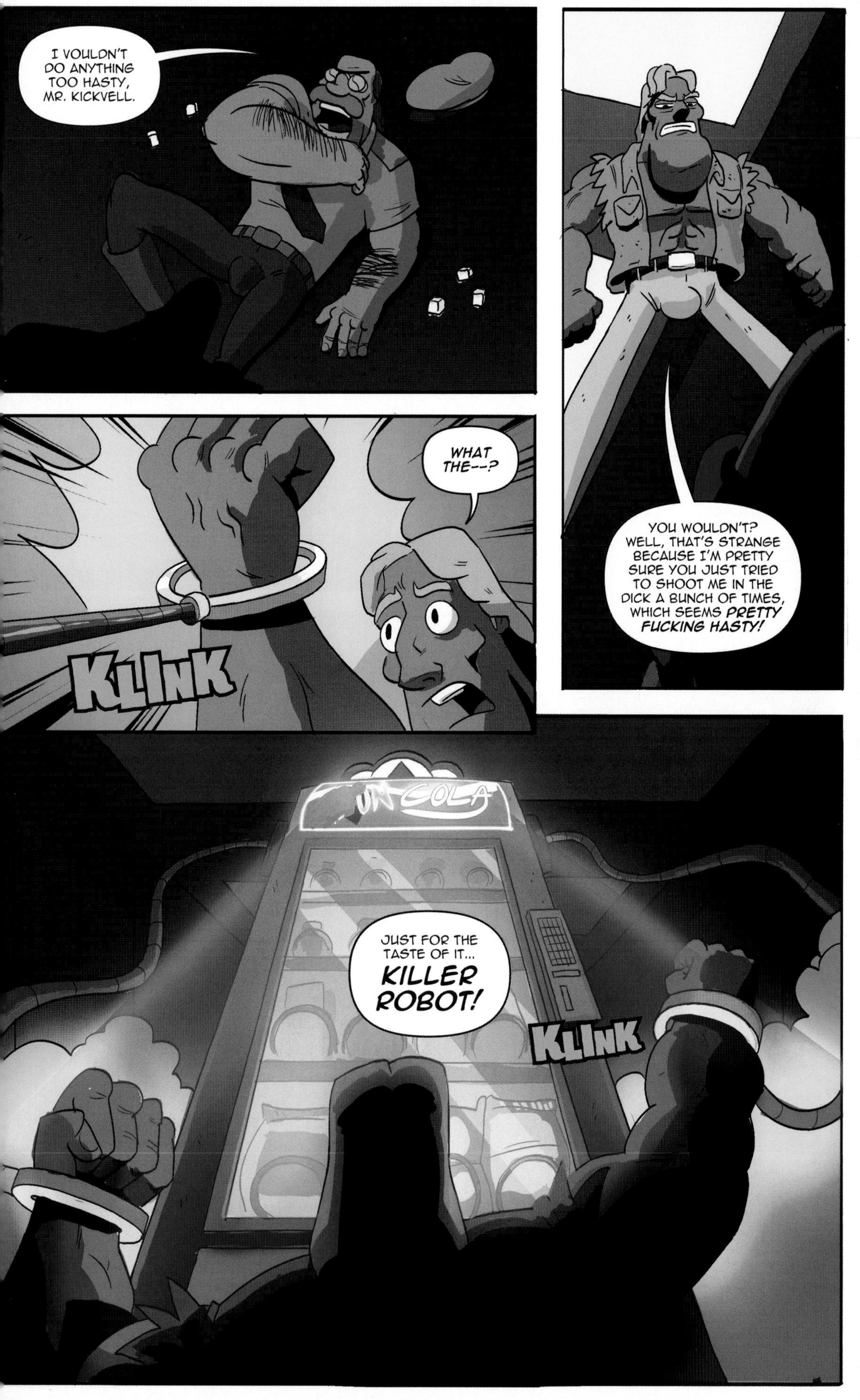
I VOULDN'T DO ANYTHING TOO HASTY, MR. KICKVELL.
YOU WOULDN'T? WELL, THAT'S STRANGE BECAUSE I'M PRETTY SURE YOU JUST TRIED TO SHOOT ME IN THE DICK A BUNCH OF TIMES, WHICH SEEMS PRETTY FUCKING HASTY!
WHAT THE--?
KLINK
JUST FOR THE TASTE OF IT... KILLER ROBOT!
KLINK

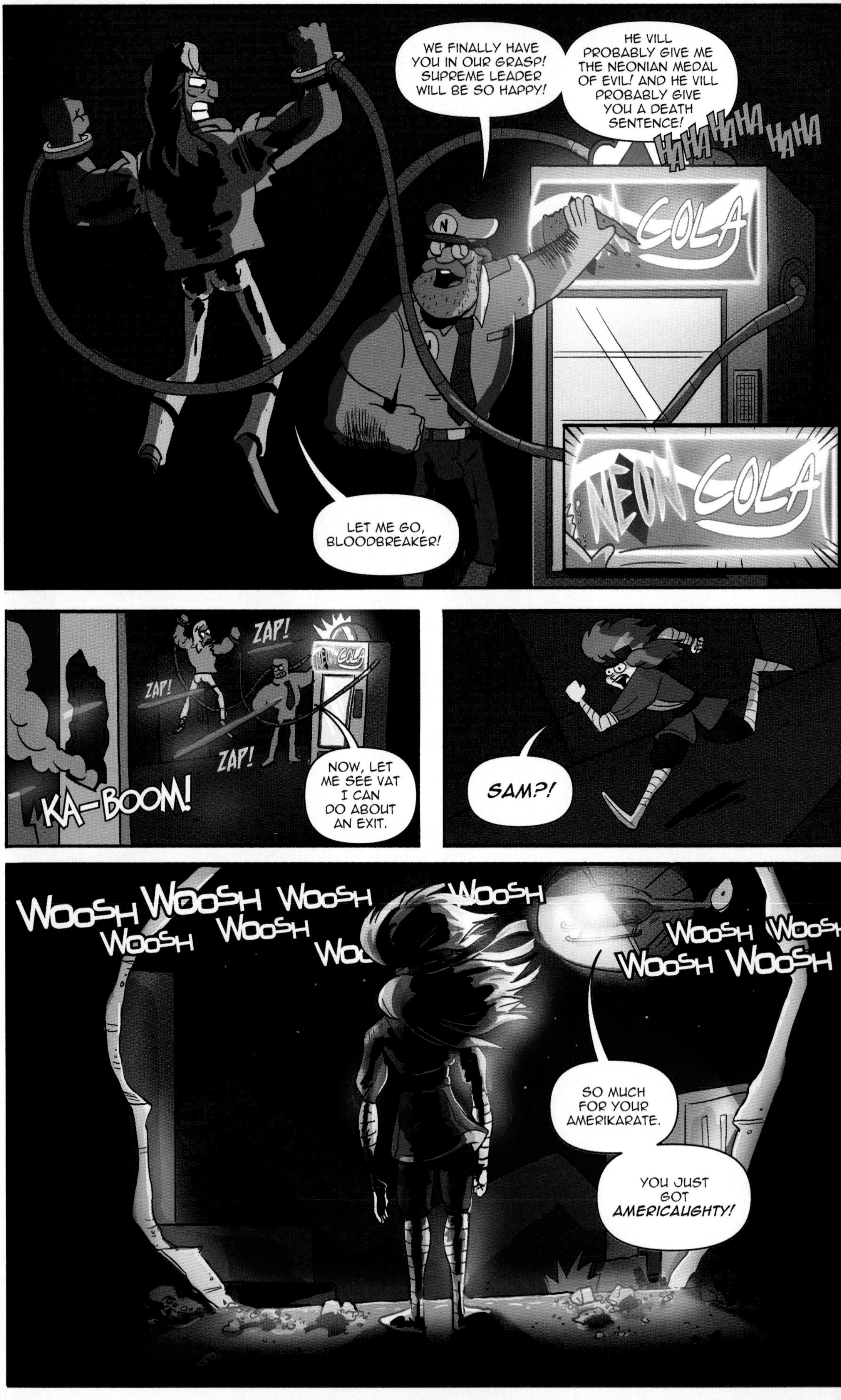
WE FINALLY HAVE YOU IN OUR GRASP! SUPREME LEADER WILL BE SO HAPPY!
HE VILL PROBABLY GIVE ME THE NEONIAN MEDAL OF EVIL! AND HE VILL PROBABLY GIVE YOU A DEATH SENTENCE!
HAHA HAHA HAHA
COLA
LET ME GO, BLOODBREAKER!
NEON COLA
ZAP!
ZAP!
ZAP!
KA-BOOM!
NOW, LET ME SEE VAT I CAN DO ABOUT AN EXIT.
SAM?!
WOOSH WOOSH WOOSH WOOSH
WOOSH WOOSH
WOOSH WOOSH
WOOSH WOOSH
SO MUCH FOR YOUR AMERIKARATE.
YOU JUST GOT AMERICAUGHTY!

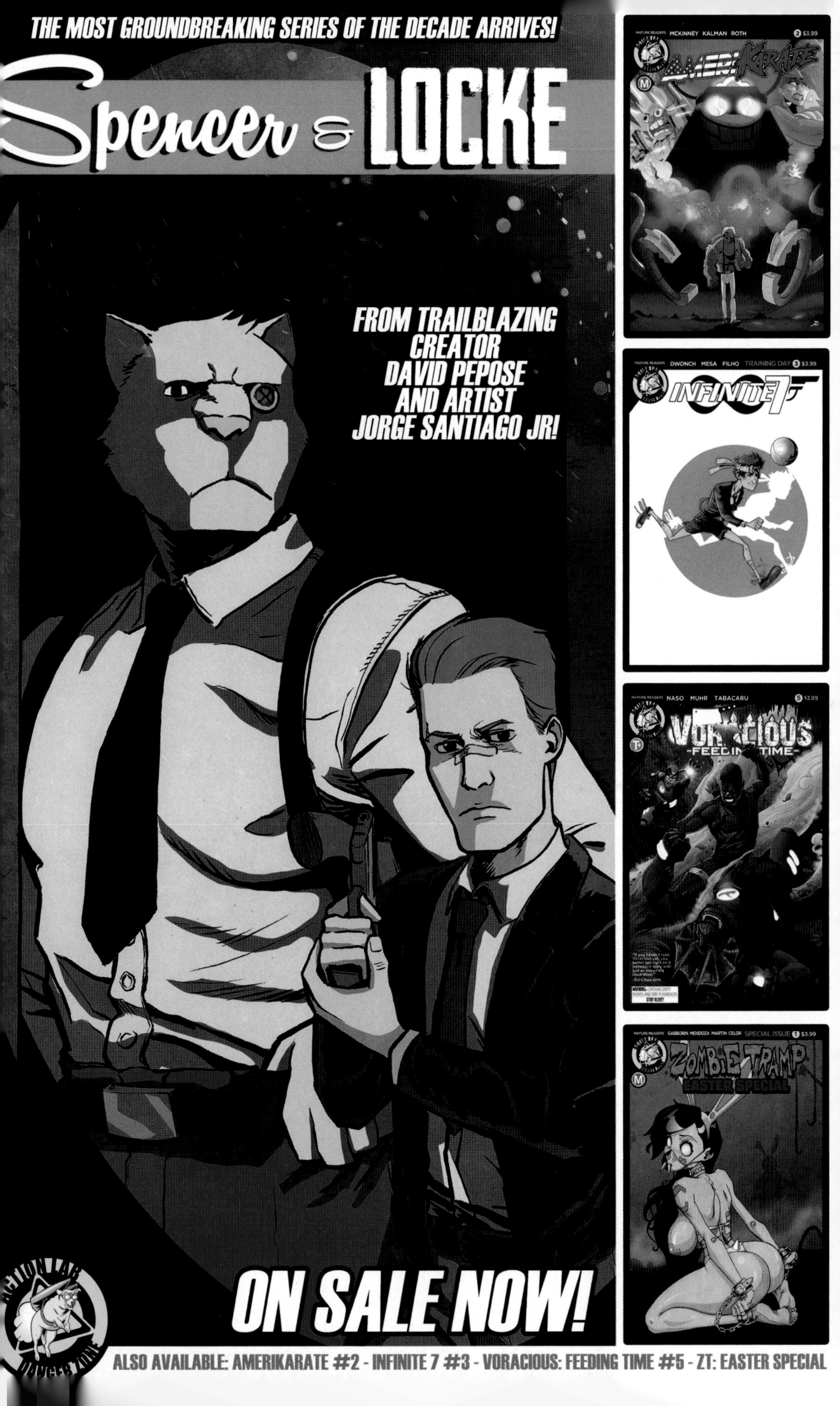
THE MOST GROUNDBREAKING SERIES OF THE DECADE ARRIVES!
Spencer & LOCKE
FROM TRAILBLAZING CREATOR DAVID PEPOSE AND ARTIST JORGE SANTIAGO JR!
ON SALE NOW!
MATURE READERS MCKINNEY KALMAN ROTH 2 $3.99
AMERIKARATE
MATURE READERS DWONCH MESA FILHO TRAINING DAY 3 $3.99
INFINITE 7
MATURE READERS NASO MUHR TABACARU 5 $3.99
VORACIOUS -FEEDING TIME-
MATURE READERS GABBORN MENDOZA MARTIN CELOR SPECIAL ISSUE 1 $3.99
ZOMBIE TRAMP EASTER SPECIAL
ACTION LAB DANGER ZONE
ALSO AVAILABLE: AMERIKARATE #2 - INFINITE 7 #3 - VORACIOUS: FEEDING TIME #5 - ZT: EASTER SPECIAL

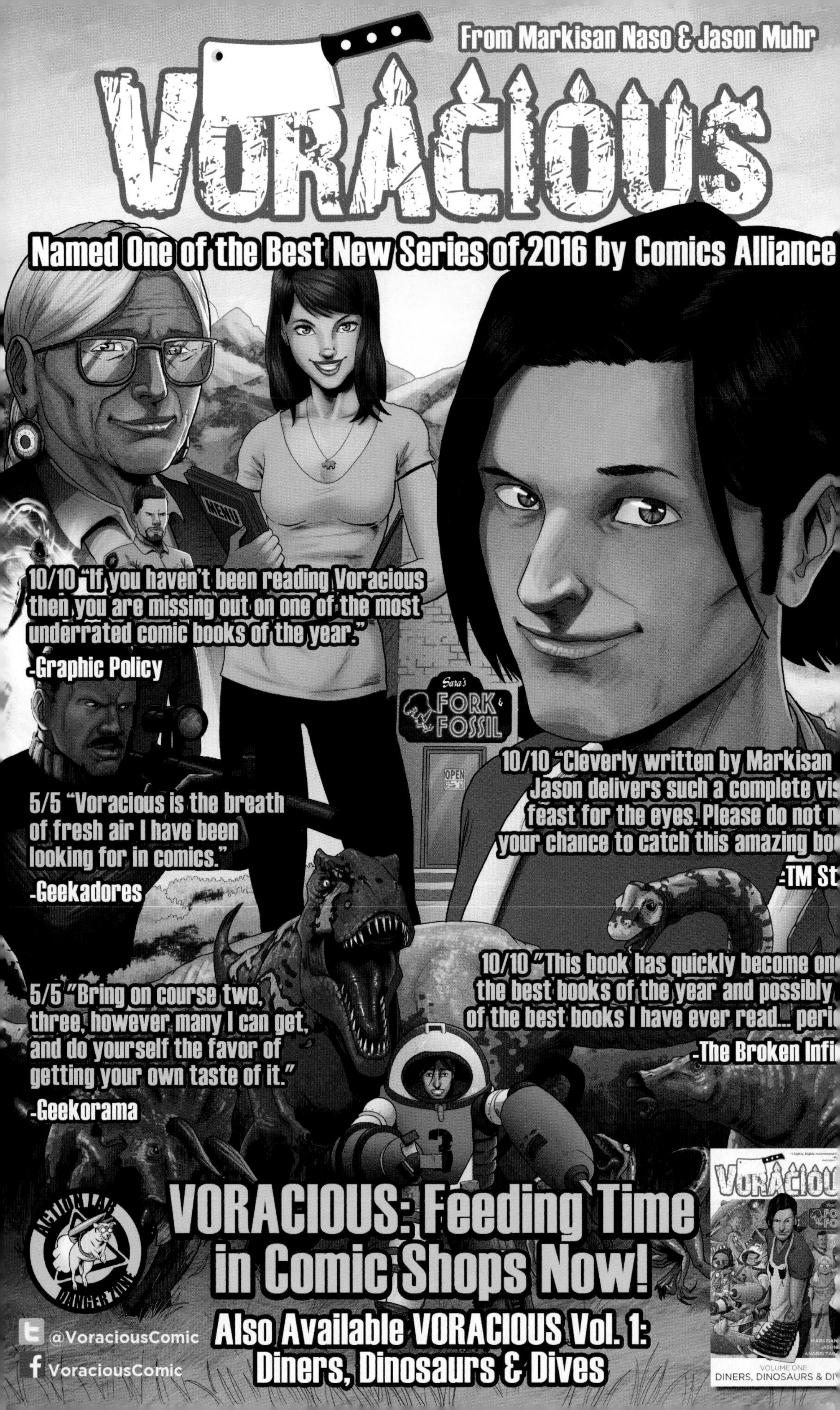

From Markisan Naso & Jason Muhr
VORACIOUS
Named One of the Best New Series of 2016 by Comics Alliance
MENU
10/10 "If you haven't been reading Voracious then you are missing out on one of the most underrated comic books of the year."
-Graphic Policy
Sara's FORK & FOSSIL
OPEN
10/10 "Cleverly written by Markisan
Jason delivers such a complete vi
feast for the eyes. Please do not
your chance to catch this amazing bo
-TM St
5/5 "Voracious is the breath of fresh air I have been looking for in comics."
-Geekadores
10/10 "This book has quickly become on
the best books of the year and possibly
of the best books I have ever read... peri
-The Broken Infi
5/5 "Bring on course two, three, however many I can get, and do yourself the favor of getting your own taste of it."
-Geekorama
ACTION LAB DANGER ZONE
VORACIOUS: Feeding Time in Comic Shops Now!
@VoraciousComic
VoraciousComic
Also Available VORACIOUS Vol. 1: Diners, Dinosaurs & Dives
VOLUME ONE: DINERS, DINOSAURS & DI

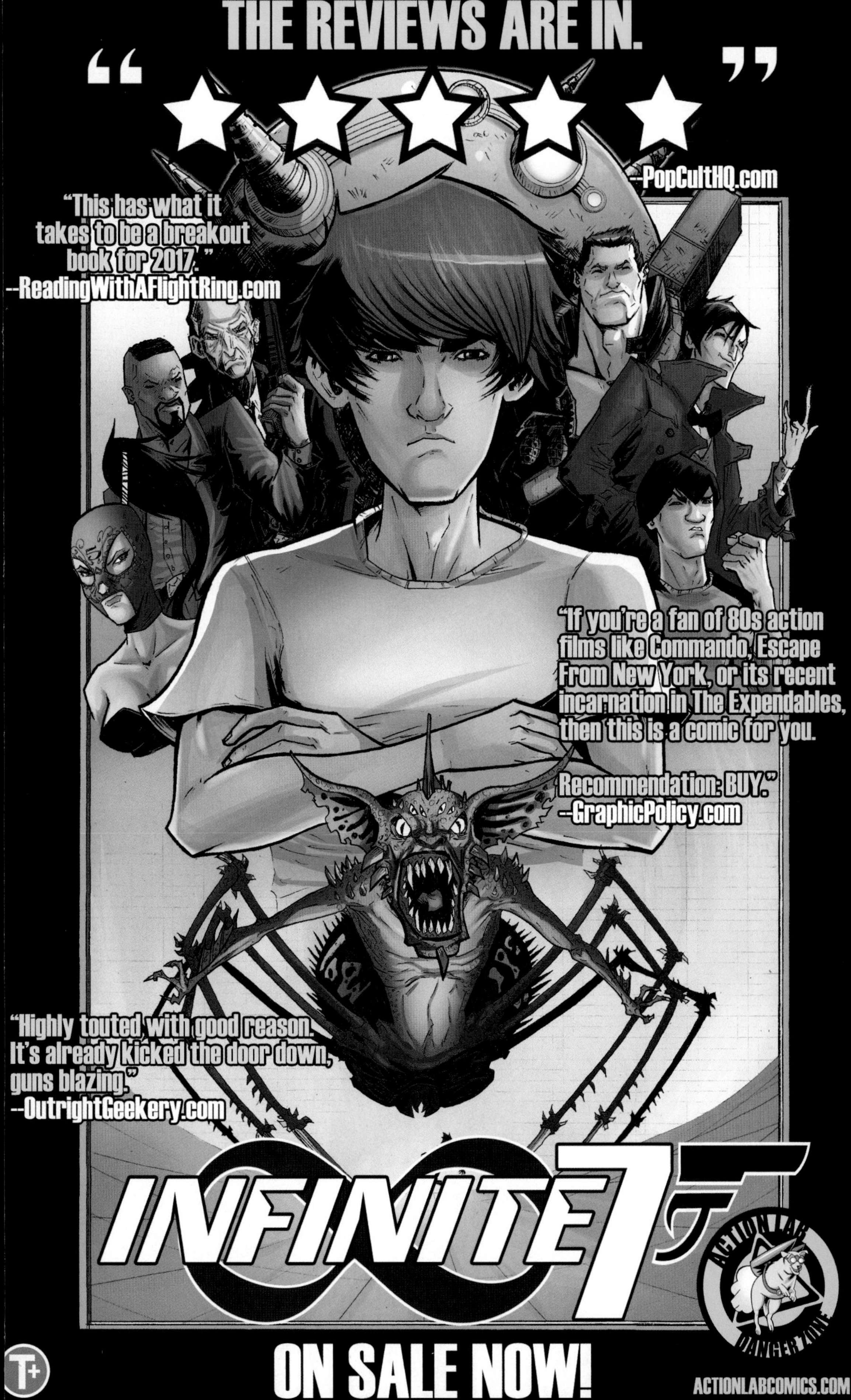
THE REVIEWS ARE IN.
“★★★★★”
--PopCultHQ.com
“This has what it takes to be a breakout book for 2017.”
--ReadingWithAFlightRing.com
“If you're a fan of 80s action films like Commando, Escape From New York, or its recent incarnation in The Expendables, then this is a comic for you.
Recommendation: BUY.”
--GraphicPolicy.com
“Highly touted with good reason. It's already kicked the door down, guns blazing.”
--OutrightGeekery.com
INFINITE 7
ACTION LAB DANGER ZONE
T+
ON SALE NOW!
ACTIONLABCOMICS.COM

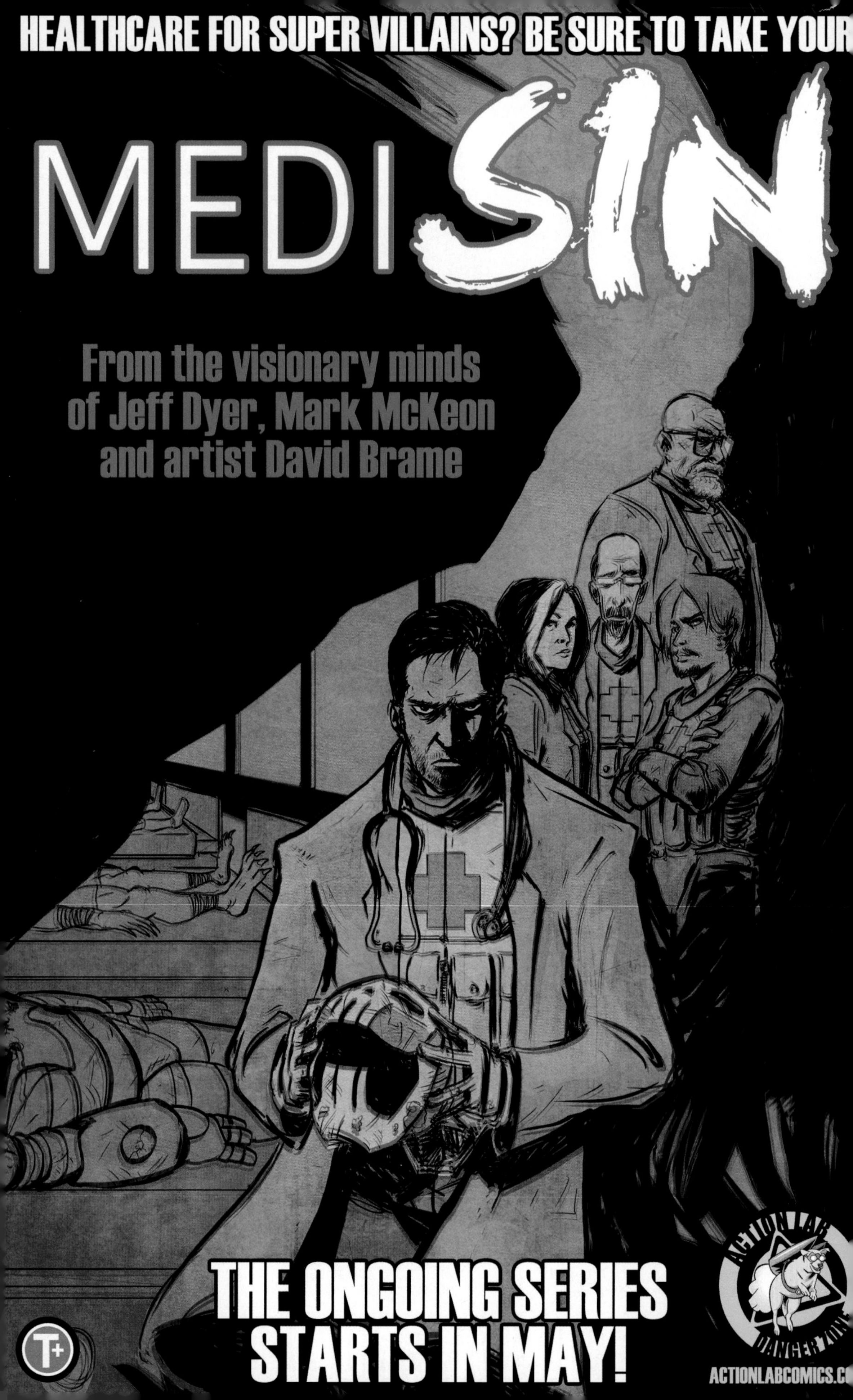
HEALTHCARE FOR SUPER VILLAINS? BE SURE TO TAKE YOUR
MEDISIN
From the visionary minds of Jeff Dyer, Mark McKeon and artist David Brame
THE ONGOING SERIES STARTS IN MAY!
T+
ACTION LAB DANGER ZONE
ACTIONLABCOMICS.C

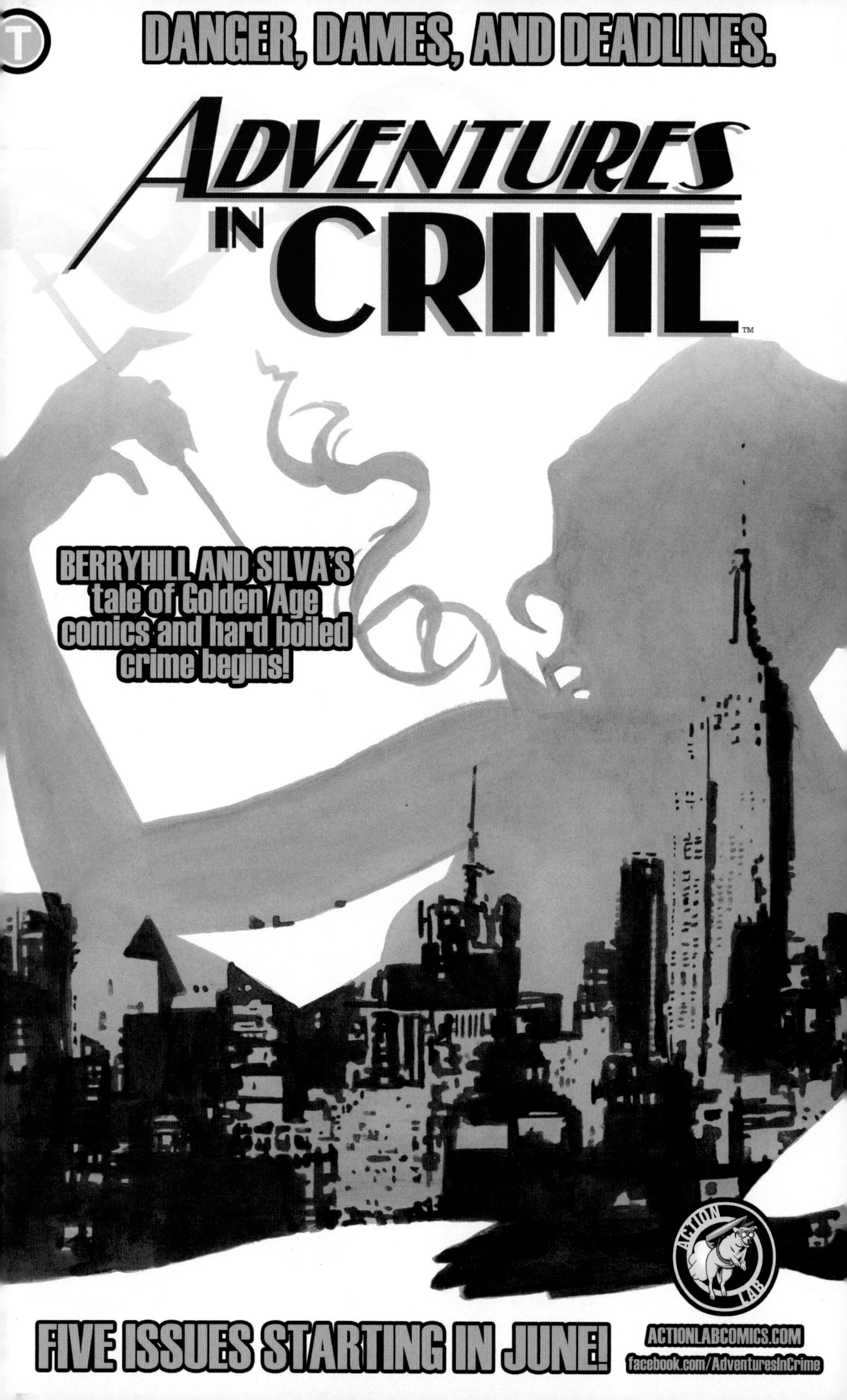
DANGER, DAMES, AND DEADLINES.
ADVENTURES IN CRIME™
BERRYHILL AND SILVA'S tale of Golden Age comics and hard boiled crime begins!
ACTION LAB
FIVE ISSUES STARTING IN JUNE!
ACTIONLABCOMICS.COM
facebook.com/AdventuresInCrime

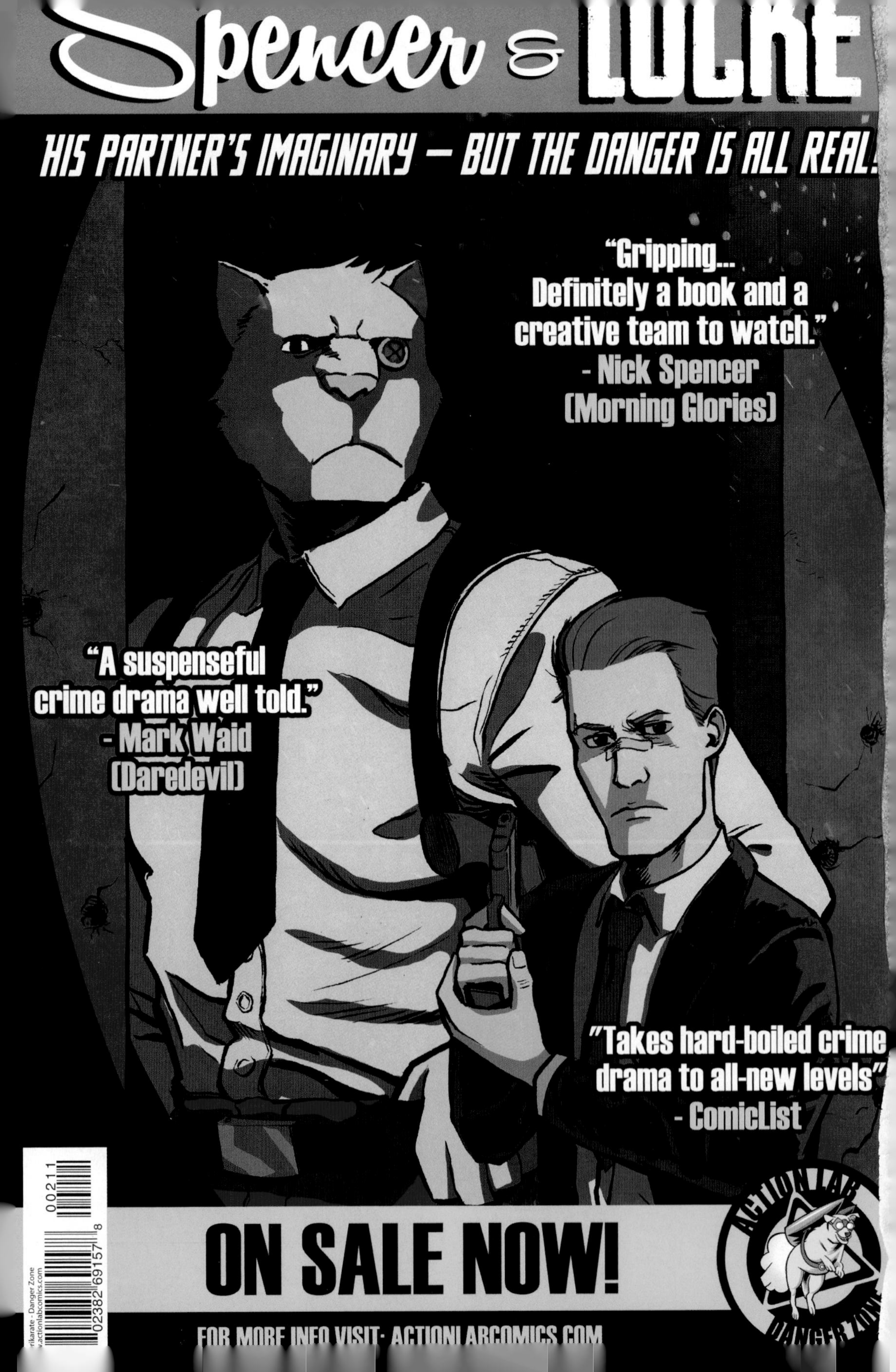
Spencer & LOCKE
HIS PARTNER'S IMAGINARY — BUT THE DANGER IS ALL REAL!
"Gripping... Definitely a book and a creative team to watch."
- Nick Spencer (Morning Glories)
"A suspenseful crime drama well told."
- Mark Waid (Daredevil)
"Takes hard-boiled crime drama to all-new levels"
- ComicList
ON SALE NOW!
ACTION LAB DANGER ZONE
FOR MORE INFO VISIT: ACTIONLABCOMICS.COM

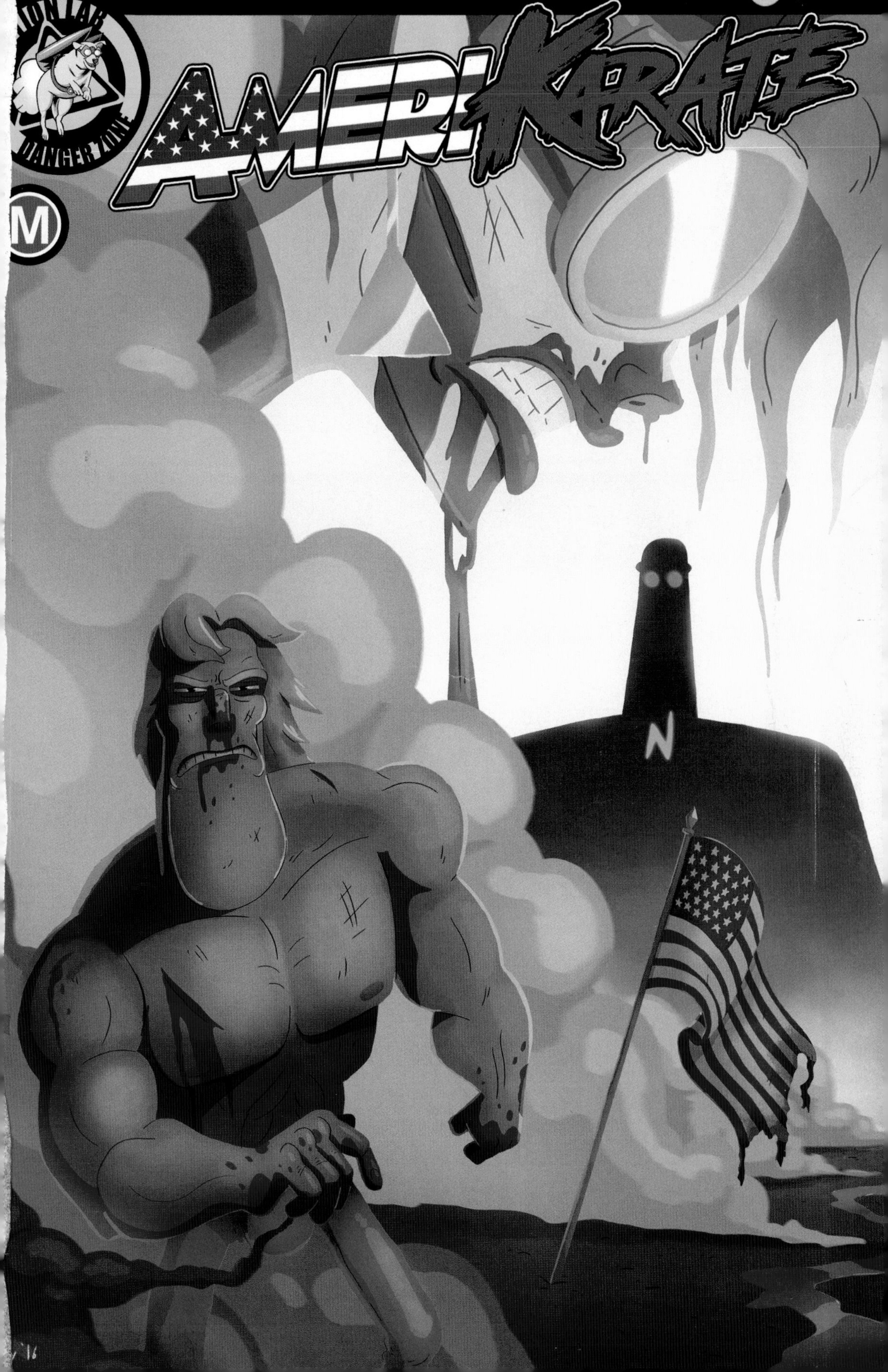
AMERIKARATE
DANGER ZONE
M

ACTION LAB: DANGER ZONE PRESENTS

Super HARD
Super KARATE

AMERIKARATE

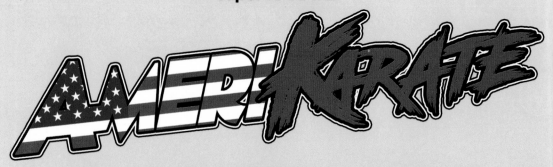

WRITTEN BY
COREY KALMAN & BROCKTON McKINNEY

ILLUSTRATED BY
DEVIN ROTH

LETTERS BY
DAVE DWONCH

MCKINNEY KALMAN ROTH
$3.99
AMERIKARATE

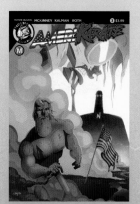

AMERIKARATE REGULAR
Devin Roth & Joey McCormick

MCKINNEY KALMAN ROTH
AmeriKarate

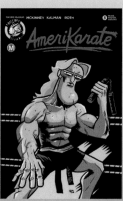

Daniel Arruda Massa ARTIST VARIANT
"Bloodsports"
Limited to 1500

MCKINNEY KALMAN ROTH
AMERIKARATE
CYNTHIA
MASTER THUNDERMOON

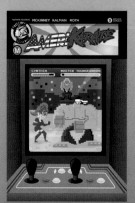

Dave Perillo ARTIST VARIANT
"16 Bit"
Limited to 1500

MCKINNEY KALMAN ROTH
AMERIKARATE

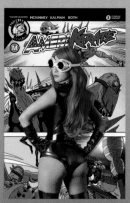

April O'Neil PHOTO VARIANT
Limited to 1500

AMERIKARATE #3 May 2017.

Published by Action Lab Comics.

Printed in Canada.
First printing.

ACTIONLABCOMICS.COM

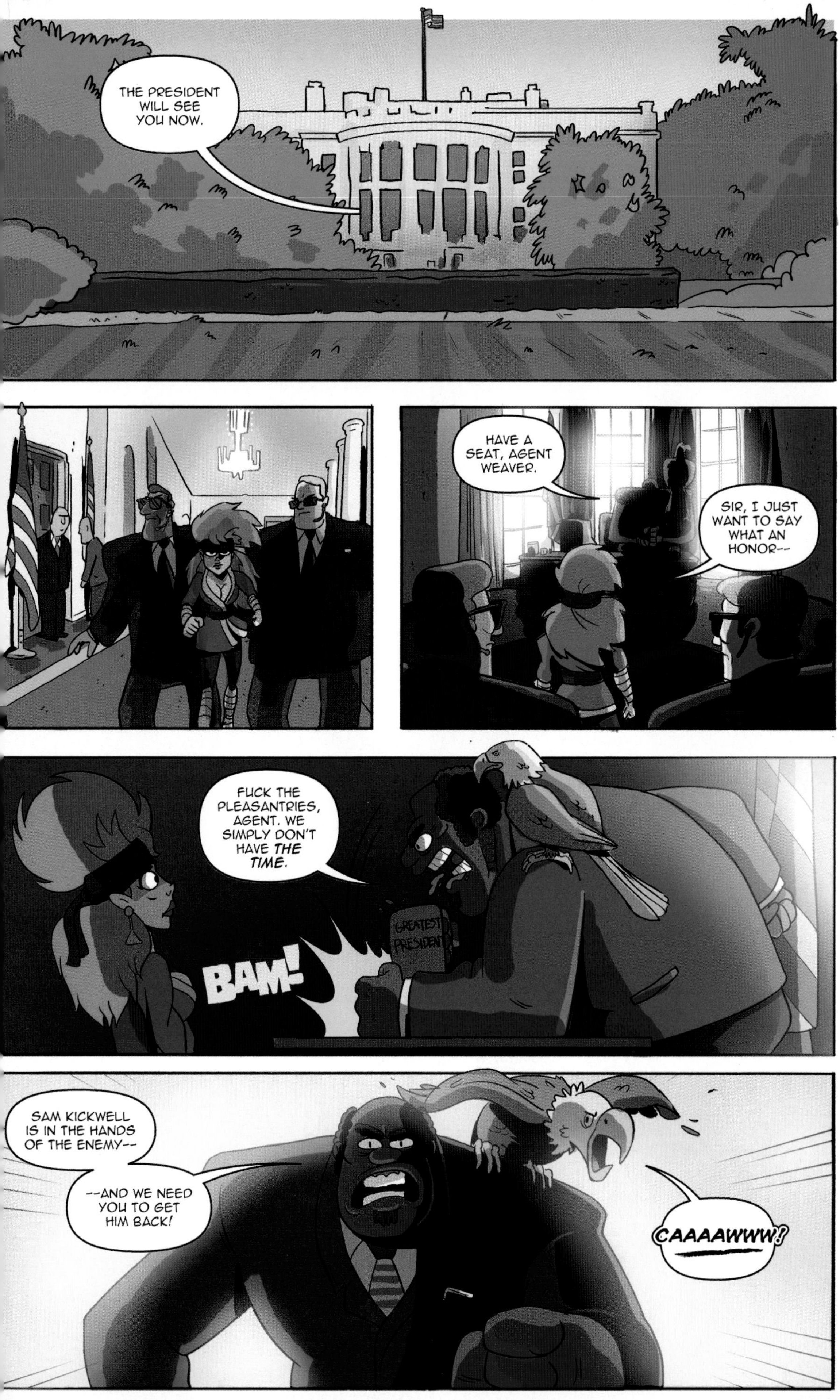
THE PRESIDENT WILL SEE YOU NOW.
HAVE A SEAT, AGENT WEAVER.
SIR, I JUST WANT TO SAY WHAT AN HONOR--
FUCK THE PLEASANTRIES, AGENT. WE SIMPLY DON'T HAVE THE TIME.
GREATEST PRESIDENT
BAM!
SAM KICKWELL IS IN THE HANDS OF THE ENEMY--
--AND WE NEED YOU TO GET HIM BACK!
CAAAAWWW!

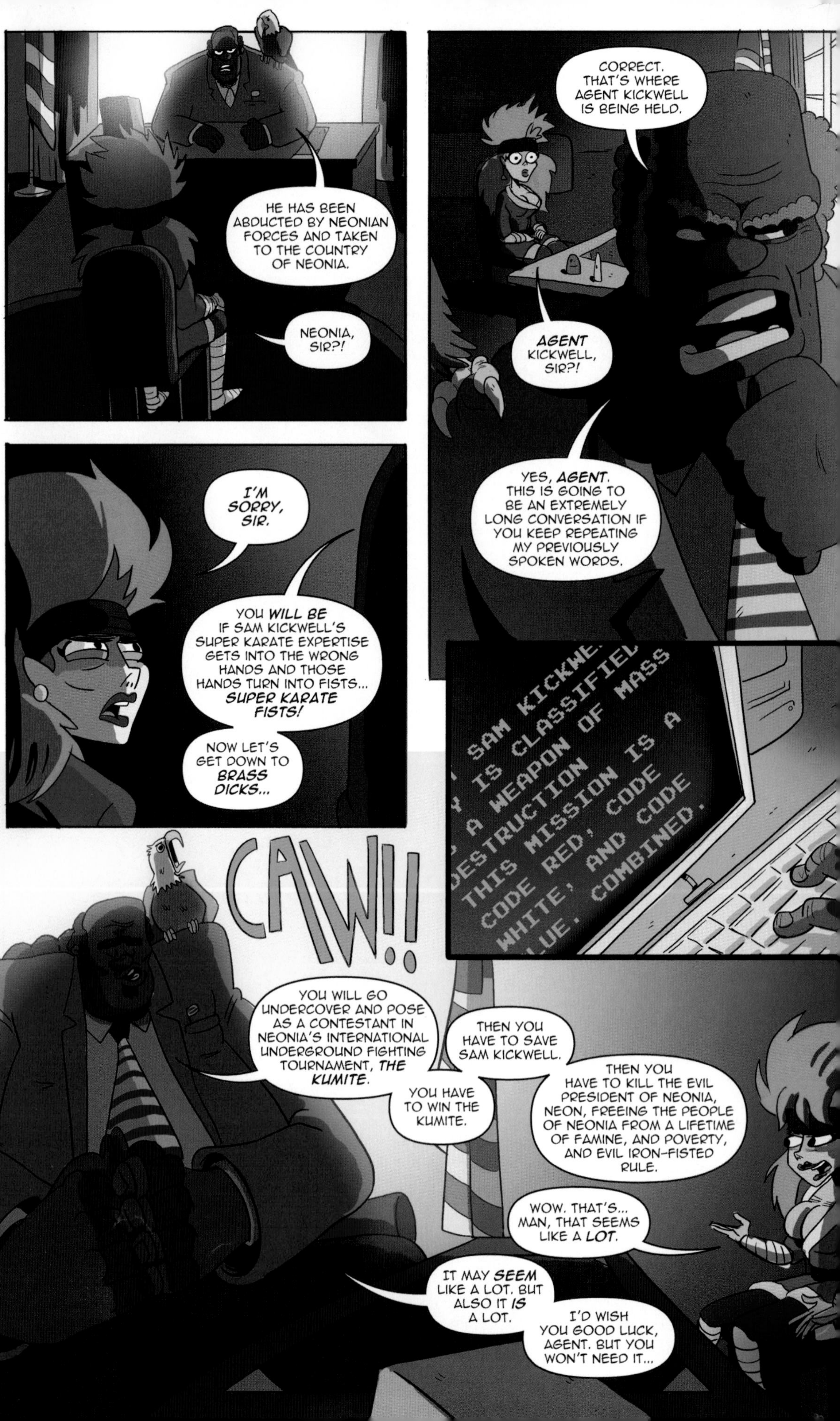
HE HAS BEEN ABDUCTED BY NEONIAN FORCES AND TAKEN TO THE COUNTRY OF NEONIA.
NEONIA, SIR?!
CORRECT. THAT'S WHERE AGENT KICKWELL IS BEING HELD.
AGENT KICKWELL, SIR?!
YES, ***AGENT***. THIS IS GOING TO BE AN EXTREMELY LONG CONVERSATION IF YOU KEEP REPEATING MY PREVIOUSLY SPOKEN WORDS.
I'M SORRY, SIR.
YOU ***WILL BE*** IF SAM KICKWELL'S SUPER KARATE EXPERTISE GETS INTO THE WRONG HANDS AND THOSE HANDS TURN INTO FISTS... ***SUPER KARATE FISTS!***
NOW LET'S GET DOWN TO ***BRASS DICKS...***
SAM KICKWE
IS CLASSIFIED
A WEAPON OF MASS
DESTRUCTION
THIS MISSION IS A
CODE RED, CODE
WHITE, AND CODE
LUE. COMBINED.
CAW!!
YOU WILL GO UNDERCOVER AND POSE AS A CONTESTANT IN NEONIA'S INTERNATIONAL UNDERGROUND FIGHTING TOURNAMENT, ***THE KUMITE***.
THEN YOU HAVE TO SAVE SAM KICKWELL.
YOU HAVE TO WIN THE KUMITE.
THEN YOU HAVE TO KILL THE EVIL PRESIDENT OF NEONIA, NEON, FREEING THE PEOPLE OF NEONIA FROM A LIFETIME OF FAMINE, AND POVERTY, AND EVIL IRON-FISTED RULE.
WOW. THAT'S... MAN, THAT SEEMS LIKE A ***LOT***.
IT MAY ***SEEM*** LIKE A LOT. BUT ALSO IT ***IS*** A LOT.
I'D WISH YOU GOOD LUCK, AGENT. BUT YOU WON'T NEED IT...

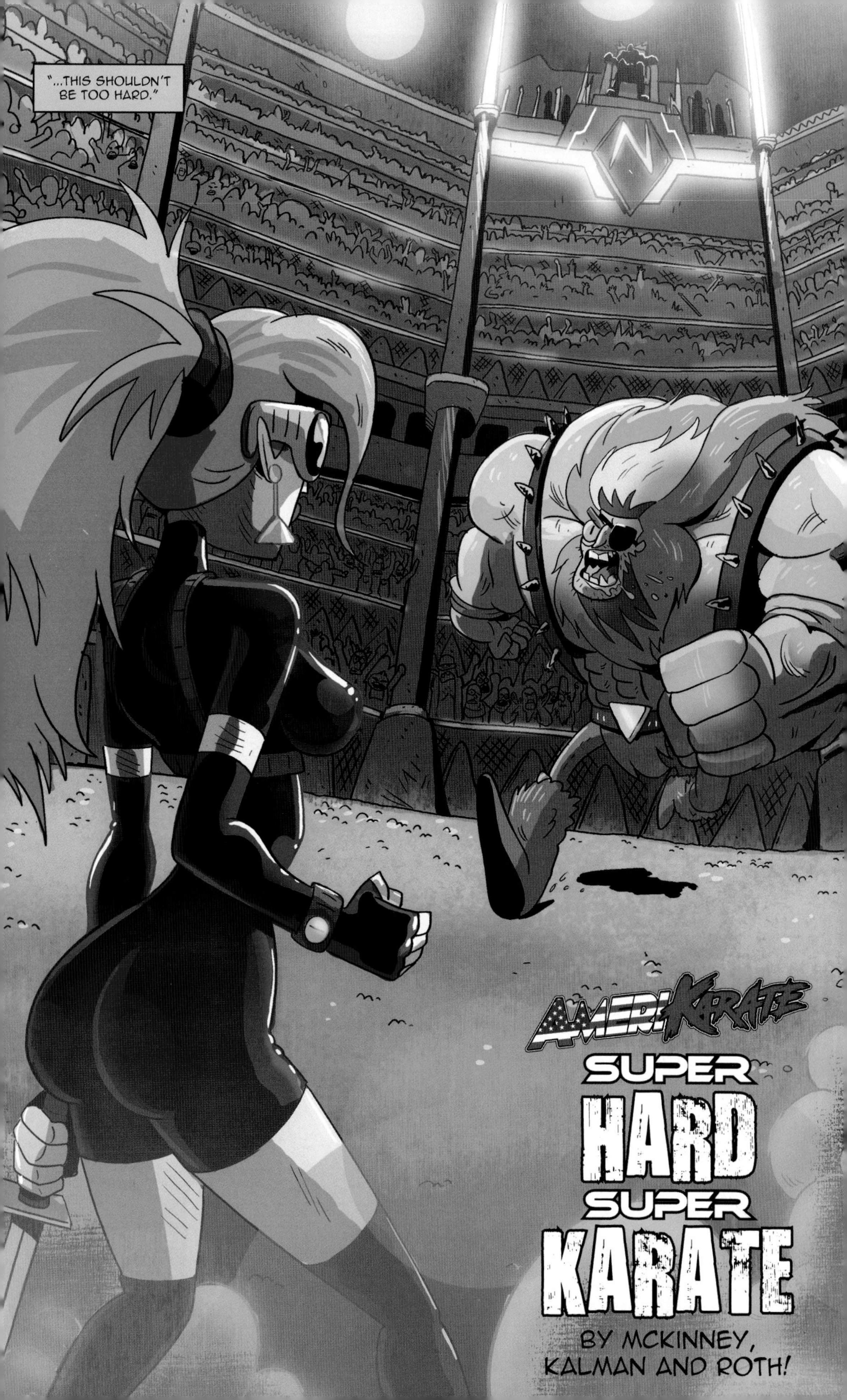
"...THIS SHOULDN'T BE TOO HARD."
AMERIKARATE
SUPER HARD SUPER KARATE
BY MCKINNEY, KALMAN AND ROTH!

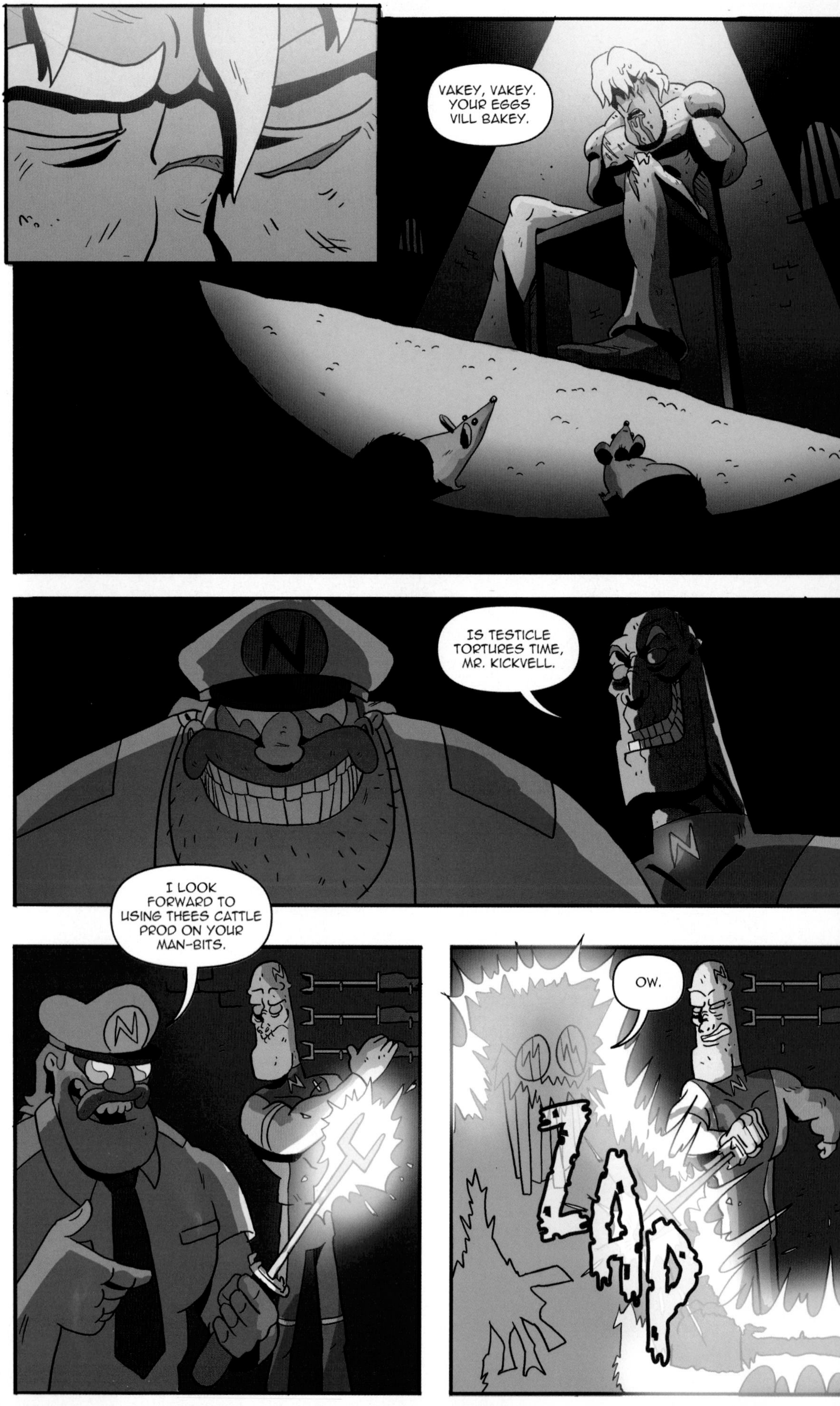
VAKEY, VAKEY. YOUR EGGS VILL BAKEY.
IS TESTICLE TORTURES TIME, MR. KICKVELL.
I LOOK FORWARD TO USING THEES CATTLE PROD ON YOUR MAN-BITS.
OW.
ZAP

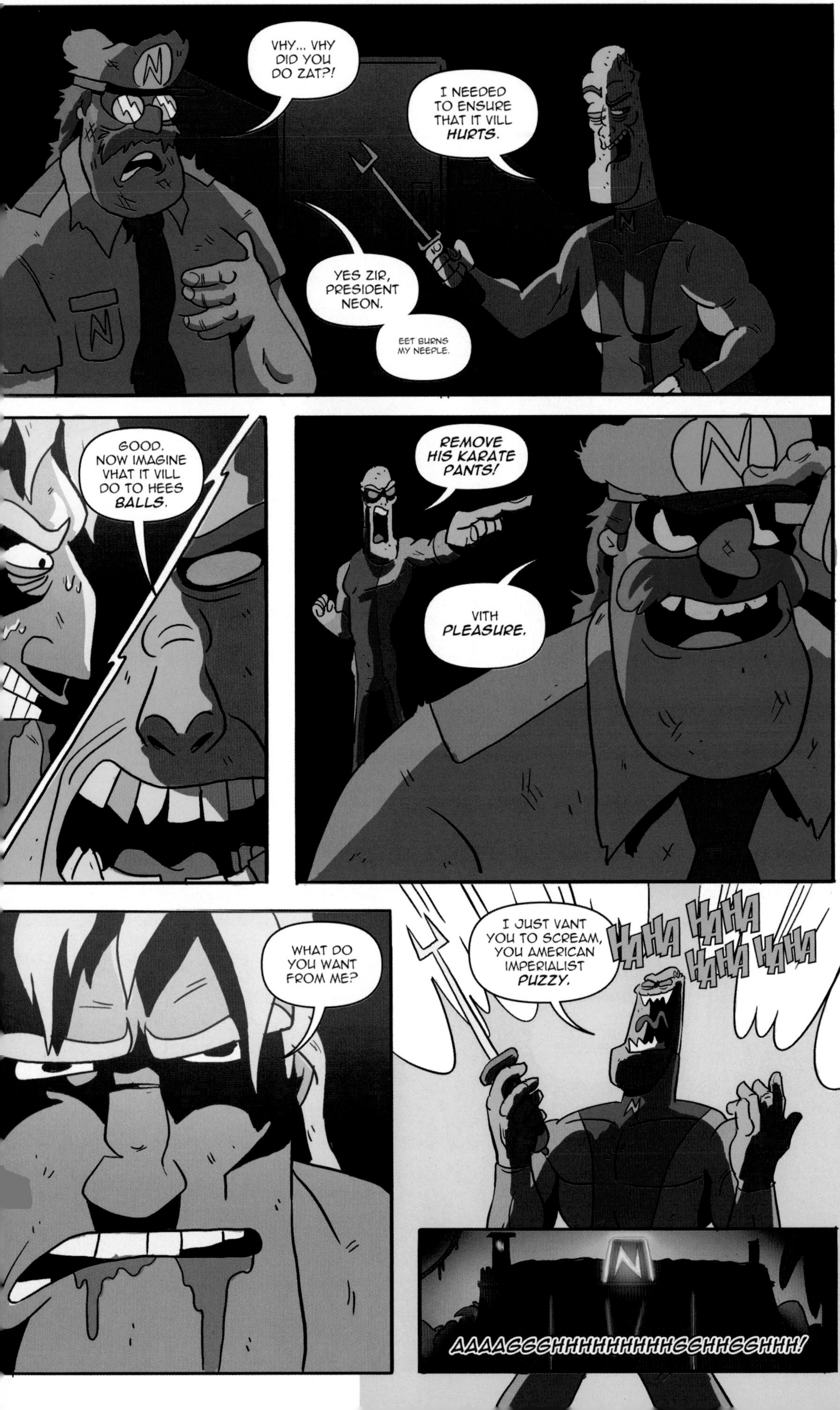
VHY... VHY DID YOU DO ZAT?!
I NEEDED TO ENSURE THAT IT VILL *HURTS*.
YES ZIR, PRESIDENT NEON.
EET BURNS MY NEEPLE.
GOOD. NOW IMAGINE VHAT IT VILL DO TO HEES *BALLS*.
REMOVE HIS KARATE PANTS!
VITH *PLEASURE*.
WHAT DO YOU WANT FROM ME?
I JUST VANT YOU TO SCREAM, YOU AMERICAN IMPERIALIST *PUZZY*.
HAHA HAHA HAHA HAHA
AAAAGGGHHHHHHHHHHGGHHGGHHH!

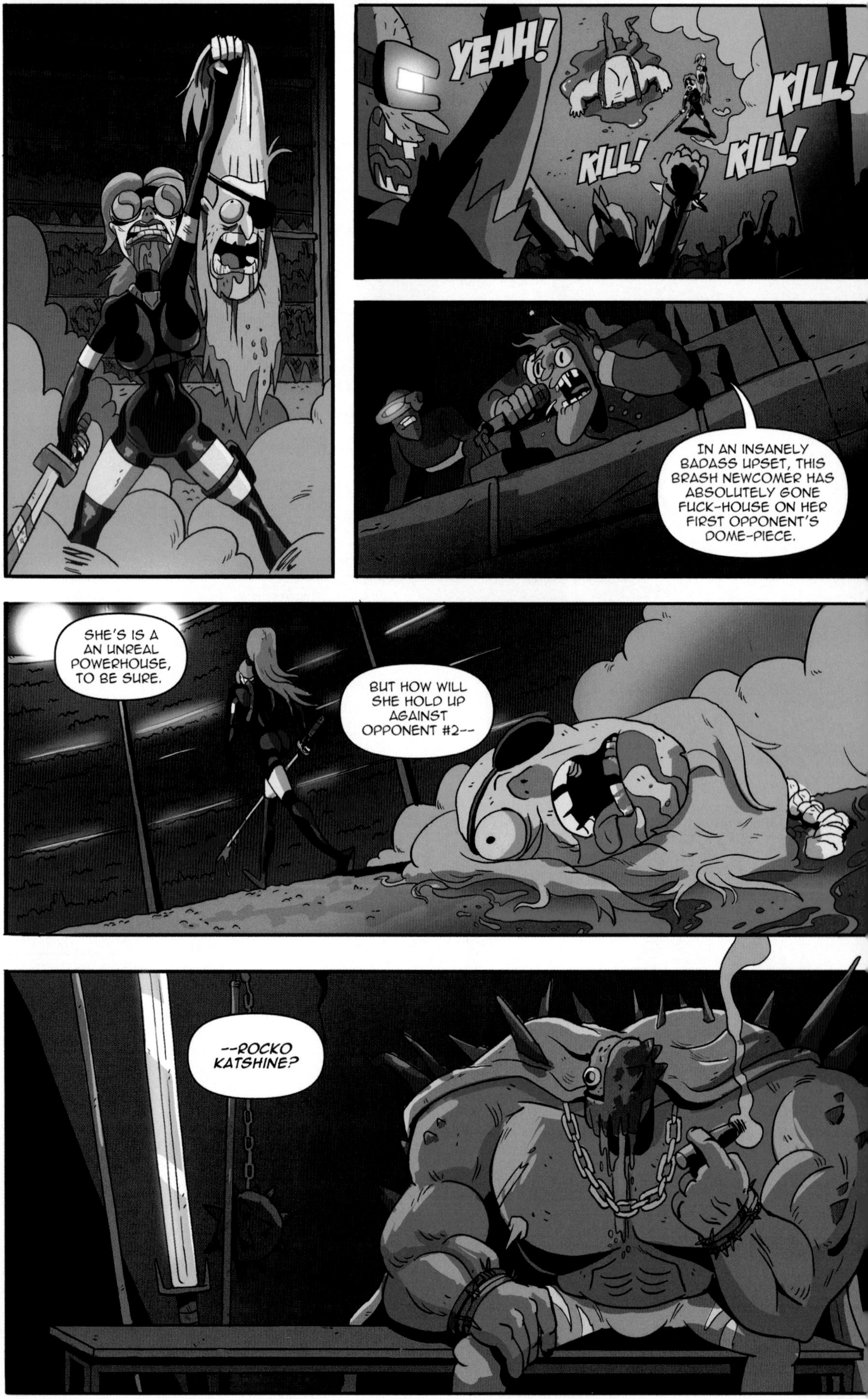

YEAH!
KILL!
KILL!
KILL!
IN AN INSANELY BADASS UPSET, THIS BRASH NEWCOMER HAS ABSOLUTELY GONE FUCK-HOUSE ON HER FIRST OPPONENT'S DOME-PIECE.
SHE'S IS A AN UNREAL POWERHOUSE, TO BE SURE.
BUT HOW WILL SHE HOLD UP AGAINST OPPONENT #2--
--ROCKO KATSHINE?

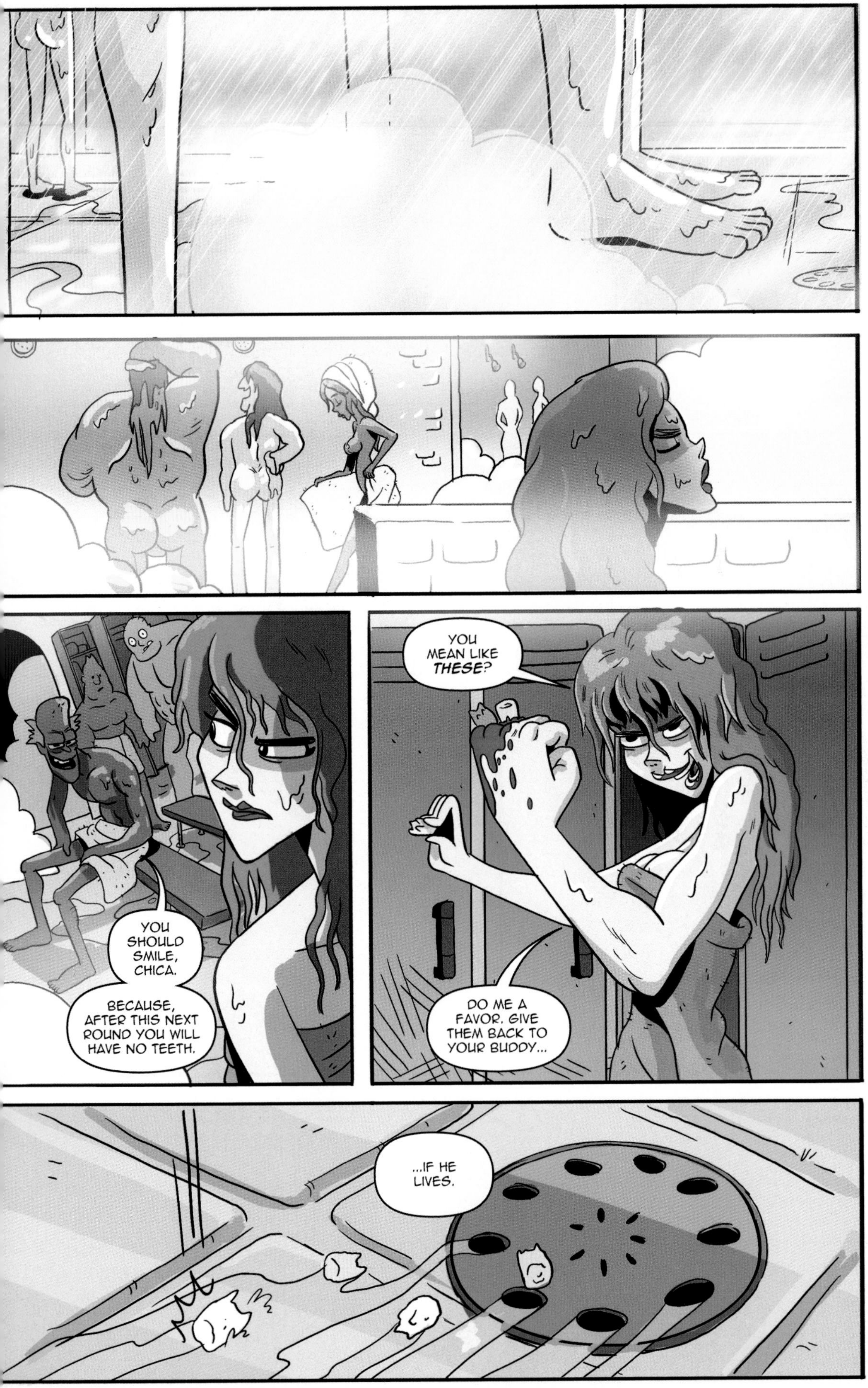
YOU SHOULD SMILE, CHICA.
BECAUSE, AFTER THIS NEXT ROUND YOU WILL HAVE NO TEETH.
YOU MEAN LIKE *THESE*?
DO ME A FAVOR. GIVE THEM BACK TO YOUR BUDDY...
...IF HE LIVES.

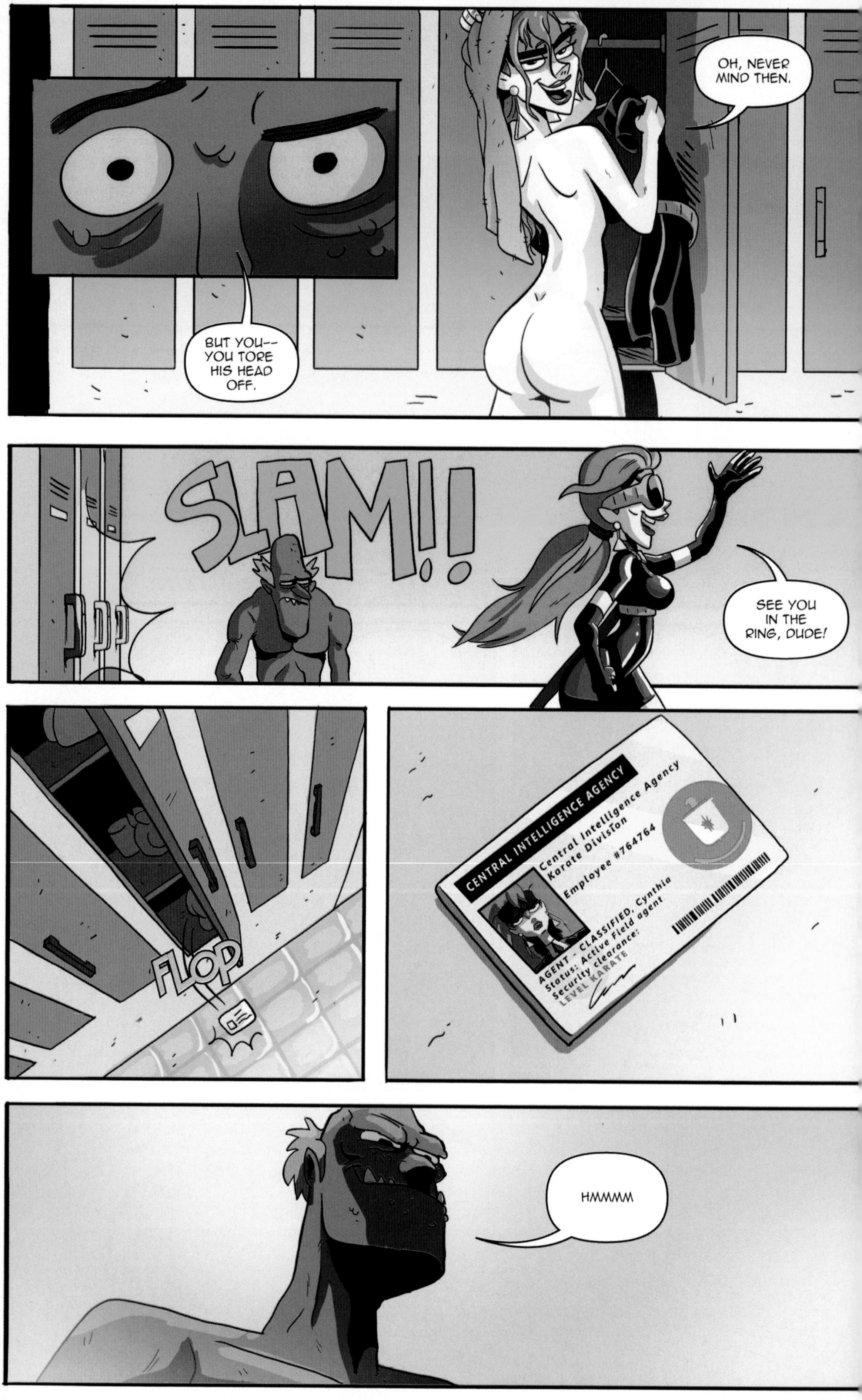
OH, NEVER MIND THEN.
BUT YOU-- YOU TORE HIS HEAD OFF.
SLAM!!
SEE YOU IN THE RING, DUDE!
FLOP
CENTRAL INTELLIGENCE AGENCY
Central Intelligence Agency
Karate Division
Employee #764764
AGENT - CLASSIFIED, Cynthia
Status: Active Field agent
Security clearance:
LEVEL KARATE
HMMMM

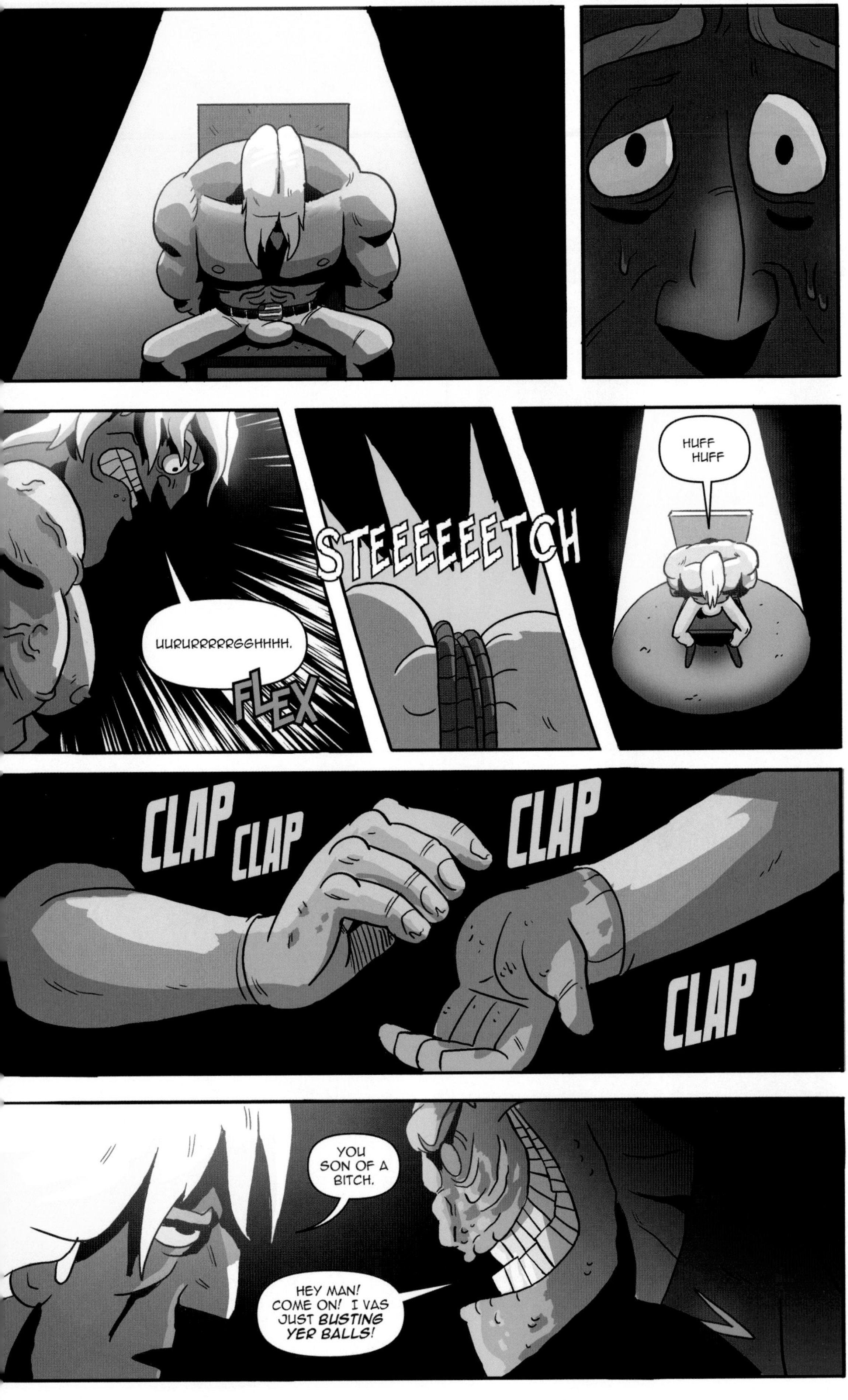
UURURRRRRGGHHHH.
FLEX
STEEEEEEETCH
HUFF HUFF
CLAP
CLAP
CLAP
CLAP
YOU SON OF A BITCH.
HEY MAN! COME ON! I VAS JUST BUSTING YER BALLS!

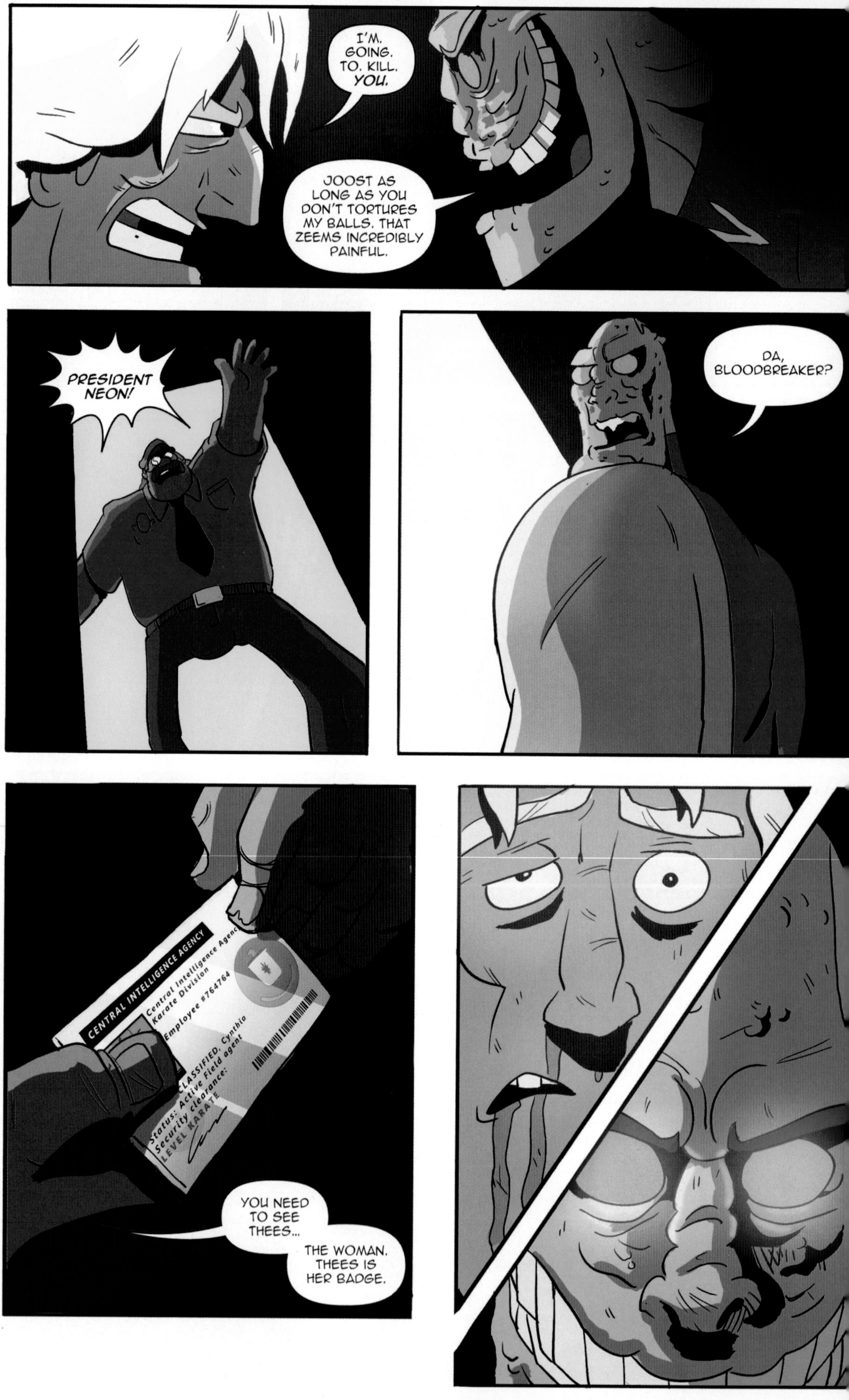
I'M. GOING. TO. KILL. YOU.
JOOST AS LONG AS YOU DON'T TORTURES MY BALLS. THAT ZEEMS INCREDIBLY PAINFUL.
PRESIDENT NEON!
DA, BLOODBREAKER?
CENTRAL INTELLIGENCE AGENCY
Central Intelligence Agenc
Karate Division
Employee #764764
CLASSIFIED, Cynthia
Status: Active Field agent
Security clearance:
LEVEL KARATE
YOU NEED TO SEE THEES...
THE WOMAN. THEES IS HER BADGE.

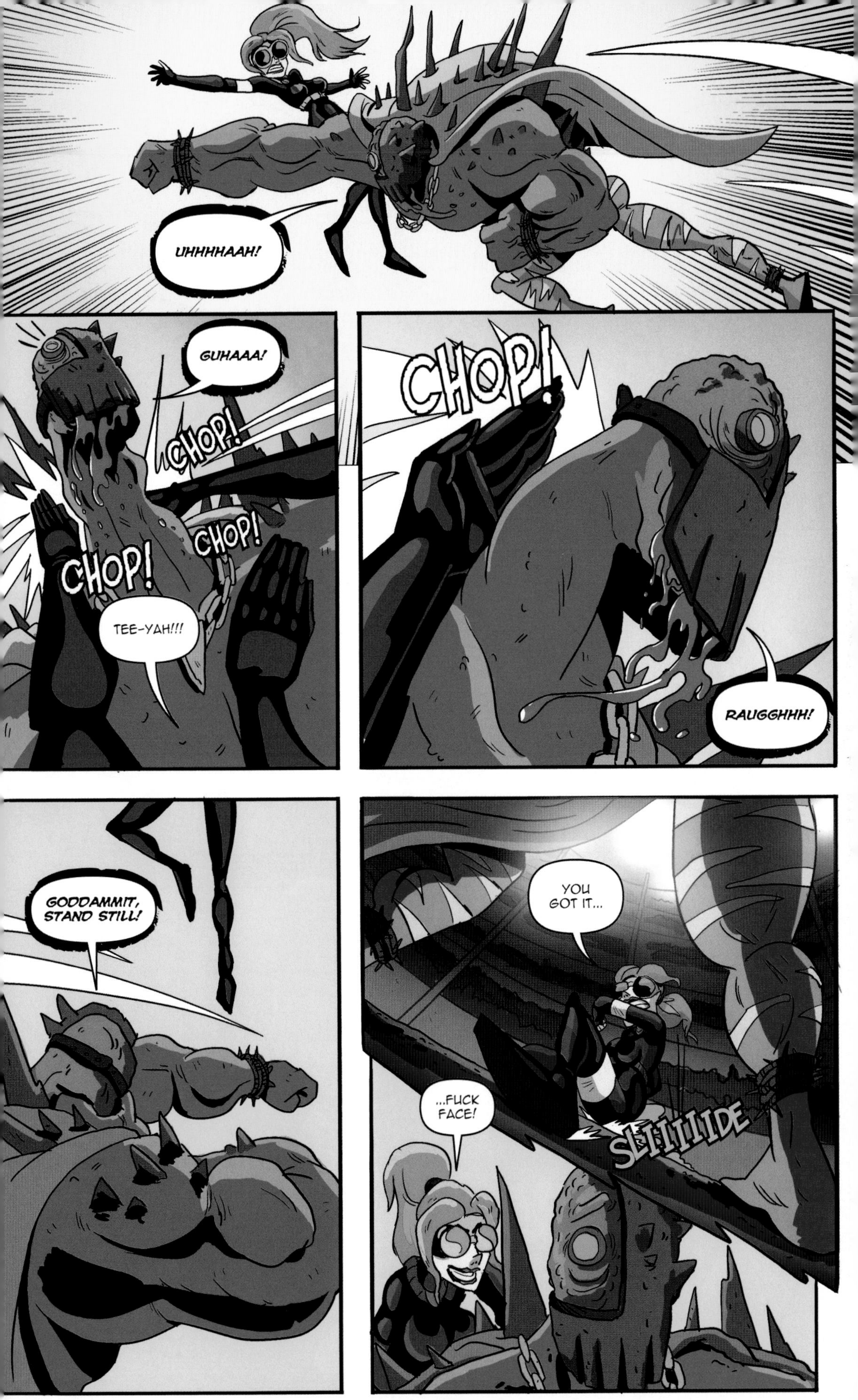
UHHHHAAH!
GUHAAA!
CHOP!
CHOP!
CHOP!
TEE-YAH!!!
CHOP!
RAUGGHHH!
GODDAMMIT, STAND STILL!
YOU GOT IT...
...FUCK FACE!
SLIIIIIDE

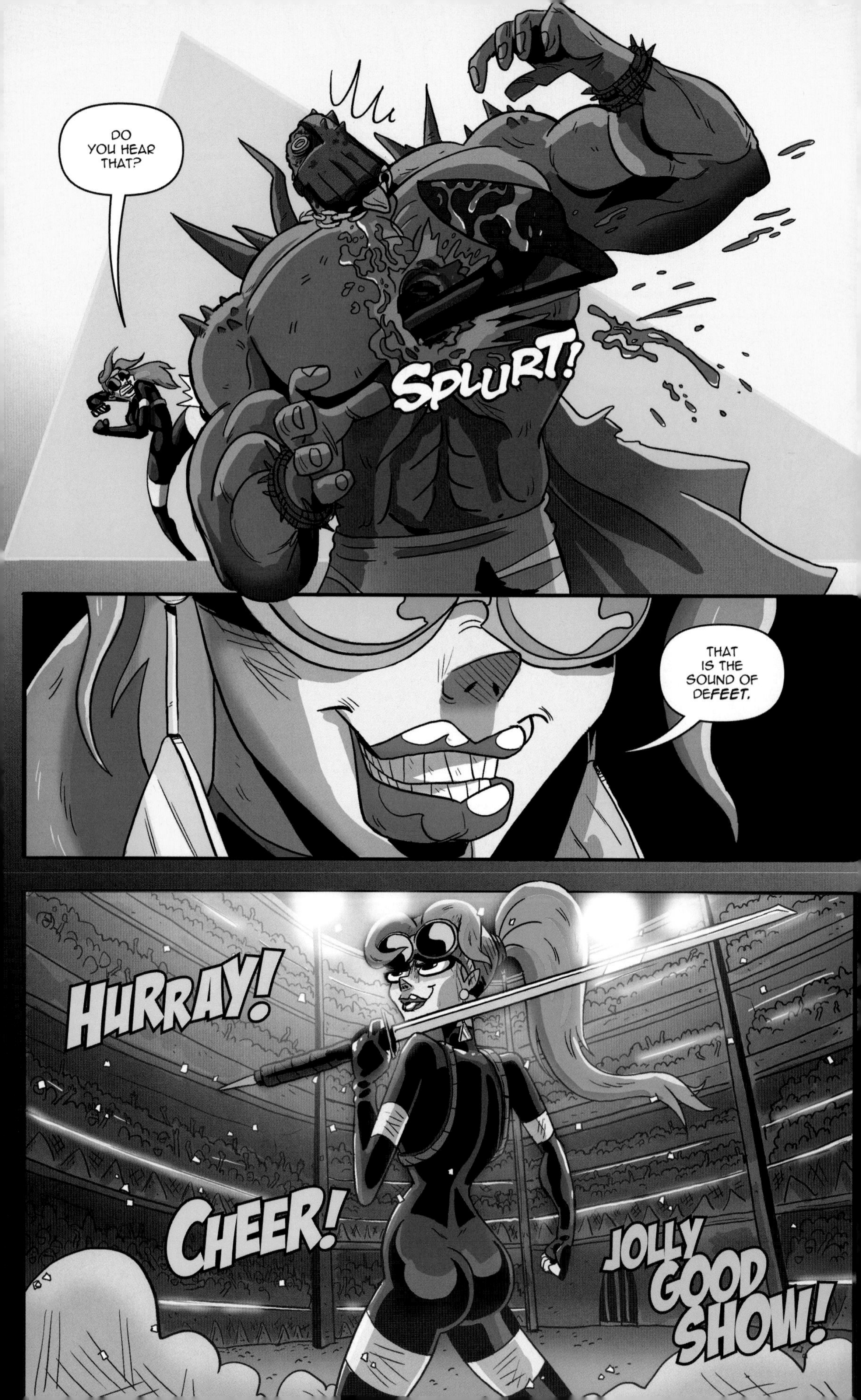
DO YOU HEAR THAT?
SPLURT!
THAT IS THE SOUND OF DEFEET.
HURRAY!
CHEER!
JOLLY GOOD SHOW!

THEES EES THIS TIED-UP HERO'S LADY FRIEND, NO?
ZAT IS CORRECT.
CYNNTHIAAAAAAA!
SHE VON'T BE ABLE TO HEAR YOU. SHE'S ABOUTS TO GET HER EARS REEPED OFF.
FLOP
CENTRAL INTELLIGENCE AGENCY
IT'S TIME SHE MET... MASTER THUNDERMOON.
MASTER THUNDERMOON?!

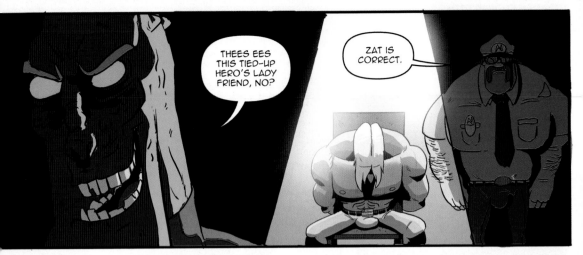

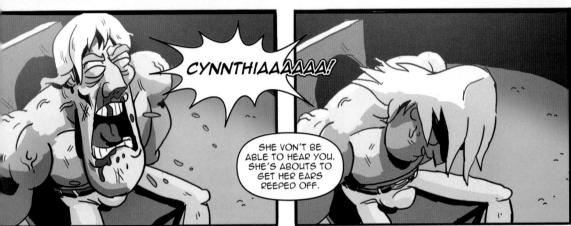

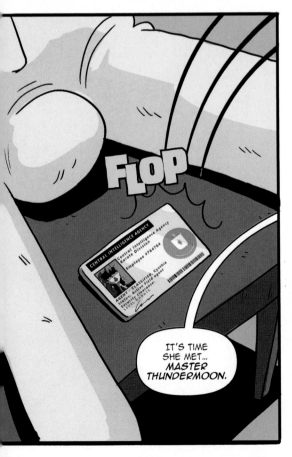

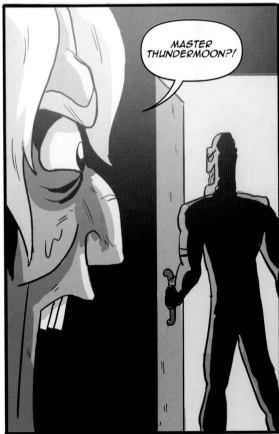

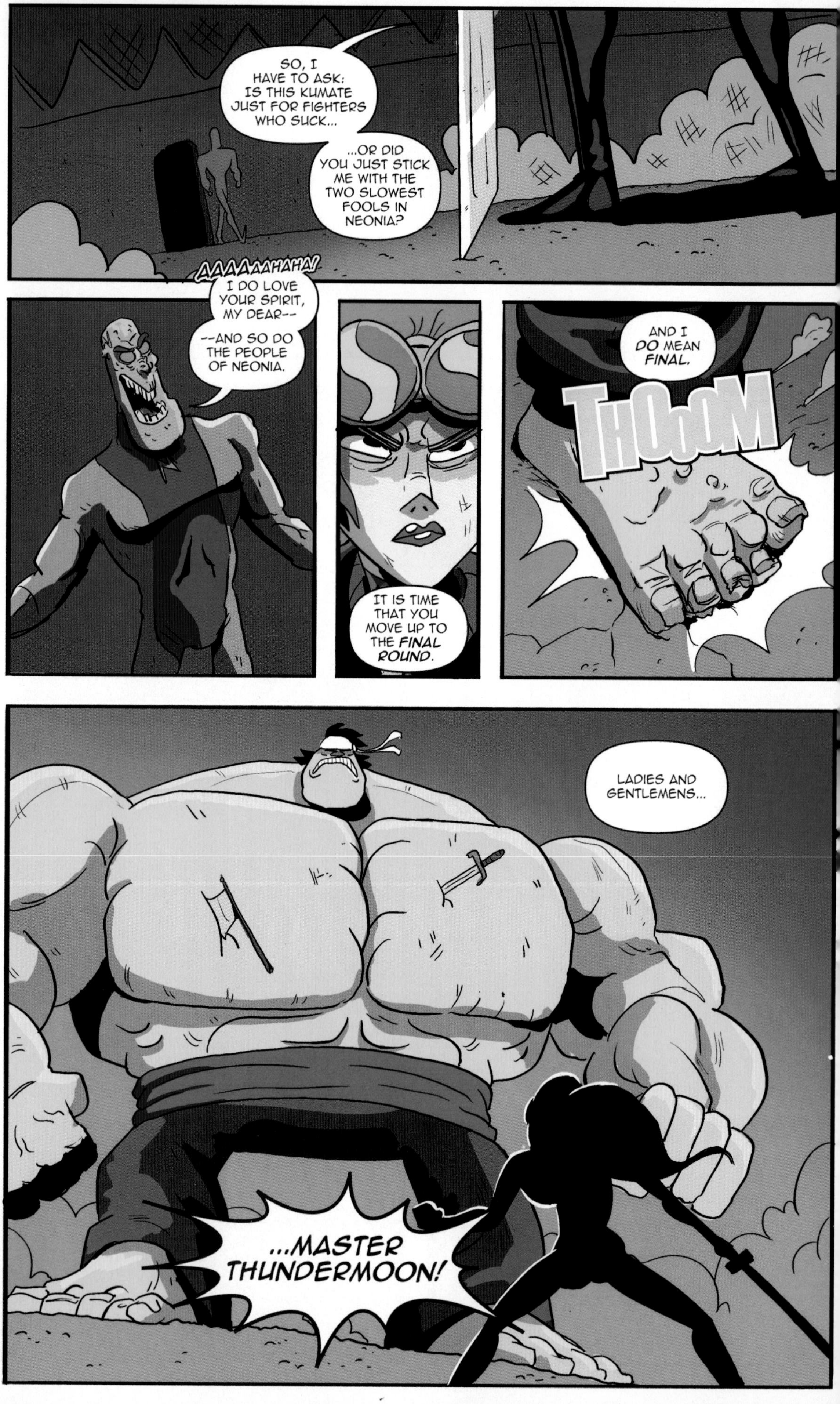
SO, I HAVE TO ASK: IS THIS KUMATE JUST FOR FIGHTERS WHO SUCK...
...OR DID YOU JUST STICK ME WITH THE TWO SLOWEST FOOLS IN NEONIA?
AAAAAAHAHA!
I DO LOVE YOUR SPIRIT, MY DEAR--
--AND SO DO THE PEOPLE OF NEONIA.
IT IS TIME THAT YOU MOVE UP TO THE FINAL ROUND.
AND I DO MEAN FINAL.
THOOOM
LADIES AND GENTLEMENS...
...MASTER THUNDERMOON!

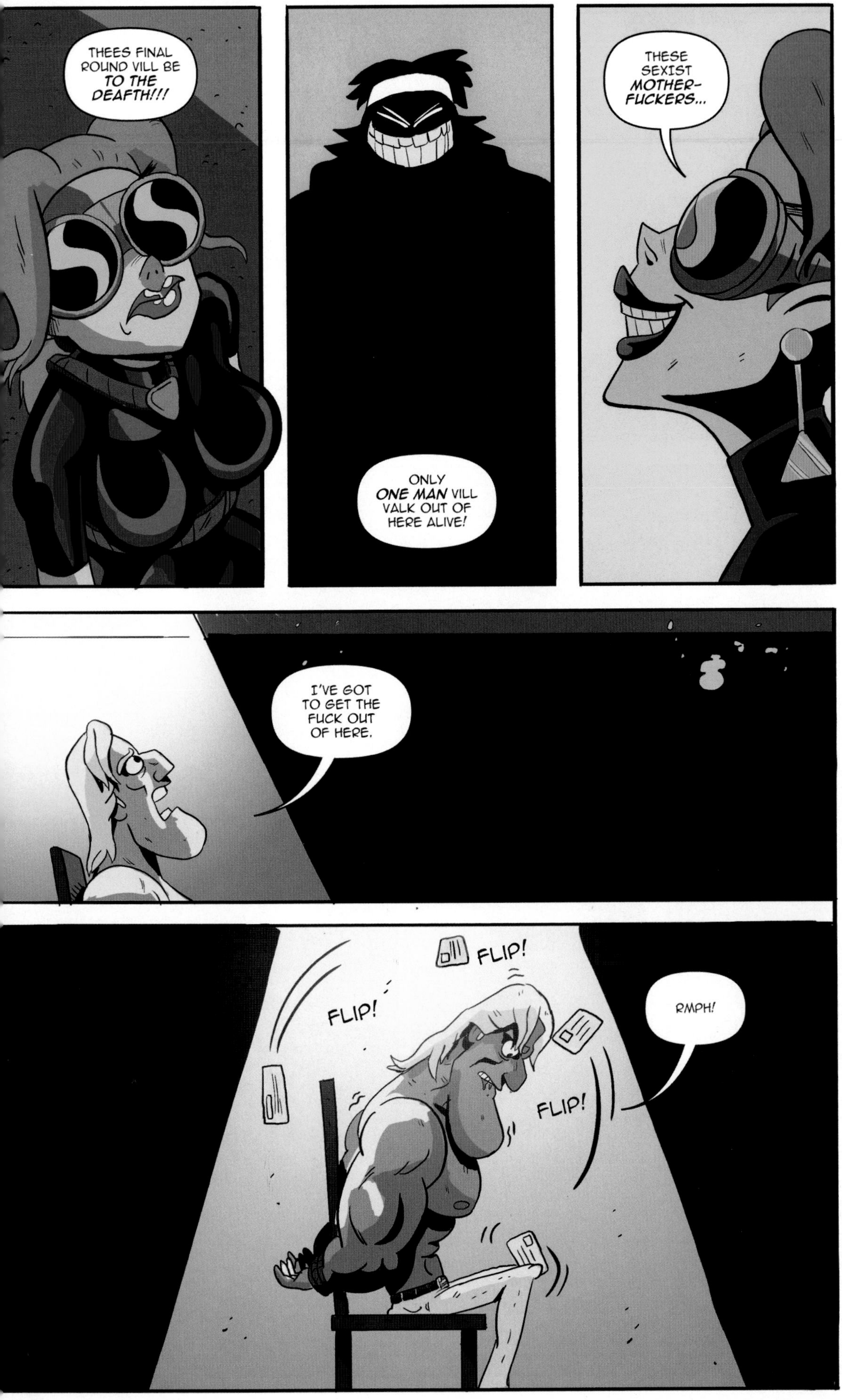
THEES FINAL ROUND VILL BE TO THE DEAFTH!!!
ONLY ONE MAN VILL VALK OUT OF HERE ALIVE!
THESE SEXIST MOTHER-FUCKERS...
I'VE GOT TO GET THE FUCK OUT OF HERE.
FLIP!
FLIP!
RMPH!
FLIP!

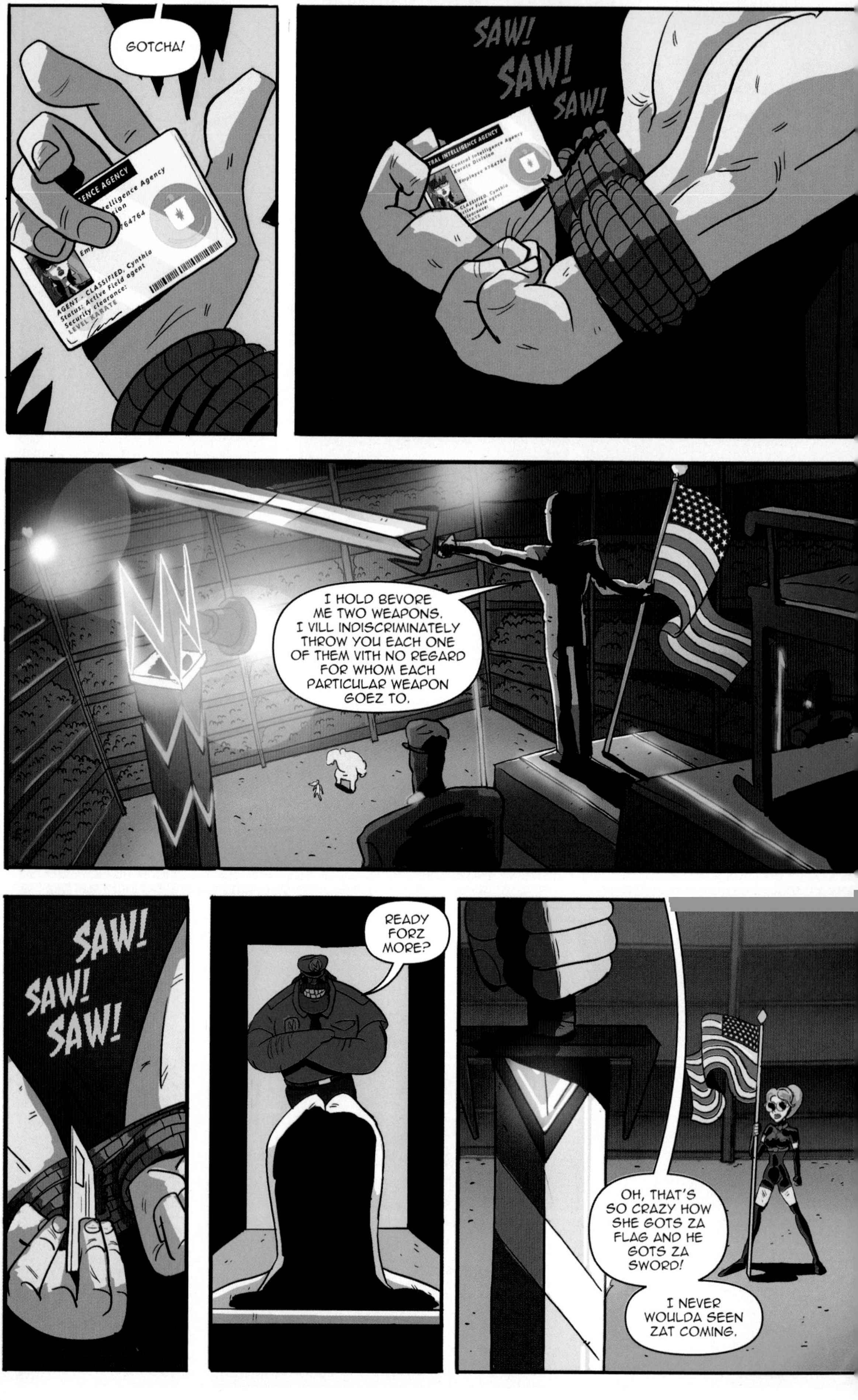
GOTCHA!
SAW! SAW! SAW!
I HOLD BEVORE ME TWO WEAPONS. I VILL INDISCRIMINATELY THROW YOU EACH ONE OF THEM VITH NO REGARD FOR WHOM EACH PARTICULAR WEAPON GOEZ TO.
SAW! SAW! SAW!
READY FORZ MORE?
OH, THAT'S SO CRAZY HOW SHE GOTS ZA FLAG AND HE GOTS ZA SWORD!
I NEVER WOULDA SEEN ZAT COMING.

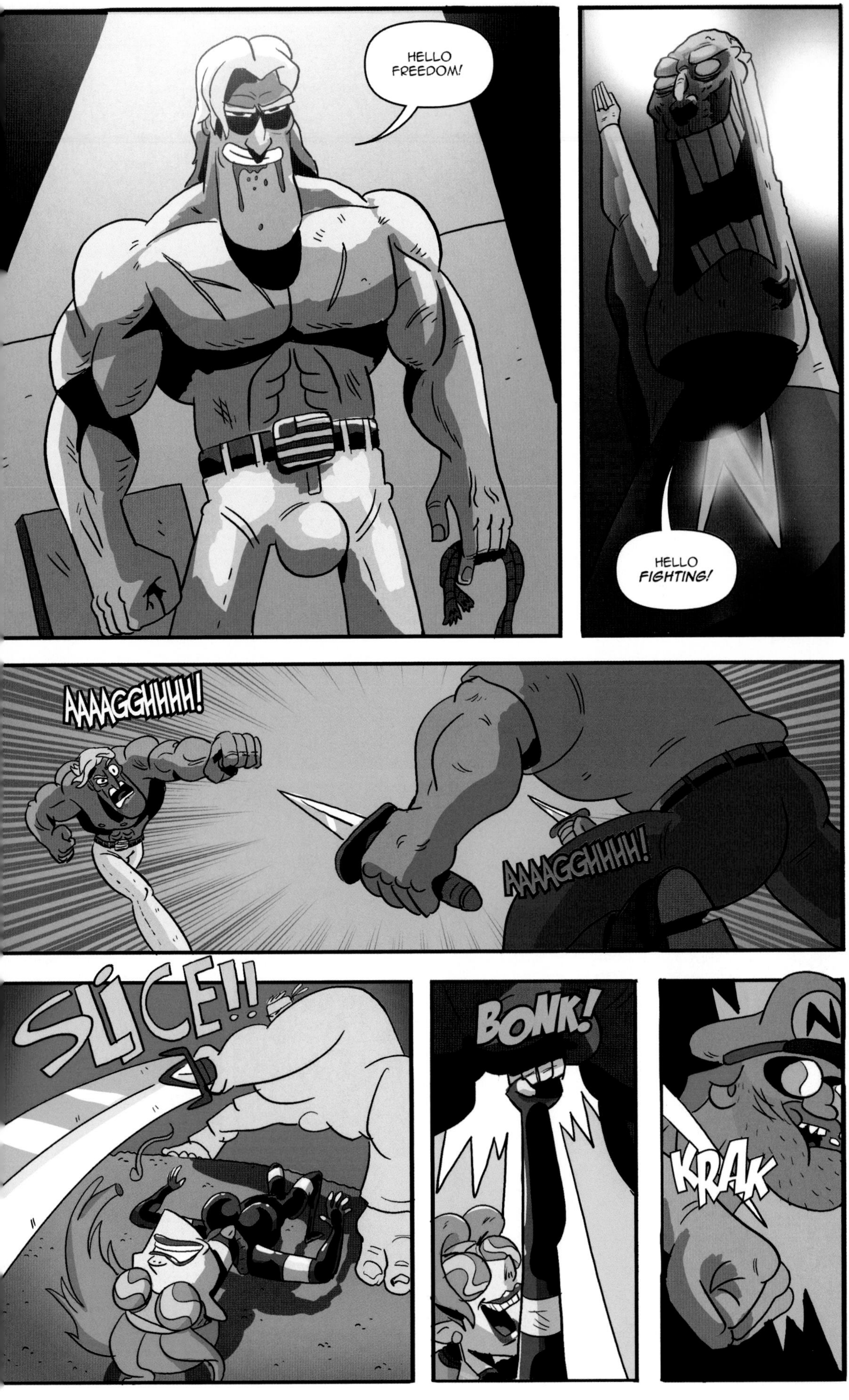
HELLO FREEDOM!
HELLO FIGHTING!
AAAAGGHHHH!
AAAAGGHHHH!
SLICE!!
BONK!
KRAK

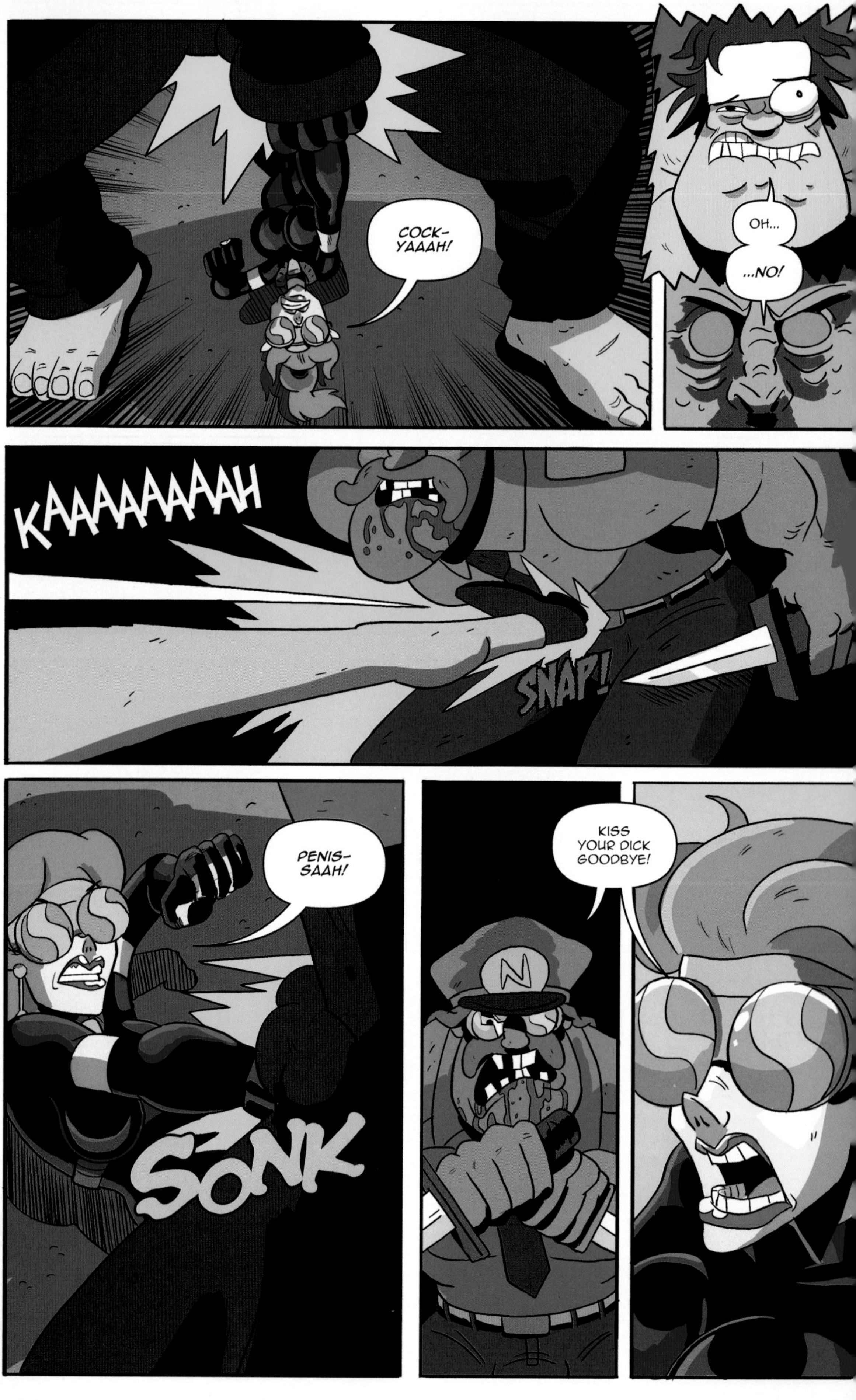
COCK-YAAAH!
OH...
...NO!
KAAAAAAAAH
SNAP!
PENIS-SAAH!
SONK
KISS YOUR DICK GOODBYE!

PUNCH!
LEG SWEEP!
ADDING TWO MORE FIGHTERS? YOU CHEATING MOTHERFUCK-
YOU WHINE JUST LIKE MY WIFE DID.
RIGHT BEFORE I EXECUTED HER FOR HIGH TREASON.
KRAK
POW

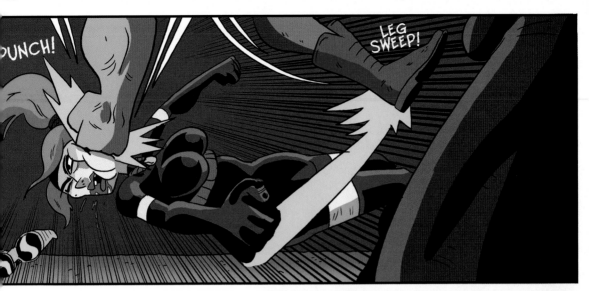

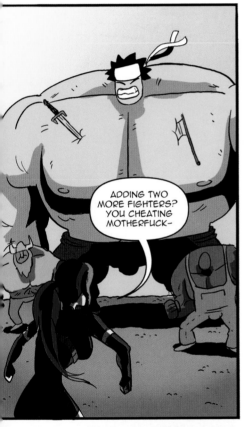

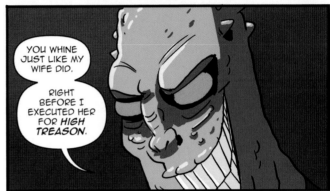

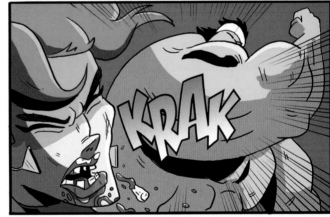

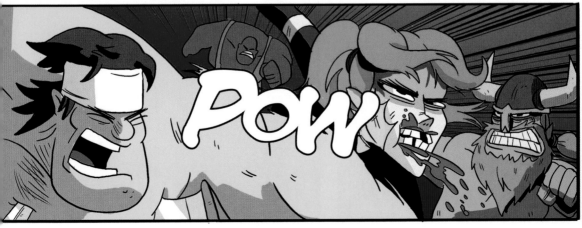

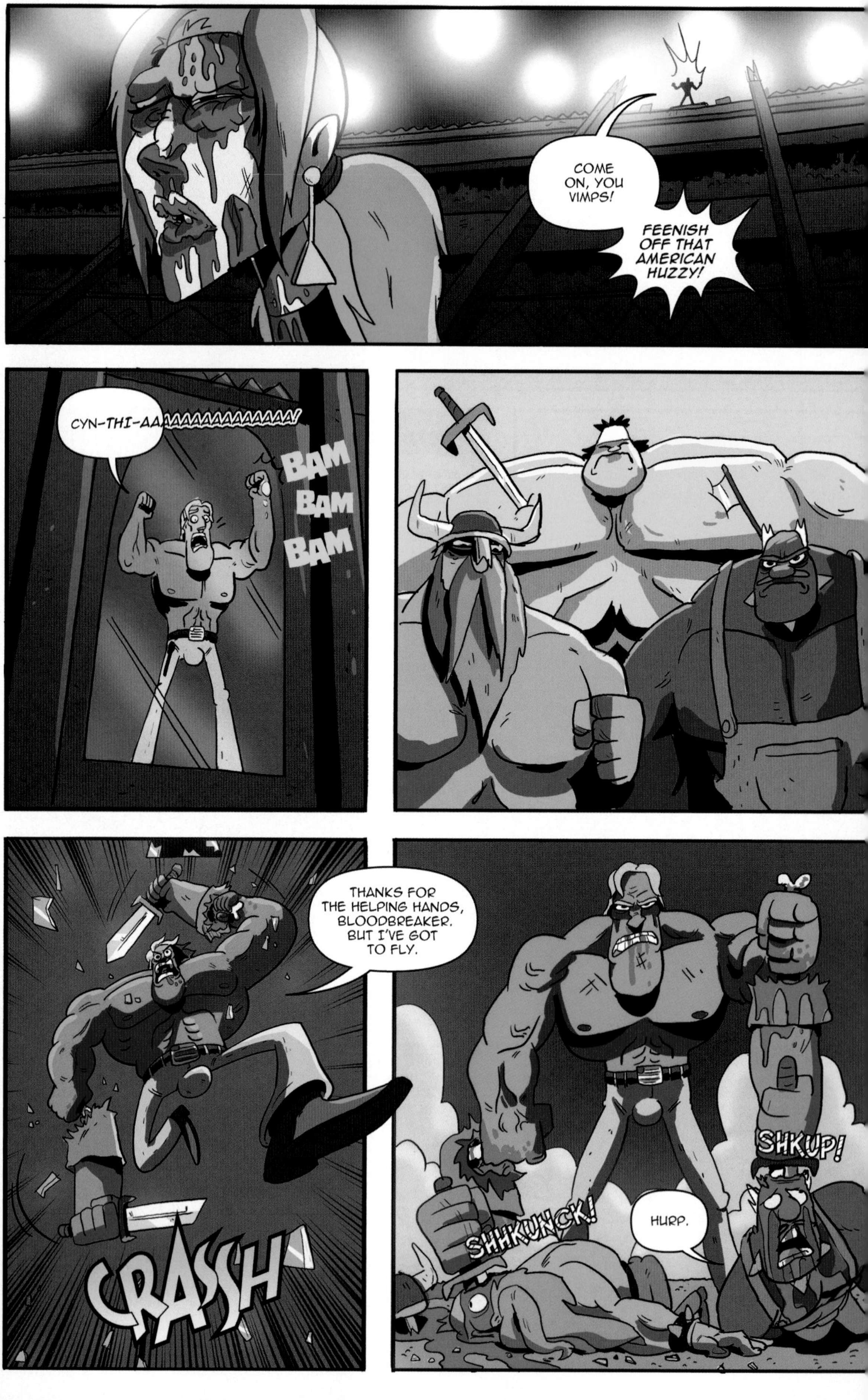

COME ON, YOU VIMPS!
FEENISH OFF THAT AMERICAN HUZZY!
CYN-THI-AAAAAAAAAAAAAAAAA!
BAM
BAM
BAM
THANKS FOR THE HELPING HANDS, BLOODBREAKER. BUT I'VE GOT TO FLY.
CRASH
SHKUP!
SHHKUNCK!
HURP.

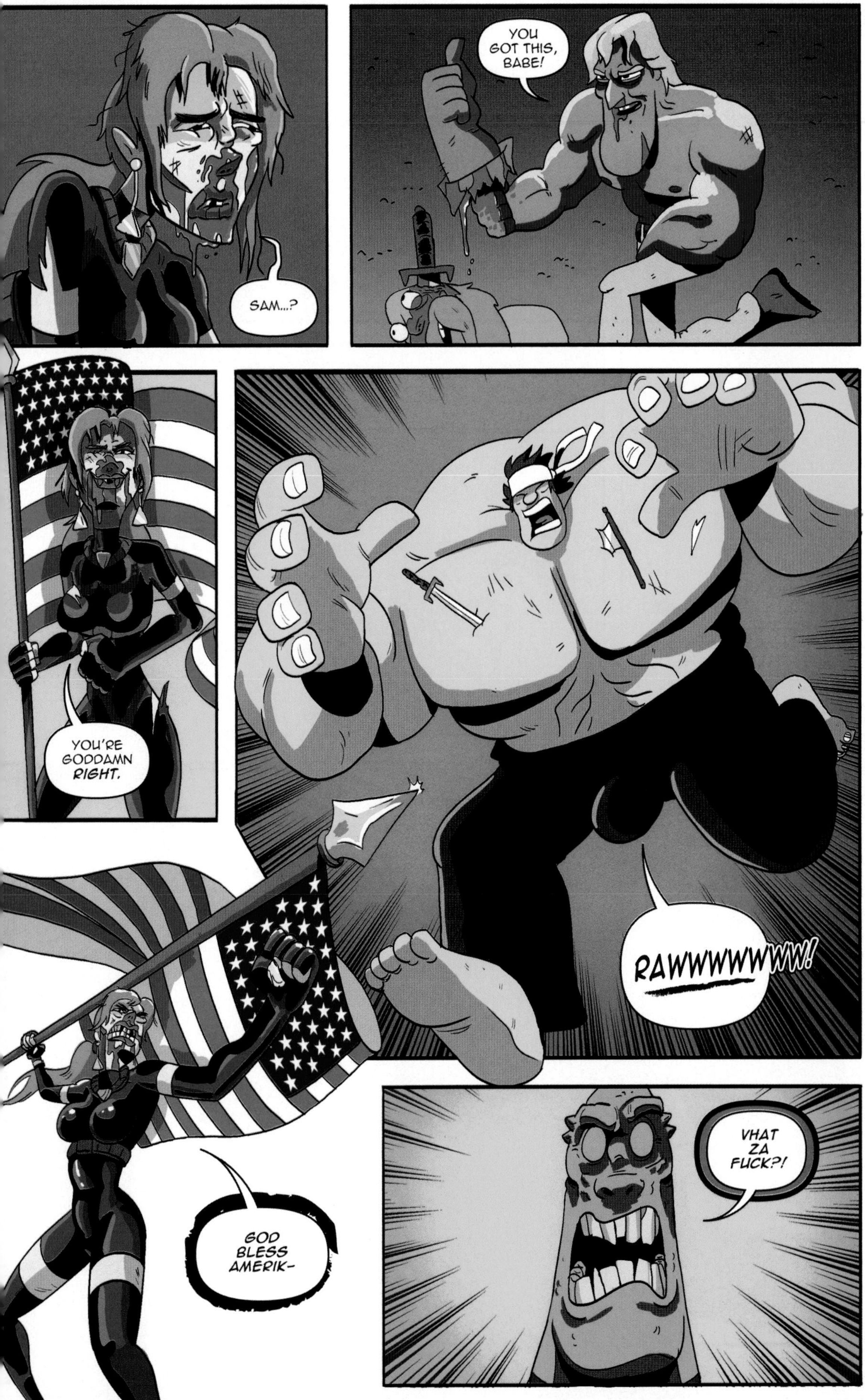
SAM...?
YOU GOT THIS, BABE!
YOU'RE GODDAMN RIGHT.
RAWWWWWWW!
GOD BLESS AMERIK-
VHAT ZA FUCK?!

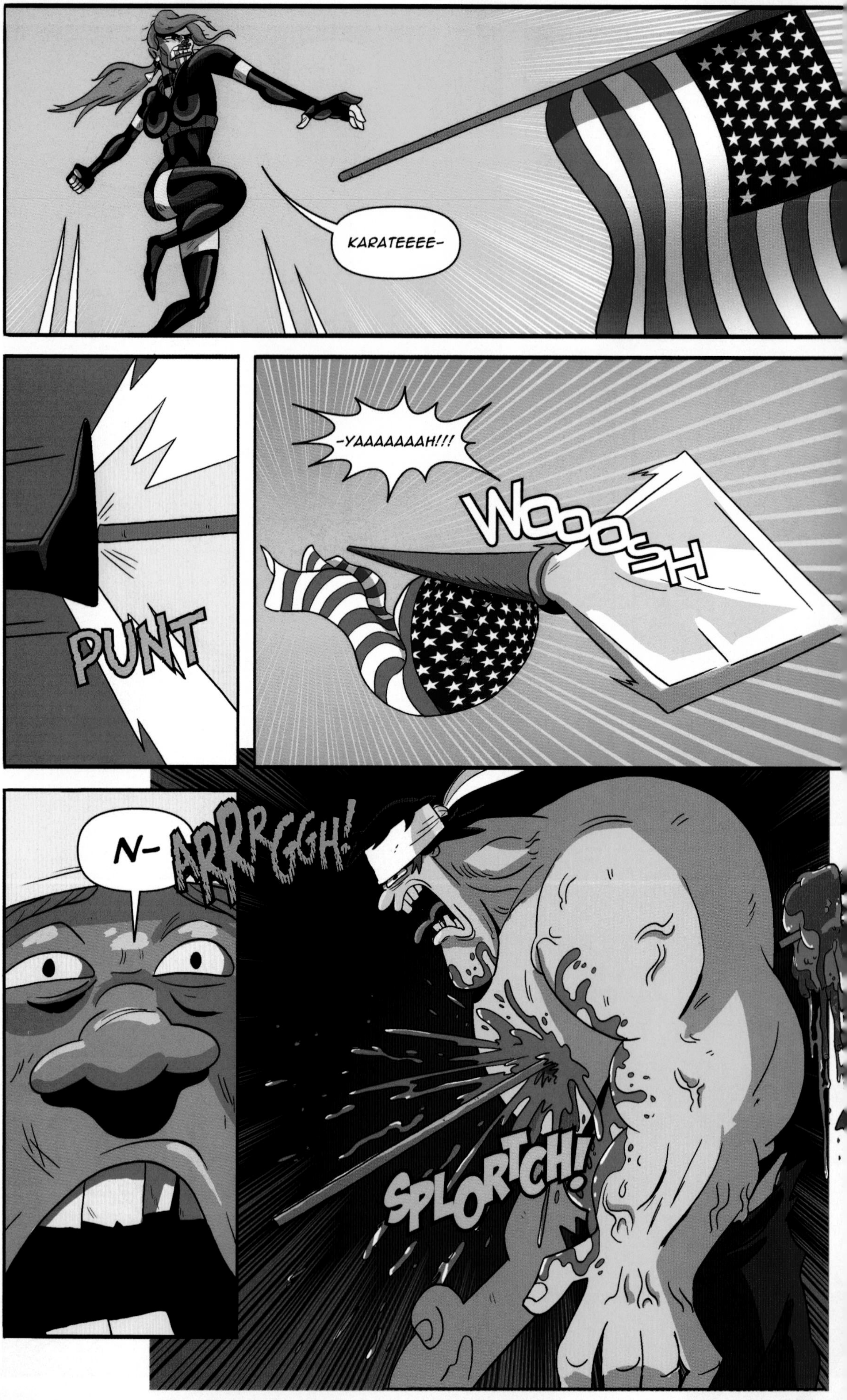
KARATEEEE-
PUNT
-YAAAAAAAH!!!
WOOOSH
N-
ARRRGGH!
SPLORTCH!

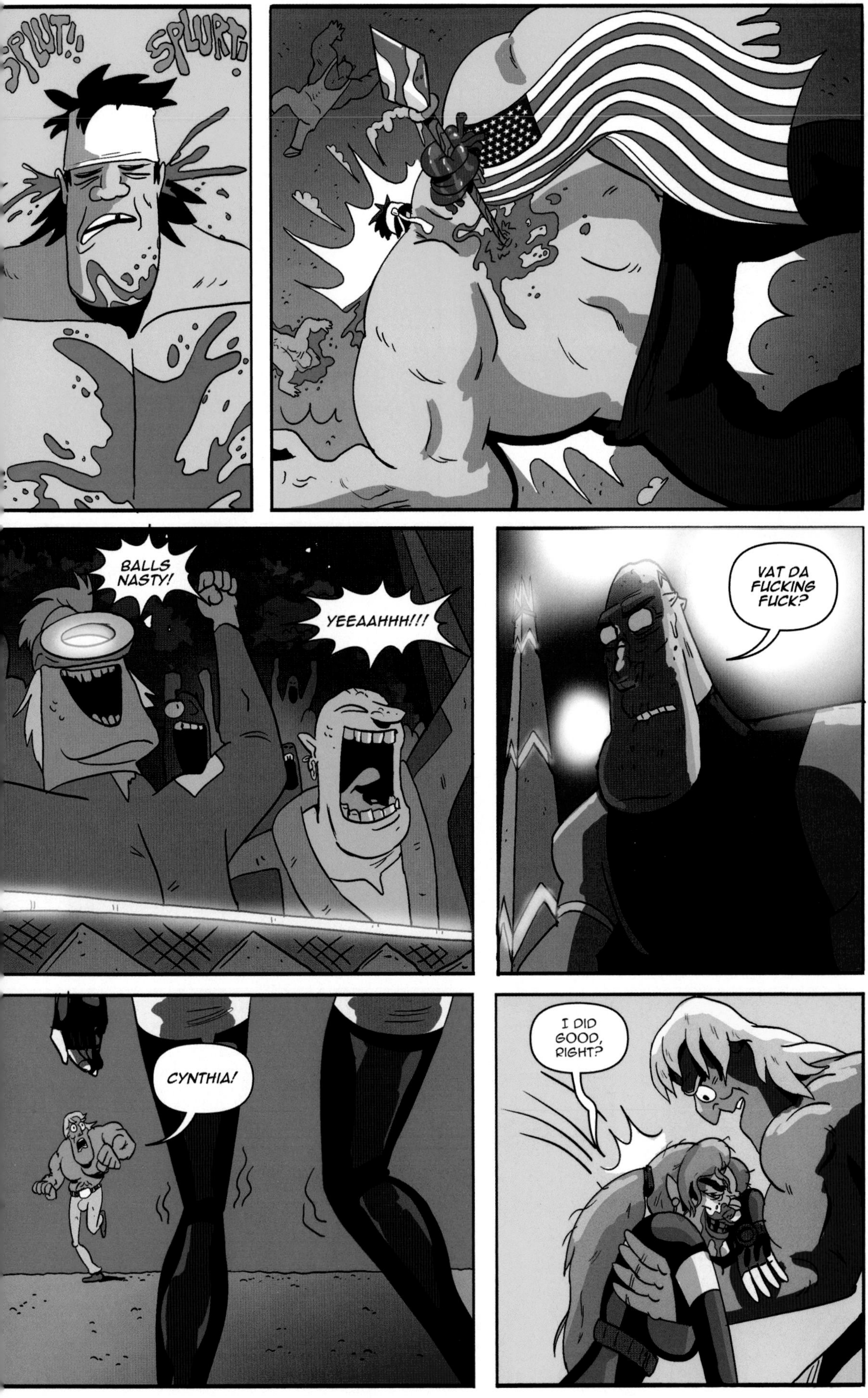
SPLUT!!
SPLURT!!
BALLS NASTY!
YEEAAHHH!!!
VAT DA FUCKING FUCK?
CYNTHIA!
I DID GOOD, RIGHT?

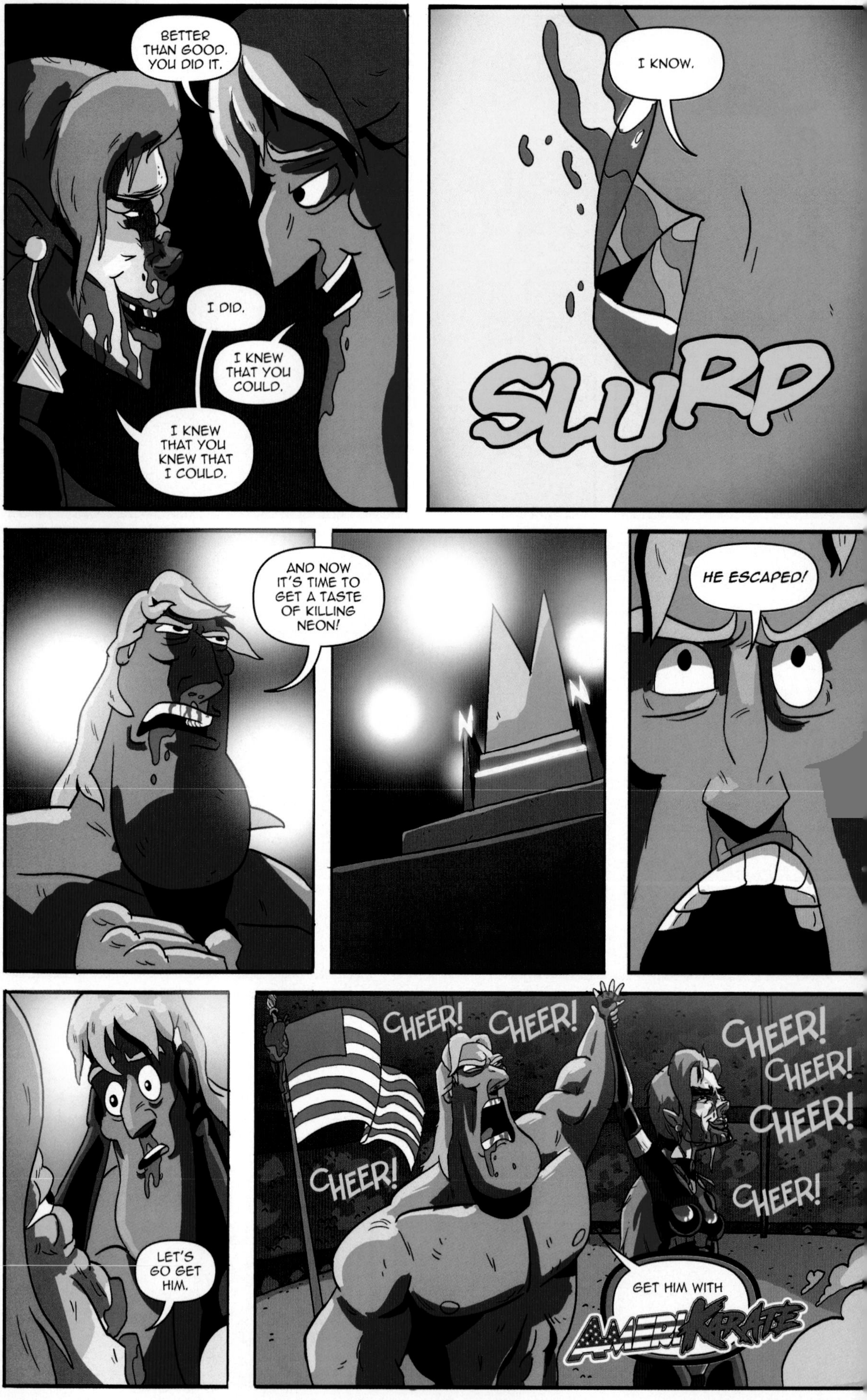
BETTER THAN GOOD. YOU DID IT.
I DID.
I KNEW THAT YOU COULD.
I KNEW THAT YOU KNEW THAT I COULD.
I KNOW.
SLURP
AND NOW IT'S TIME TO GET A TASTE OF KILLING NEON!
HE ESCAPED!
LET'S GO GET HIM.
CHEER! CHEER!
CHEER! CHEER! CHEER!
CHEER!
CHEER!
GET HIM WITH AMERIKARATE

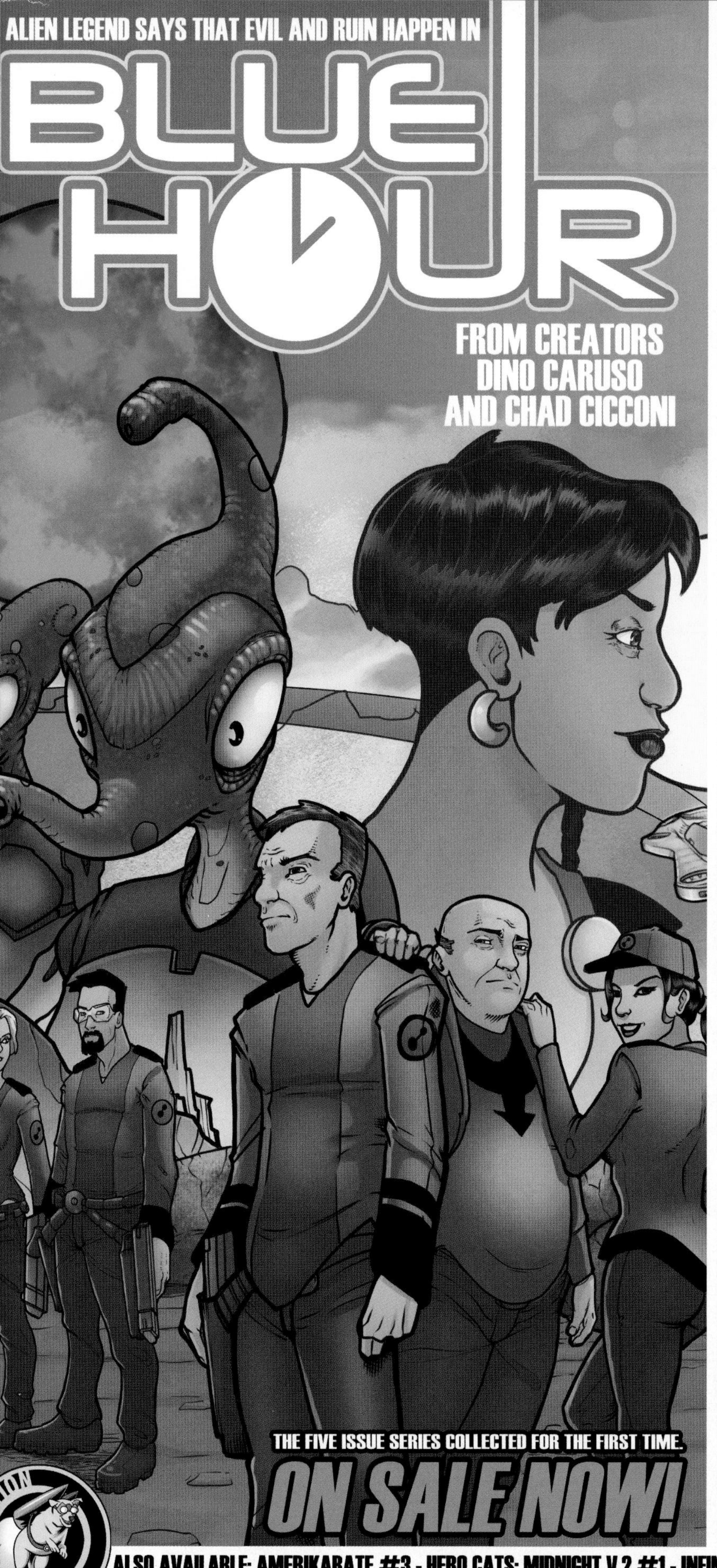
ALIEN LEGEND SAYS THAT EVIL AND RUIN HAPPEN IN
BLUE HOUR
FROM CREATORS
DINO CARUSO
AND CHAD CICCONI
THE FIVE ISSUE SERIES COLLECTED FOR THE FIRST TIME.
ON SALE NOW!

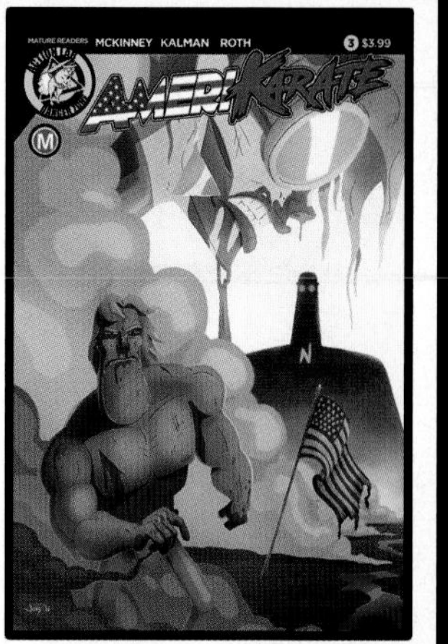
MATURE READERS MCKINNEY KALMAN ROTH
3 $3.99
AMERIKARATE

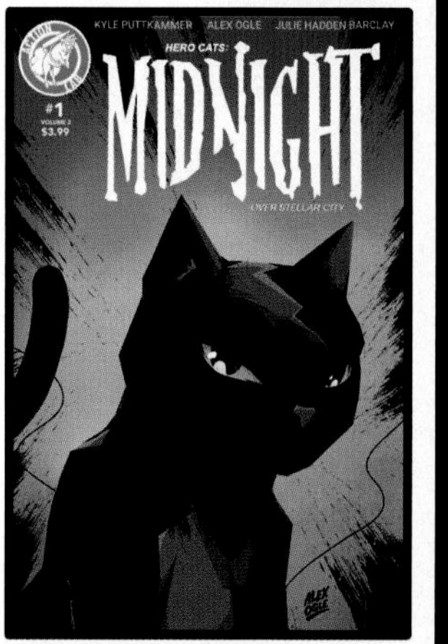
KYLE PUTTKAMMER ALEX OGLE JULIE HADDEN BARCLAY
HERO CATS:
MIDNIGHT
#1
$3.99
OVER STELLAR CITY

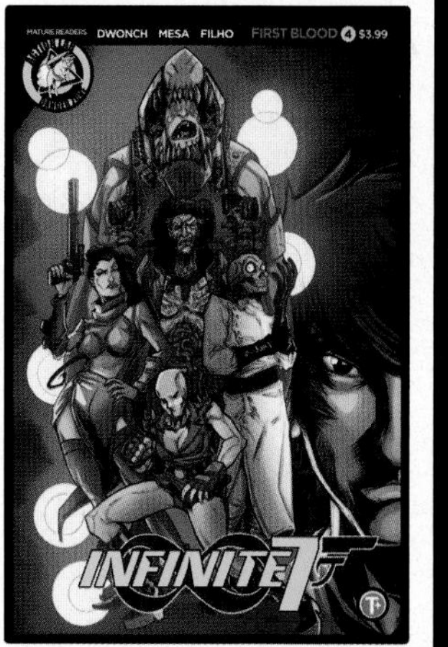
MATURE READERS DWONCH MESA FILHO FIRST BLOOD 4 $3.99
INFINITE7

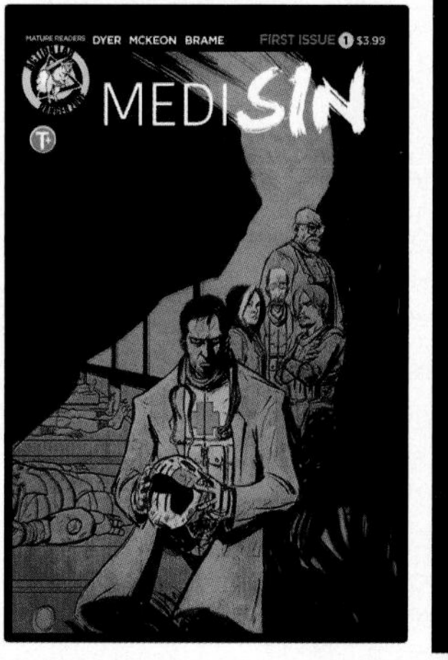
MATURE READERS DYER MCKEON BRAME FIRST ISSUE 1 $3.99
MEDISIN

ALSO AVAILABLE: AMERIKARATE #3 - HERO CATS: MIDNIGHT V.2 #1 - INFINITE SEVEN #4 - MEDISIN #1

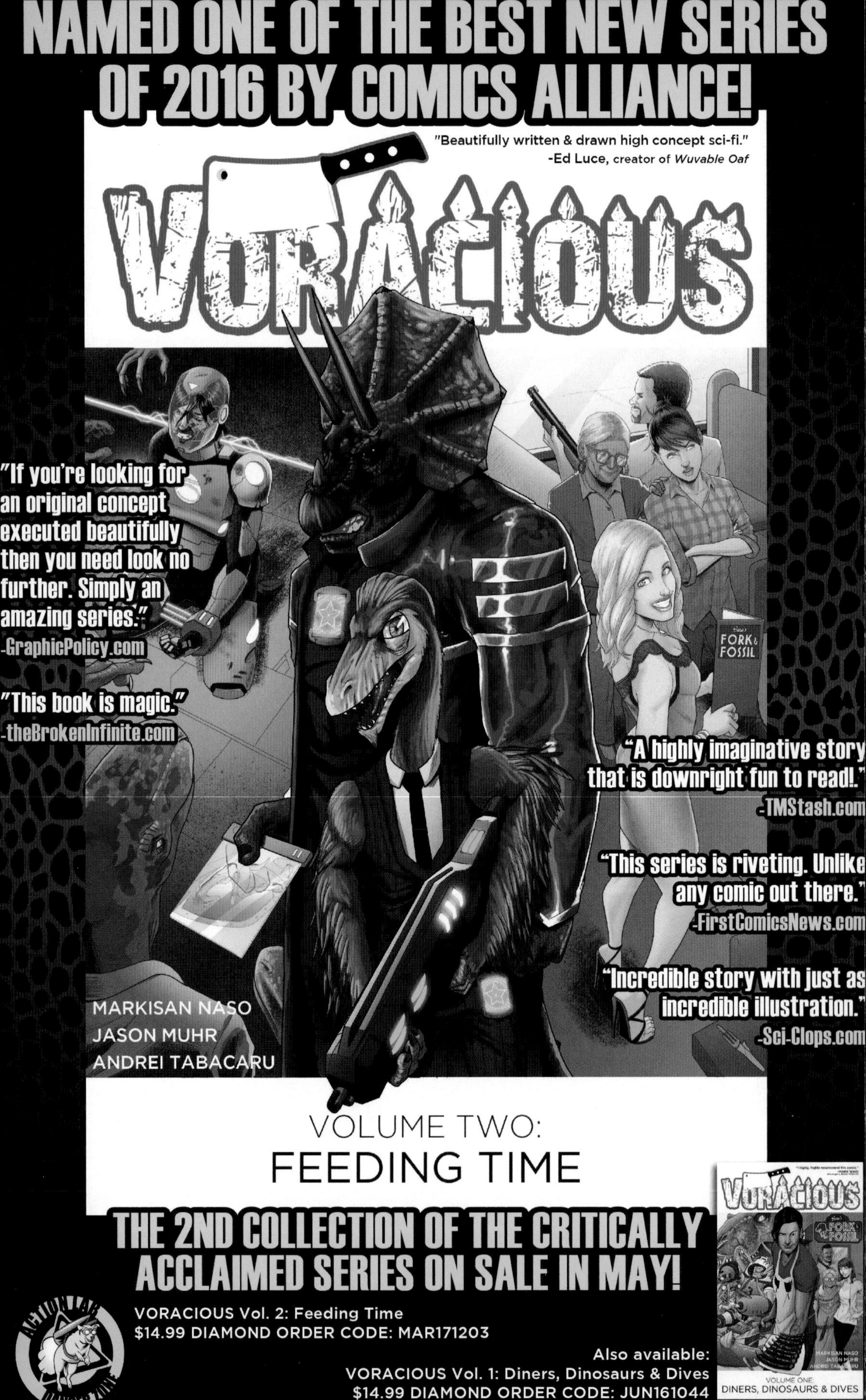
NAMED ONE OF THE BEST NEW SERIES OF 2016 BY COMICS ALLIANCE!
"Beautifully written & drawn high concept sci-fi." -Ed Luce, creator of *Wuvable Oaf*
VORACIOUS
"If you're looking for an original concept executed beautifully then you need look no further. Simply an amazing series." -GraphicPolicy.com
"This book is magic." -theBrokenInfinite.com
FORK & FOSSIL
"A highly imaginative story that is downright fun to read!." -TMStash.com
"This series is riveting. Unlike any comic out there." -FirstComicsNews.com
"Incredible story with just as incredible illustration." -Sci-Clops.com
MARKISAN NASO
JASON MUHR
ANDREI TABACARU
VOLUME TWO:
FEEDING TIME
THE 2ND COLLECTION OF THE CRITICALLY ACCLAIMED SERIES ON SALE IN MAY!
ACTION LAB
VORACIOUS Vol. 2: Feeding Time
$14.99 DIAMOND ORDER CODE: MAR171203
Also available:
VORACIOUS Vol. 1: Diners, Dinosaurs & Dives
$14.99 DIAMOND ORDER CODE: JUN161044
VORACIOUS
FORK & FOSSIL
MARKISAN NASO
JASON MUHR
ANDREI TABACARU
VOLUME ONE:
DINERS, DINOSAURS & DIVES

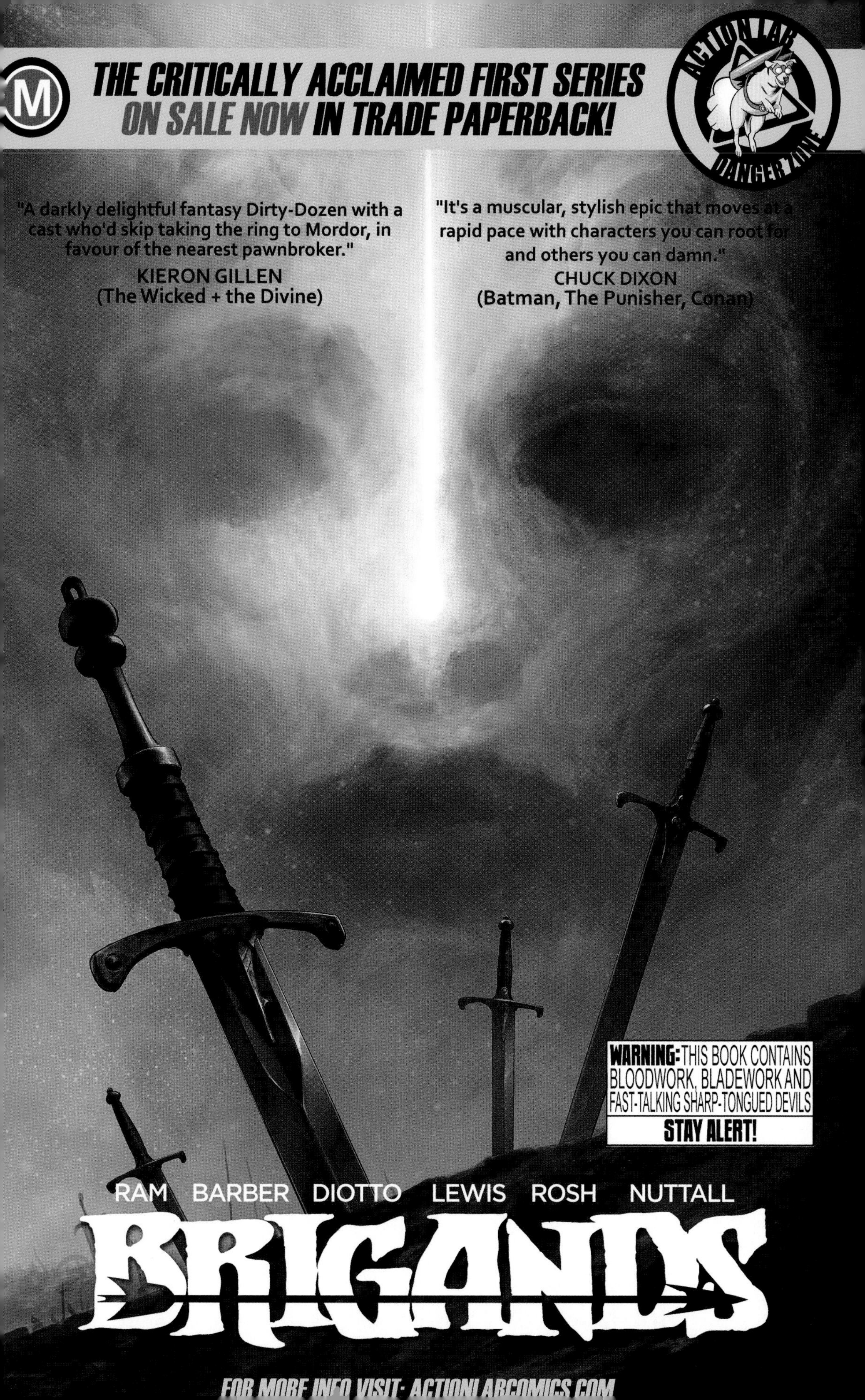
THE CRITICALLY ACCLAIMED FIRST SERIES
ON SALE NOW IN TRADE PAPERBACK!
ACTION LAB DANGER ZONE
"A darkly delightful fantasy Dirty-Dozen with a cast who'd skip taking the ring to Mordor, in favour of the nearest pawnbroker."
KIERON GILLEN
(The Wicked + the Divine)
"It's a muscular, stylish epic that moves at a rapid pace with characters you can root for and others you can damn."
CHUCK DIXON
(Batman, The Punisher, Conan)
WARNING: THIS BOOK CONTAINS BLOODWORK, BLADEWORK AND FAST-TALKING SHARP-TONGUED DEVILS
STAY ALERT!
RAM BARBER DIOTTO LEWIS ROSH NUTTALL
BRIGANDS
FOR MORE INFO VISIT: ACTIONLABCOMICS.COM

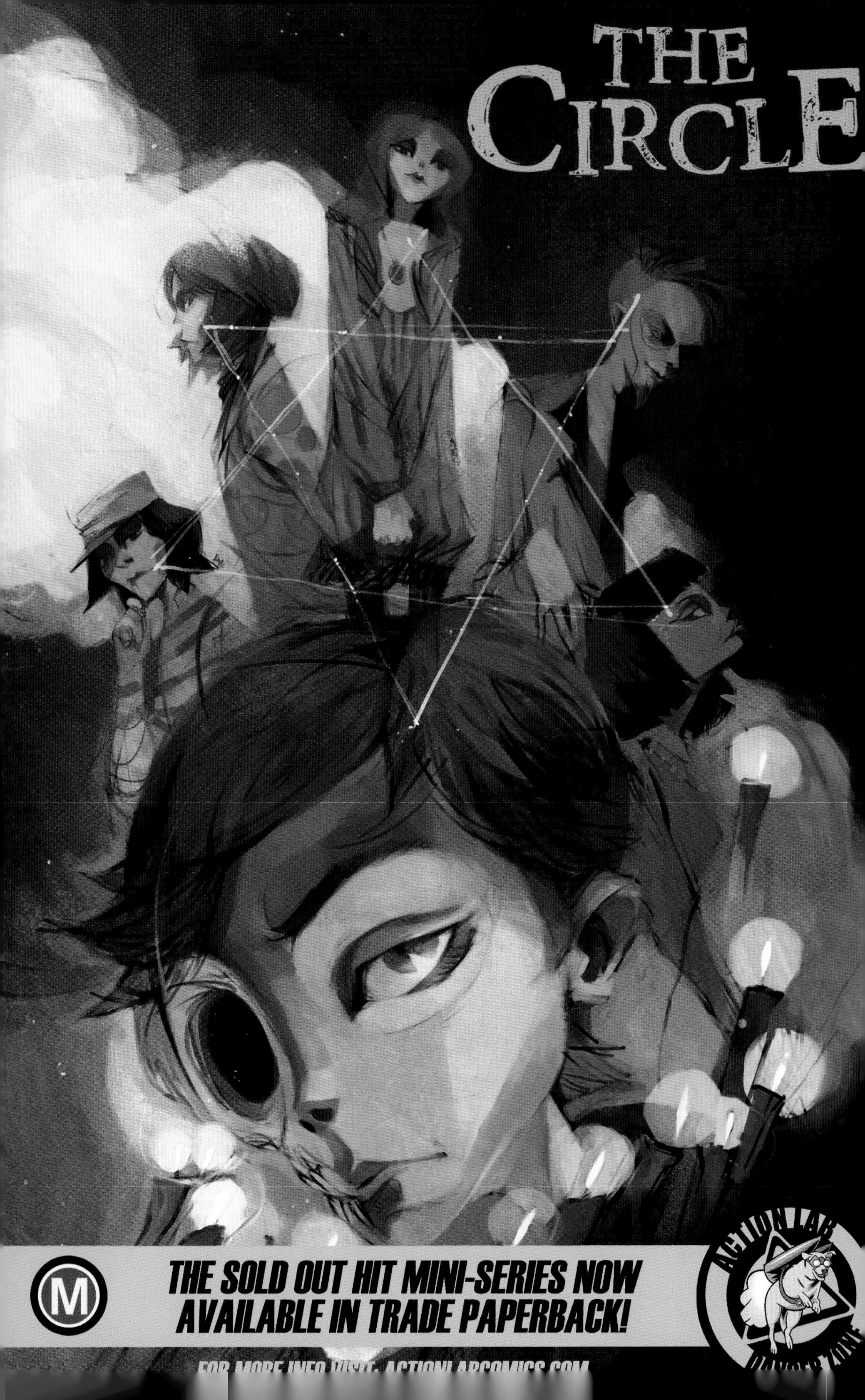

THE CIRCLE
M
THE SOLD OUT HIT MINI-SERIES NOW
AVAILABLE IN TRADE PAPERBACK!
FOR MORE INFO VISIT: ACTIONLABCOMICS.COM
ACTION LAB
DANGER ZONE

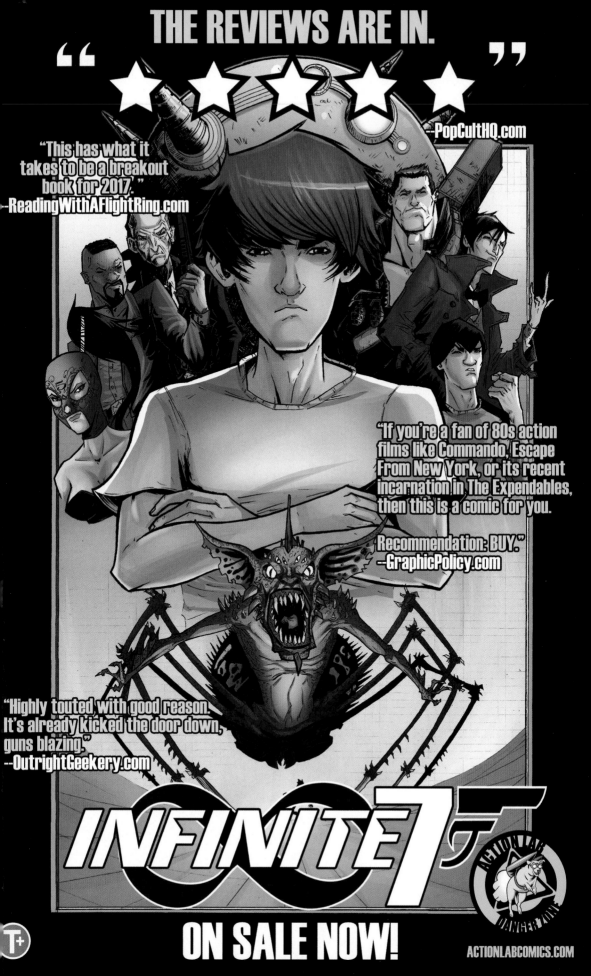

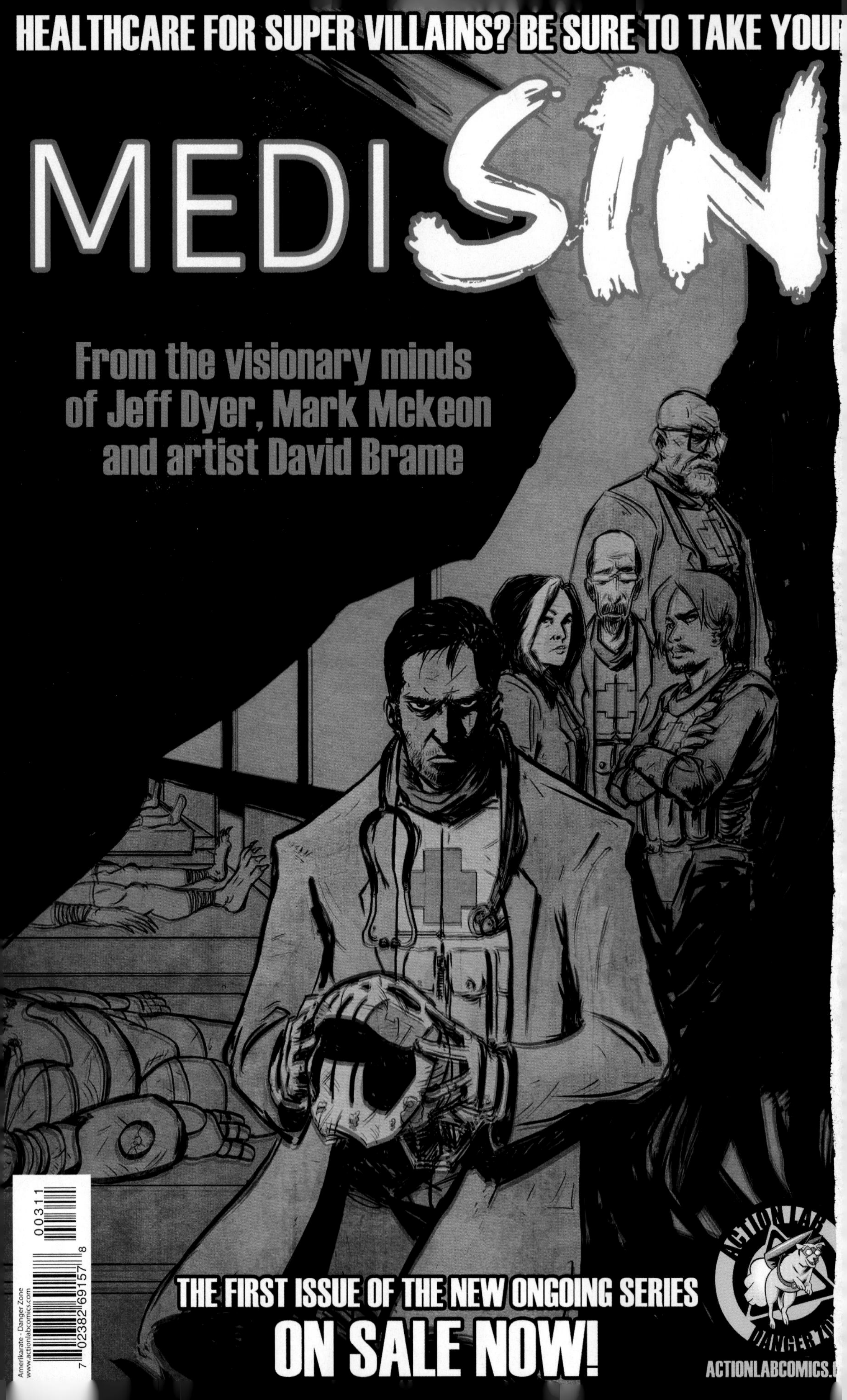
HEALTHCARE FOR SUPER VILLAINS? BE SURE TO TAKE YOUR
MEDISIN
From the visionary minds of Jeff Dyer, Mark Mckeon and artist David Brame
Amerikarate - Danger Zone
www.actionlabcomics.com
THE FIRST ISSUE OF THE NEW ONGOING SERIES
ON SALE NOW!
ACTIONLABCOMICS.

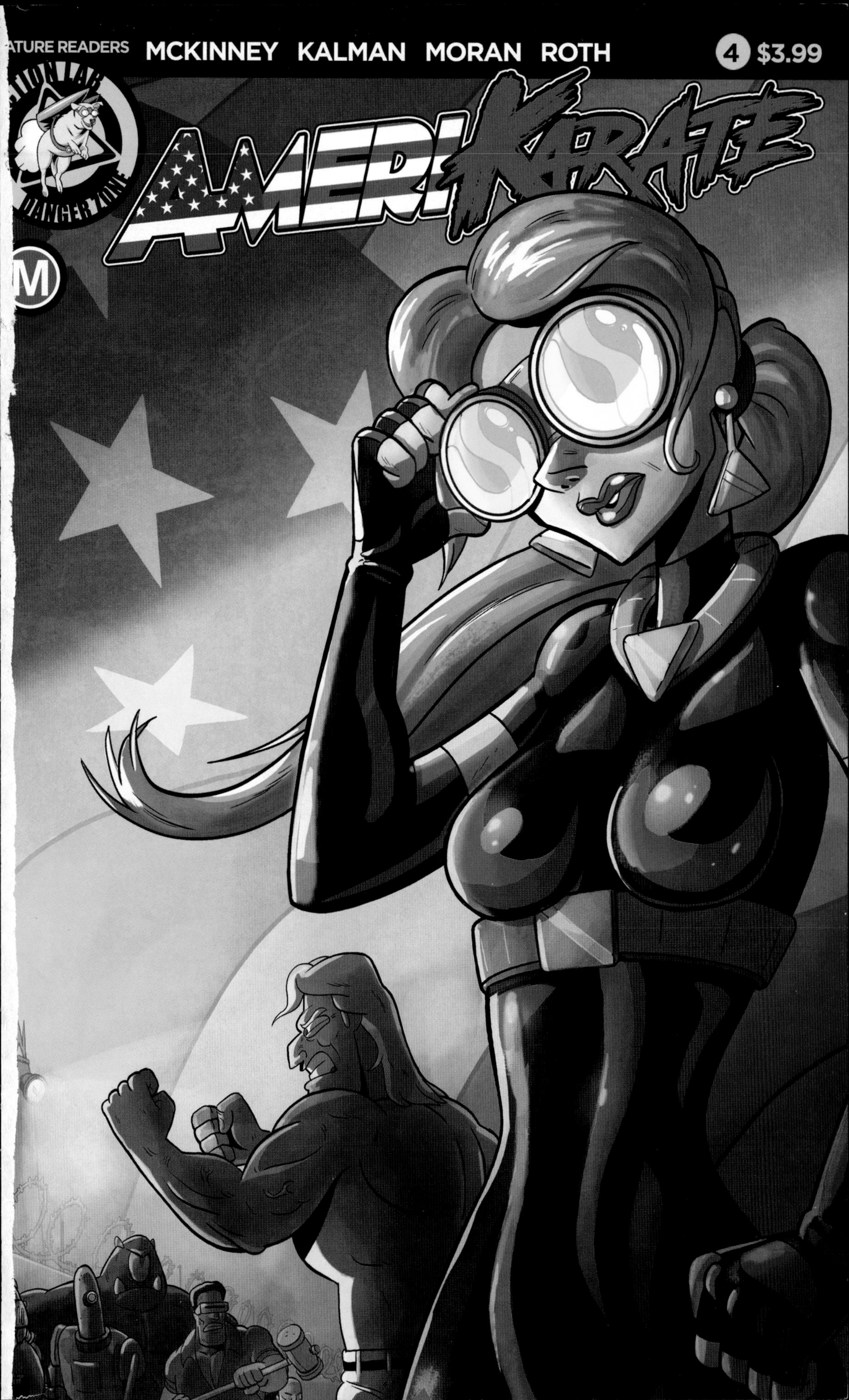
ATURE READERS
MCKINNEY KALMAN MORAN ROTH
4 $3.99
AMERIKARATE

ACTION LAB: DANGER ZONE PRESENTS

Varriors, come out and plaaaaaayyyyyyy!

AMERIKARATE

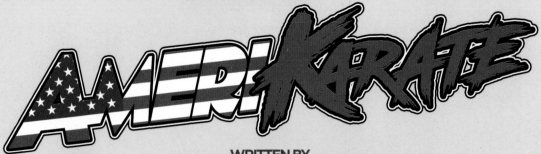

WRITTEN BY
COREY KALMAN & BROCKTON McKINNEY
& CHRISTIAN MORAN

ILLUSTRATED BY
DEVIN ROTH

LETTERS BY
DAVE DWONCH

SPLASH PAGE COLORS BY
YAOYAO MA VAN AS

MATURE READERS MCKINNEY KALMAN MORAN ROTH
4 $3.99
AMERIKARATE

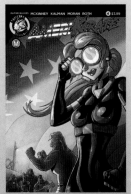

AMERIKARATE REGULAR
Devin Roth & Yaoyao Ma Van As

MCKINNEY KALMAN MORAN ROTH
AmeriKarate

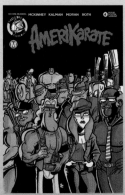

Daniel Arruda Massa MOVIE POSTER VARIANT
"Warriors"
Limited to 1500

MATURE READERS MCKINNEY KALMAN MORAN ROTH
AMERIKARATE

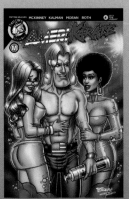

Bill McKay ARTIST VARIANT
"Sexy Time"
Limited to 1500

MATURE READERS MCKINNEY KALMAN MORAN ROTH
AMERIKARATE

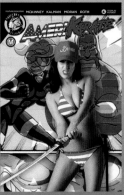

April O'Neil PHOTO VARIANT
Limited to 1500

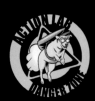

AMERIKARATE #4 June 2017.

Published by Action Lab Comics.

Printed in Canada.
First printing.

ACTIONLABCOMICS.COM

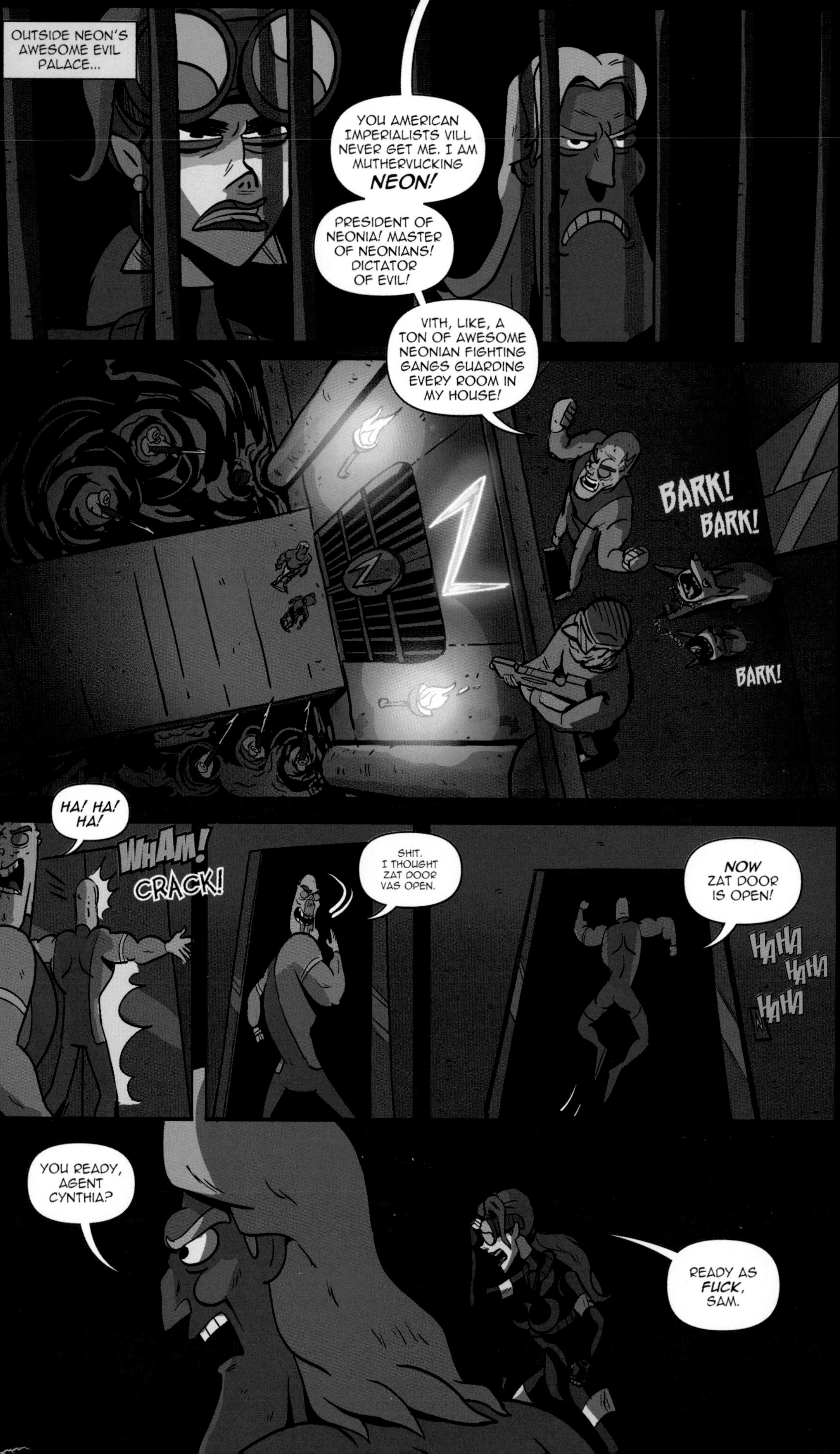
OUTSIDE NEON'S AWESOME EVIL PALACE...
YOU AMERICAN IMPERIALISTS VILL NEVER GET ME. I AM MUTHERVUCKING NEON!
PRESIDENT OF NEONIA! MASTER OF NEONIANS! DICTATOR OF EVIL!
VITH, LIKE, A TON OF AWESOME NEONIAN FIGHTING GANGS GUARDING EVERY ROOM IN MY HOUSE!
BARK!
BARK!
BARK!
HA! HA! HA!
WHAM!
CRACK!
SHIT. I THOUGHT ZAT DOOR VAS OPEN.
NOW ZAT DOOR IS OPEN!
HAHA HAHA HAHA
YOU READY, AGENT CYNTHIA?
READY AS FUCK, SAM.

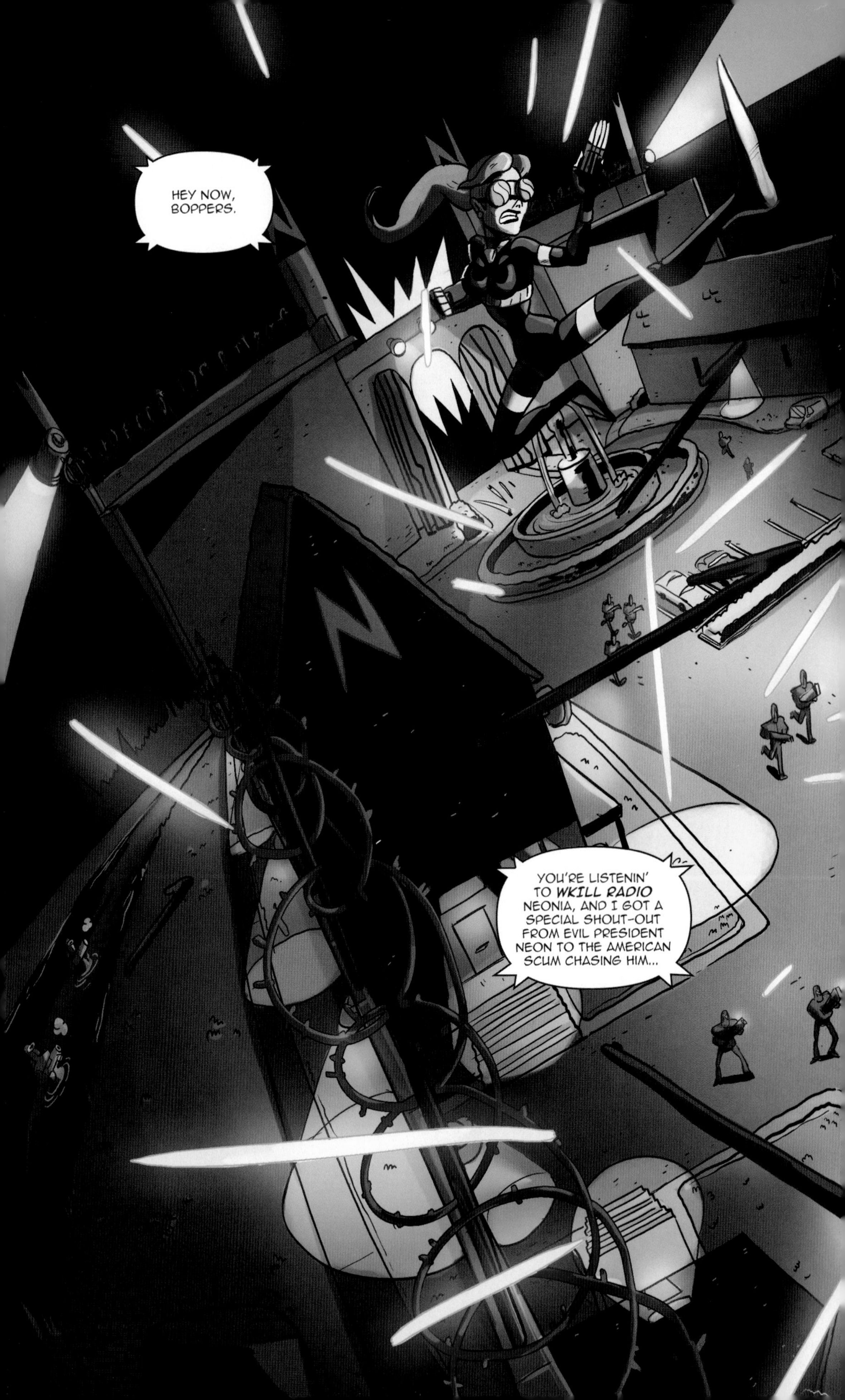
HEY NOW, BOPPERS.
YOU'RE LISTENIN' TO WKILL RADIO NEONIA, AND I GOT A SPECIAL SHOUT-OUT FROM EVIL PRESIDENT NEON TO THE AMERICAN SCUM CHASING HIM...

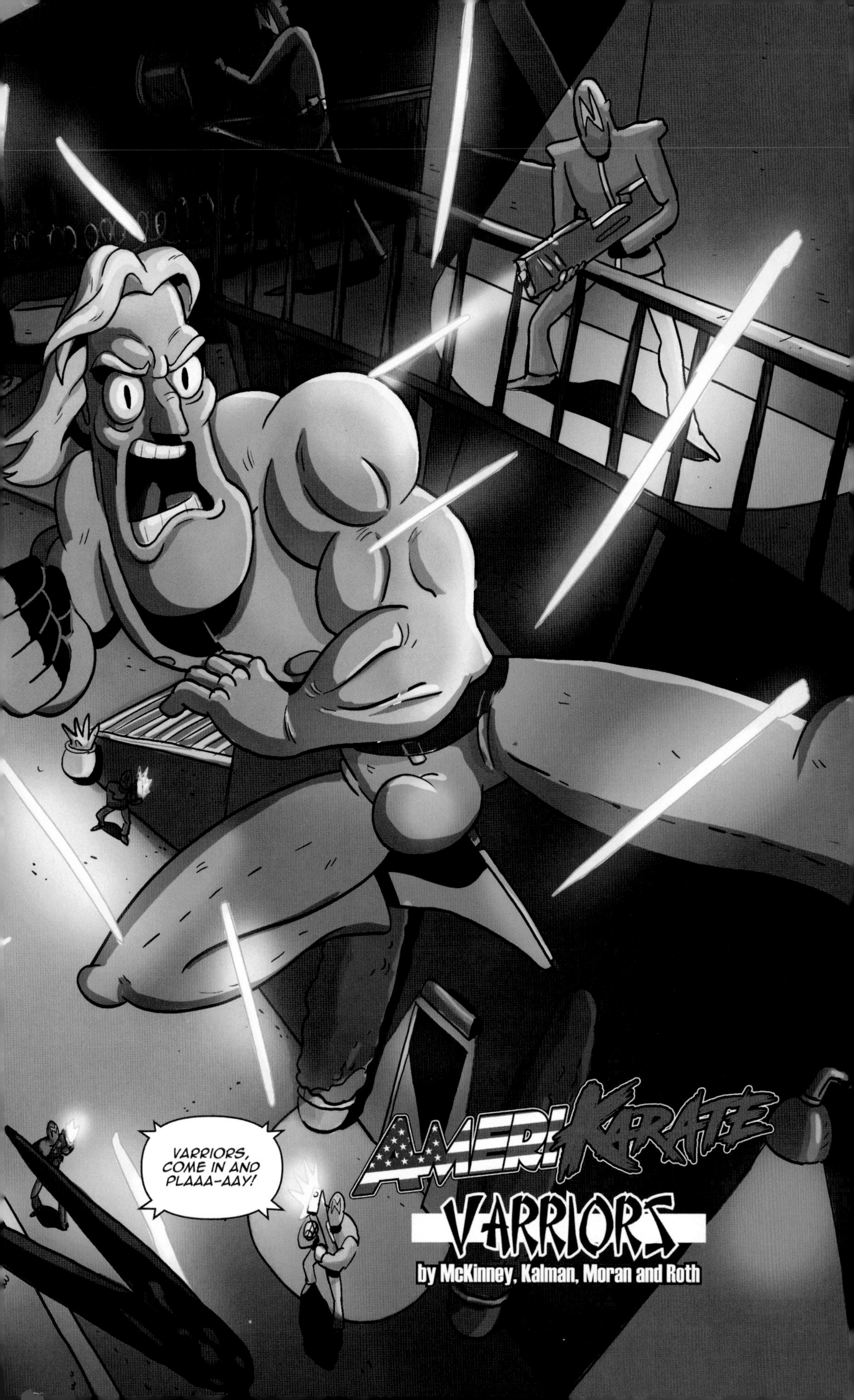
VARRIORS, COME IN AND PLAAA-AAY!
AMERIKARATE
VARRIORS
by McKinney, Kalman, Moran and Roth

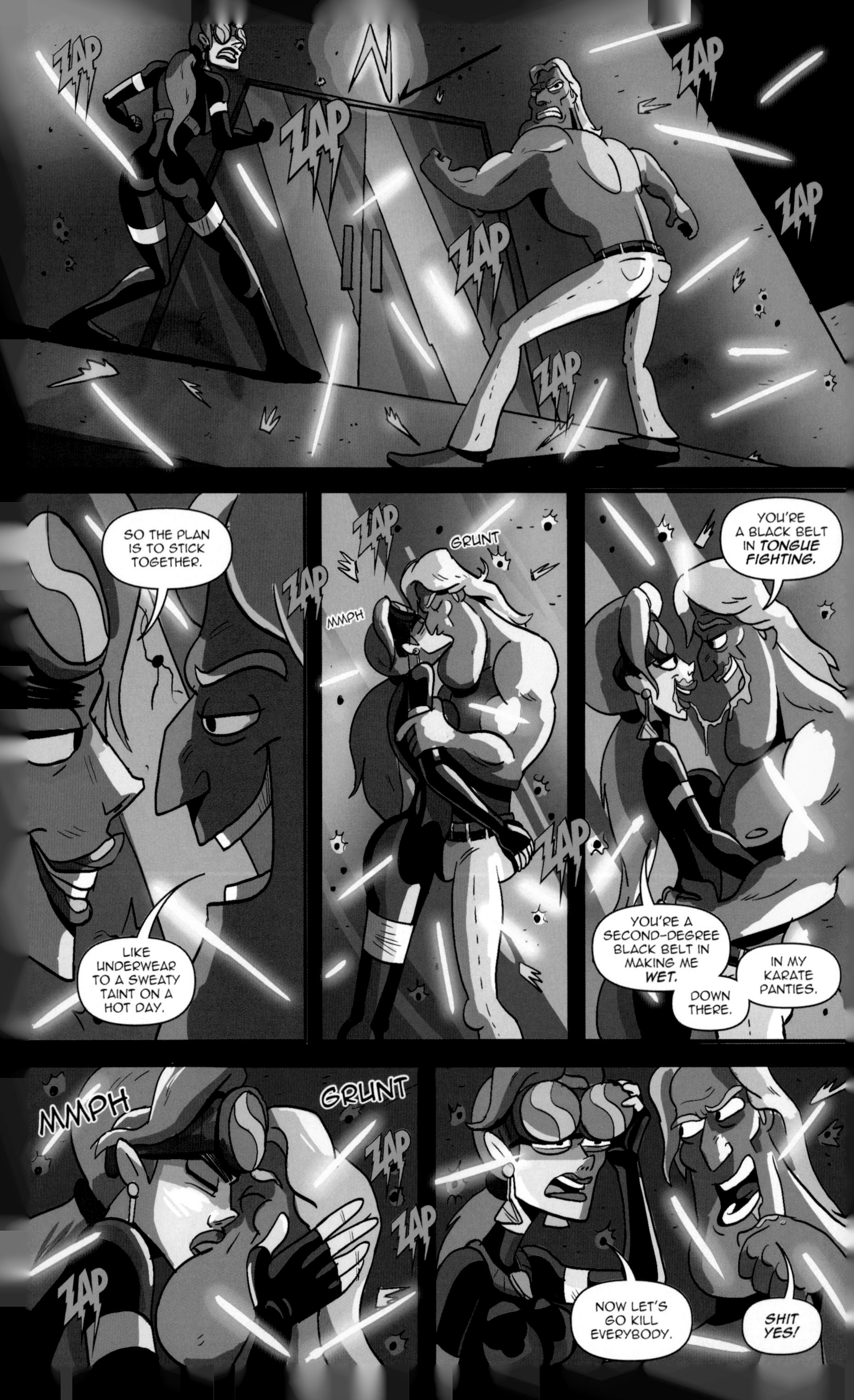
ZAP
ZAP
ZAP
ZAP
ZAP
ZAP
SO THE PLAN IS TO STICK TOGETHER.
LIKE UNDERWEAR TO A SWEATY TAINT ON A HOT DAY.
ZAP
ZAP
GRUNT
MMPH
ZAP
YOU'RE A BLACK BELT IN *TONGUE FIGHTING.*
YOU'RE A SECOND-DEGREE BLACK BELT IN MAKING ME *WET.*
DOWN THERE.
IN MY KARATE PANTIES.
MMPH
GRUNT
ZAP
ZAP
ZAP
NOW LET'S GO KILL EVERYBODY.
SHIT YES!

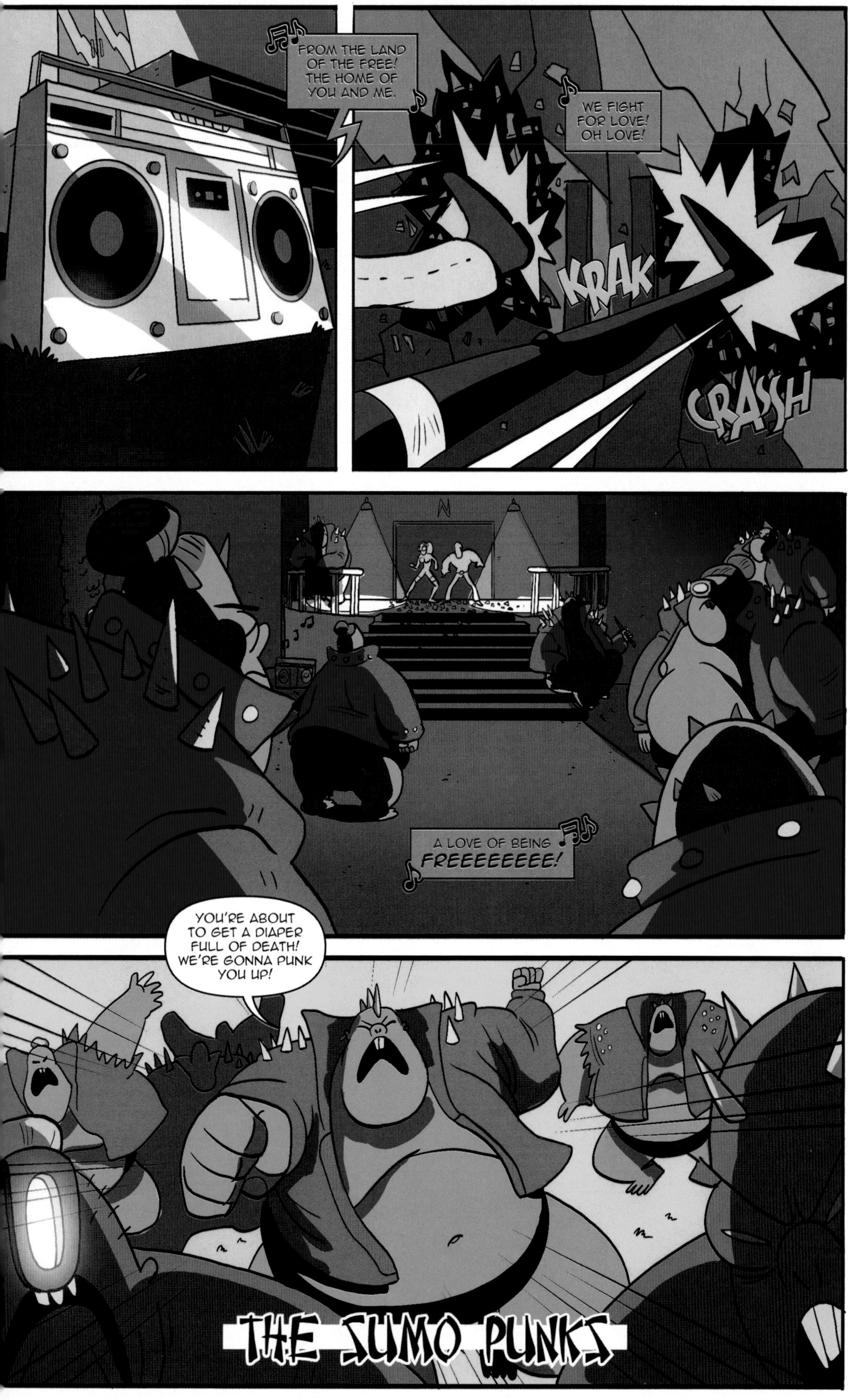
FROM THE LAND OF THE FREE! THE HOME OF YOU AND ME.
WE FIGHT FOR LOVE! OH LOVE!
KRAK
CRASSH
A LOVE OF BEING FREEEEEEEE!
YOU'RE ABOUT TO GET A DIAPER FULL OF DEATH! WE'RE GONNA PUNK YOU UP!
THE SUMO PUNKS

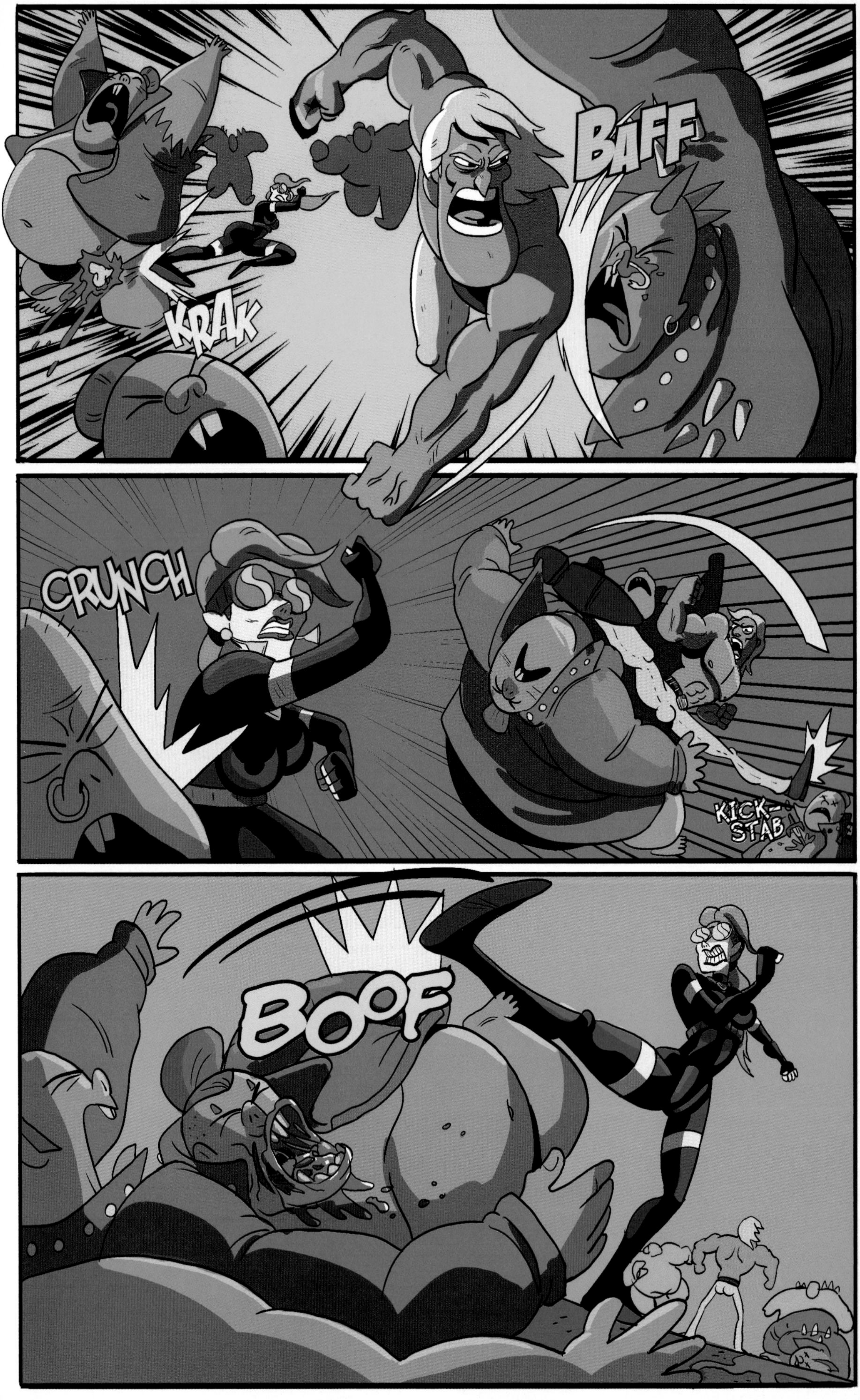
BAFF
KRAK
CRUNCH
KICK-
STAB
BOOF

CRACK!

LEAP!

BAP!

BAP!

BAP!

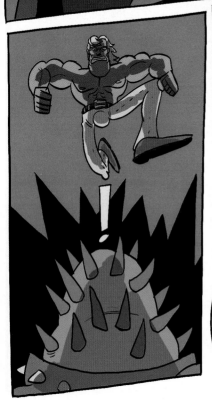

EAT MY BELLY, BITCH!

OOOOOOOF!

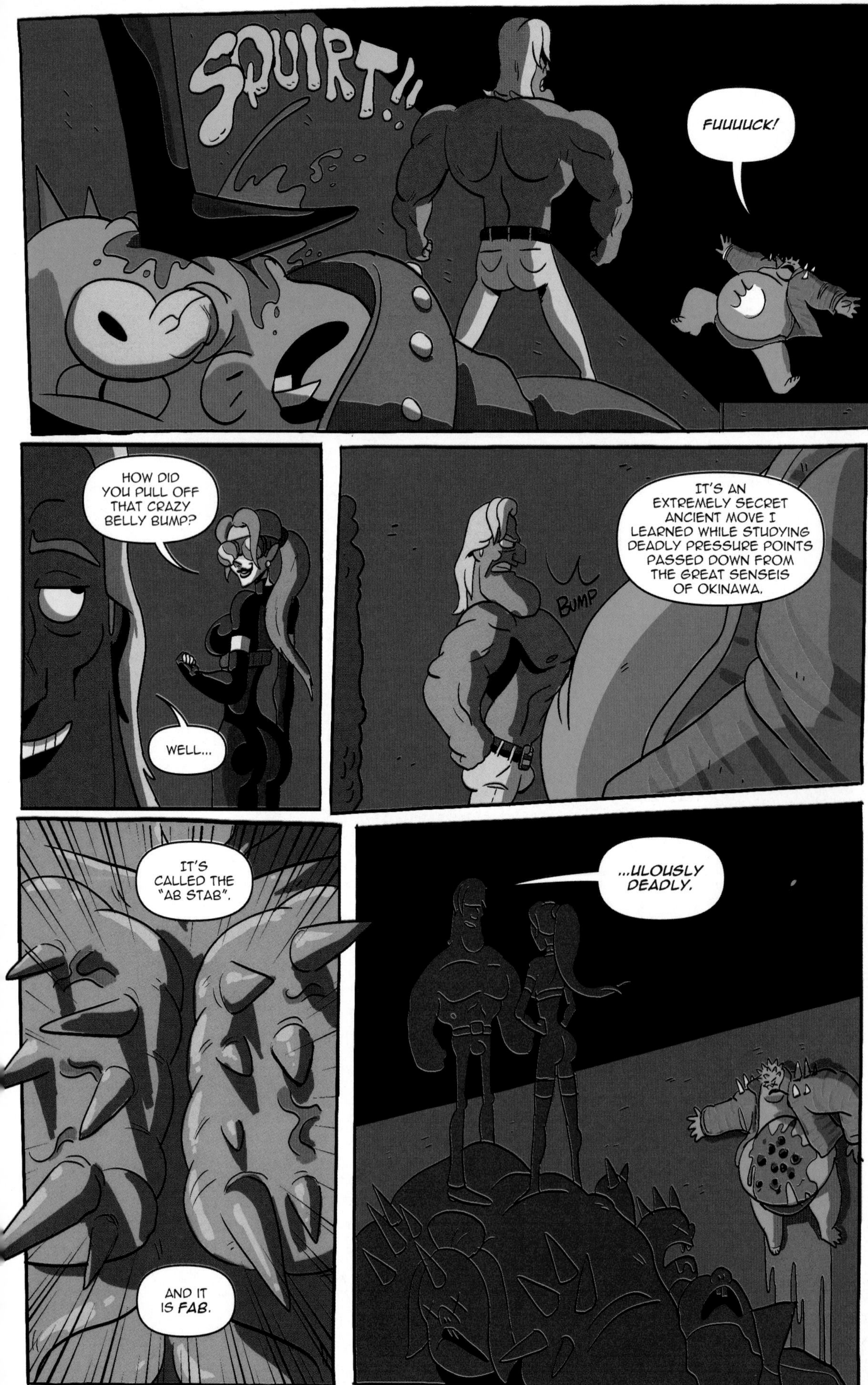
SQUIRT!!
FUUUUCK!
HOW DID YOU PULL OFF THAT CRAZY BELLY BUMP?
WELL...
BUMP
IT'S AN EXTREMELY SECRET ANCIENT MOVE I LEARNED WHILE STUDYING DEADLY PRESSURE POINTS PASSED DOWN FROM THE GREAT SENSEIS OF OKINAWA.
IT'S CALLED THE "AB STAB".
AND IT IS FAB.
...ULOUSLY DEADLY.

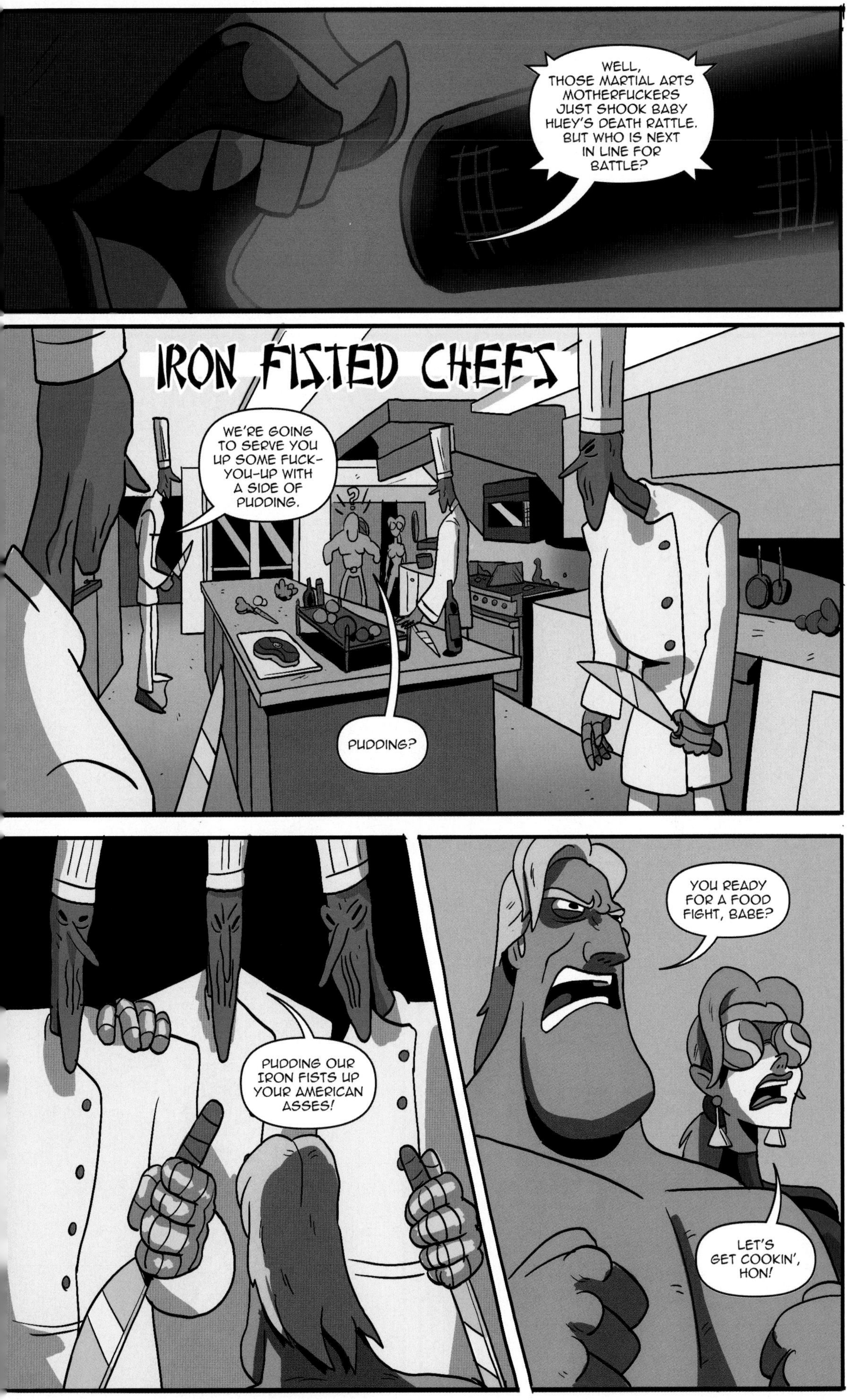
WELL, THOSE MARTIAL ARTS MOTHERFUCKERS JUST SHOOK BABY HUEY'S DEATH RATTLE. BUT WHO IS NEXT IN LINE FOR BATTLE?
IRON FISTED CHEFS
WE'RE GOING TO SERVE YOU UP SOME FUCK-YOU-UP WITH A SIDE OF PUDDING.
PUDDING?
PUDDING OUR IRON FISTS UP YOUR AMERICAN ASSES!
YOU READY FOR A FOOD FIGHT, BABE?
LET'S GET COOKIN', HON!

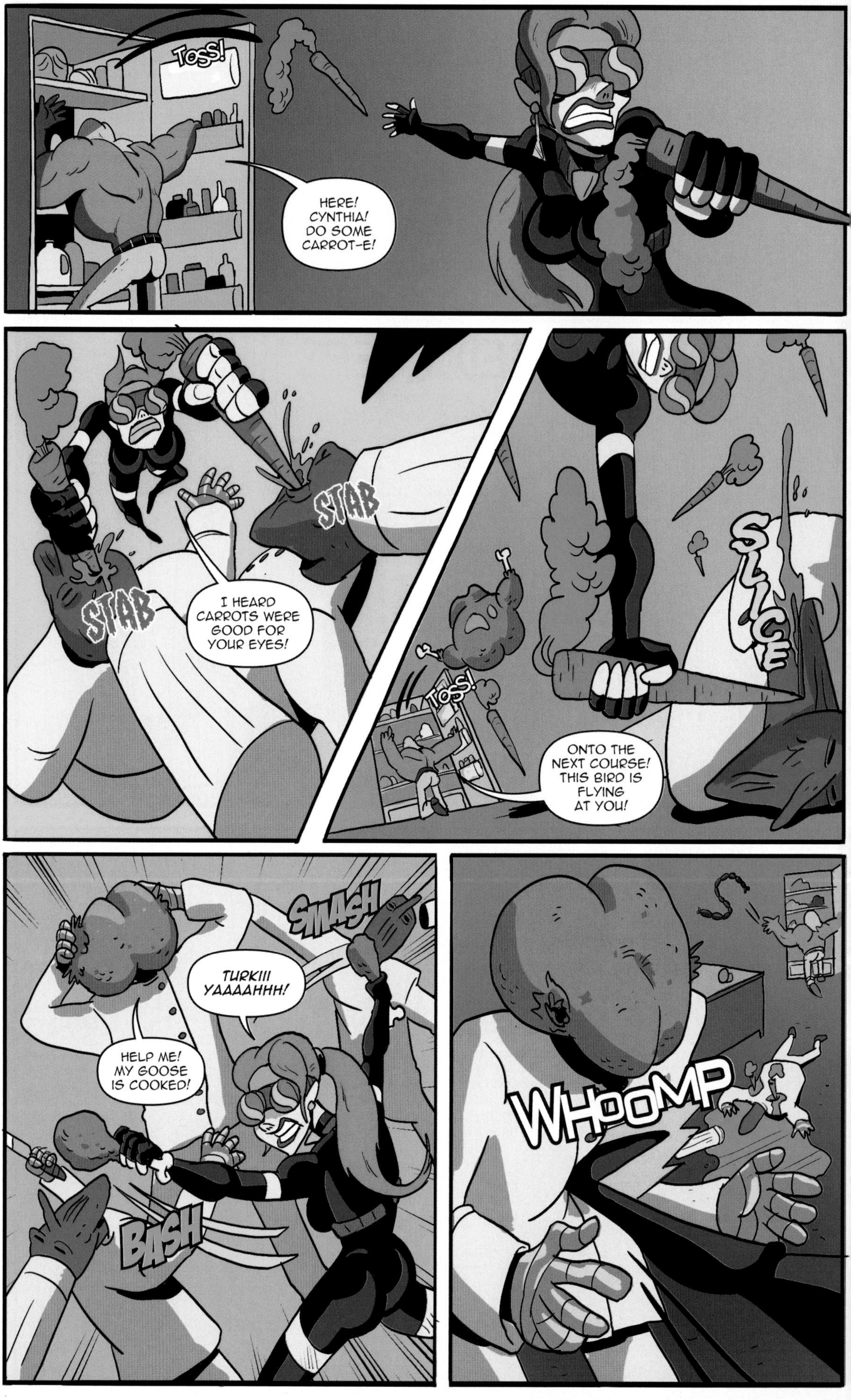
TOSS!
HERE! CYNTHIA! DO SOME CARROT-E!
STAB
STAB
I HEARD CARROTS WERE GOOD FOR YOUR EYES!
SLICE
TOSS!
ONTO THE NEXT COURSE! THIS BIRD IS FLYING AT YOU!
SMASH
TURKIII YAAAAHHH!
HELP ME! MY GOOSE IS COOKED!
BASH
WHOOMP

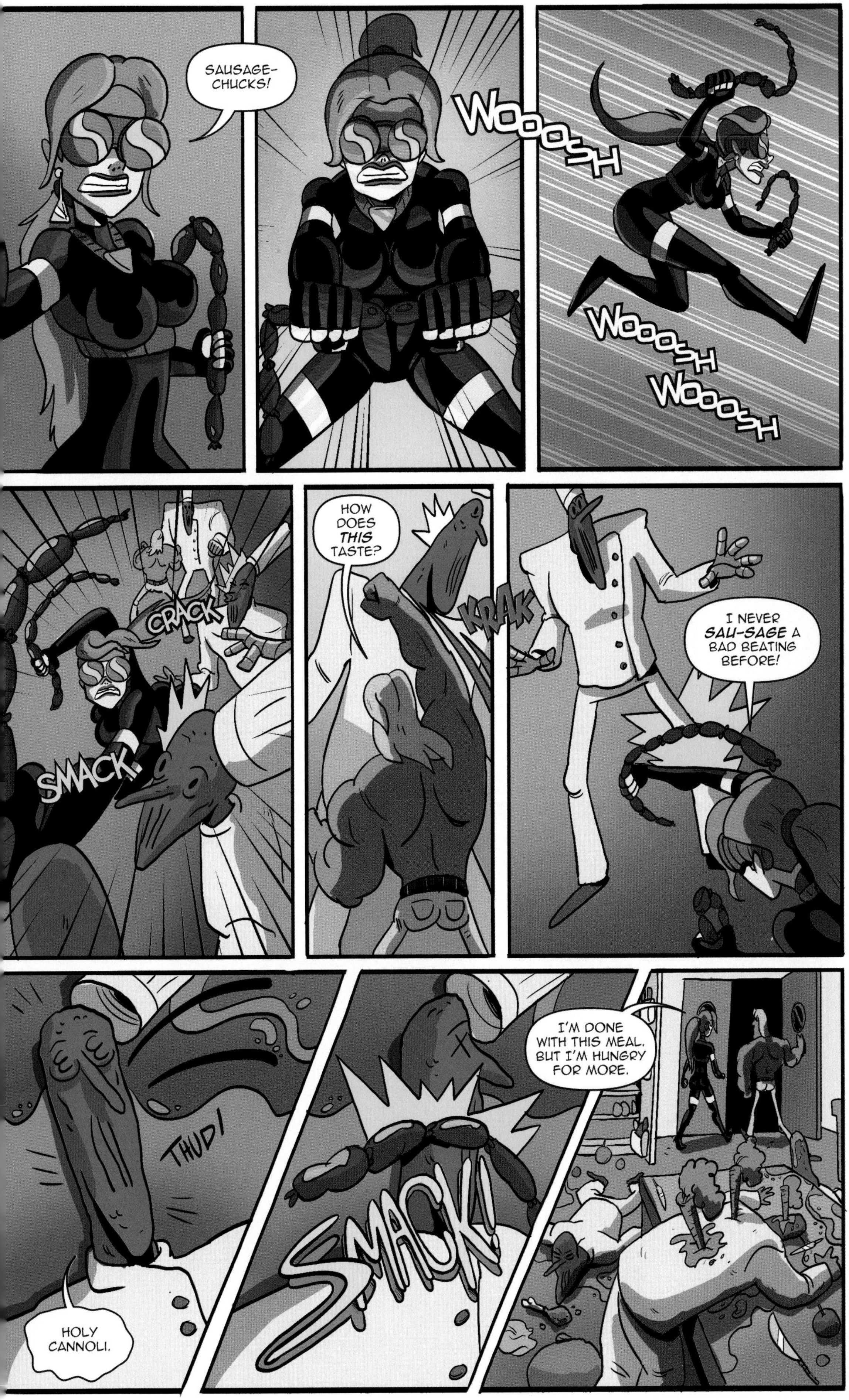
SAUSAGE-CHUCKS!
WOOOSH
WOOOSH
WOOOSH
WOOOSH
CRACK
SMACK
HOW DOES THIS TASTE?
KRAK
I NEVER SAU-SAGE A BAD BEATING BEFORE!
THUD!
HOLY CANNOLI.
SMACK!
I'M DONE WITH THIS MEAL. BUT I'M HUNGRY FOR MORE.

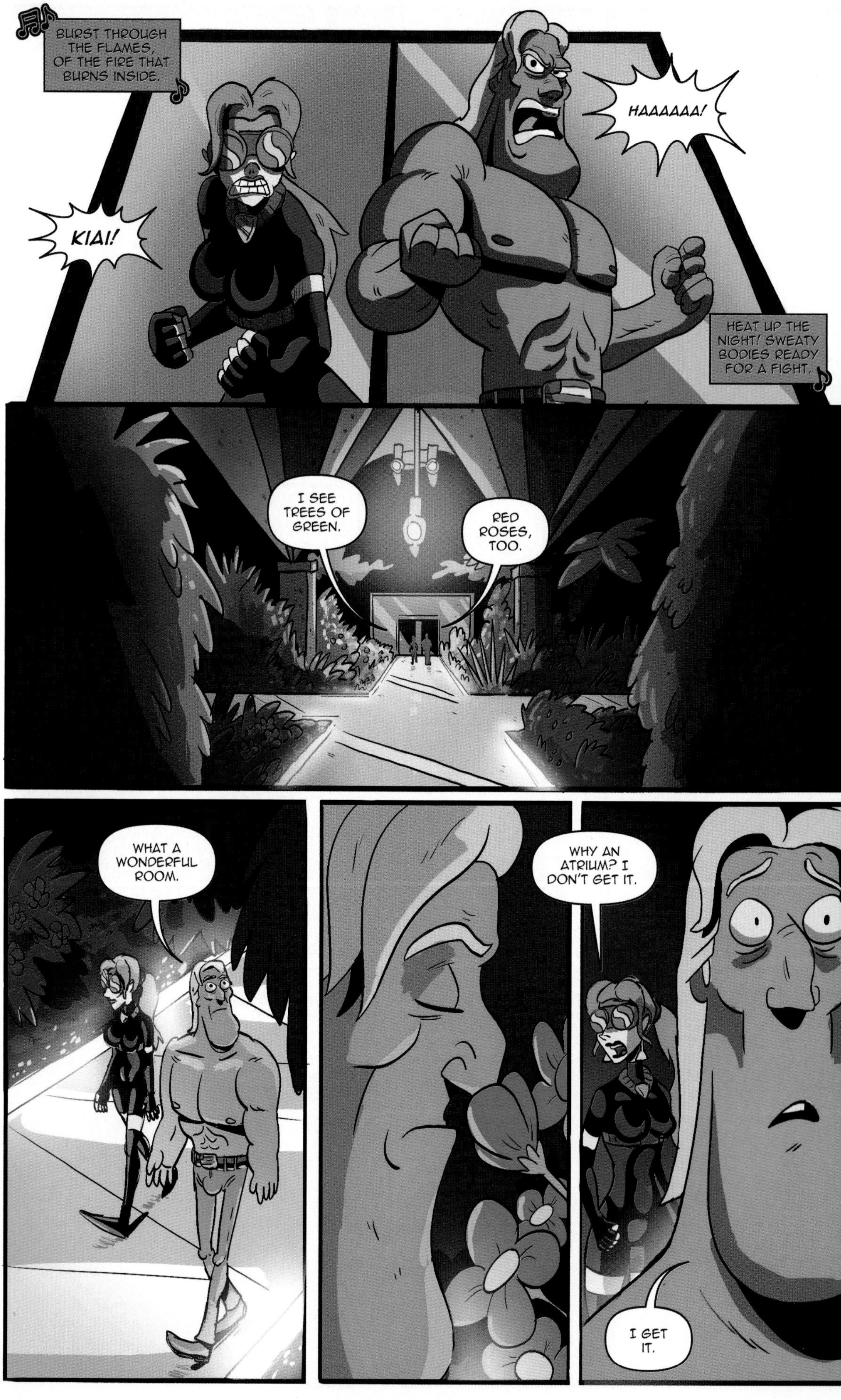
BURST THROUGH THE FLAMES, OF THE FIRE THAT BURNS INSIDE.
HAAAAAAA!
KIAI!
HEAT UP THE NIGHT! SWEATY BODIES READY FOR A FIGHT.
I SEE TREES OF GREEN.
RED ROSES, TOO.
WHAT A WONDERFUL ROOM.
WHY AN ATRIUM? I DON'T GET IT.
I GET IT.

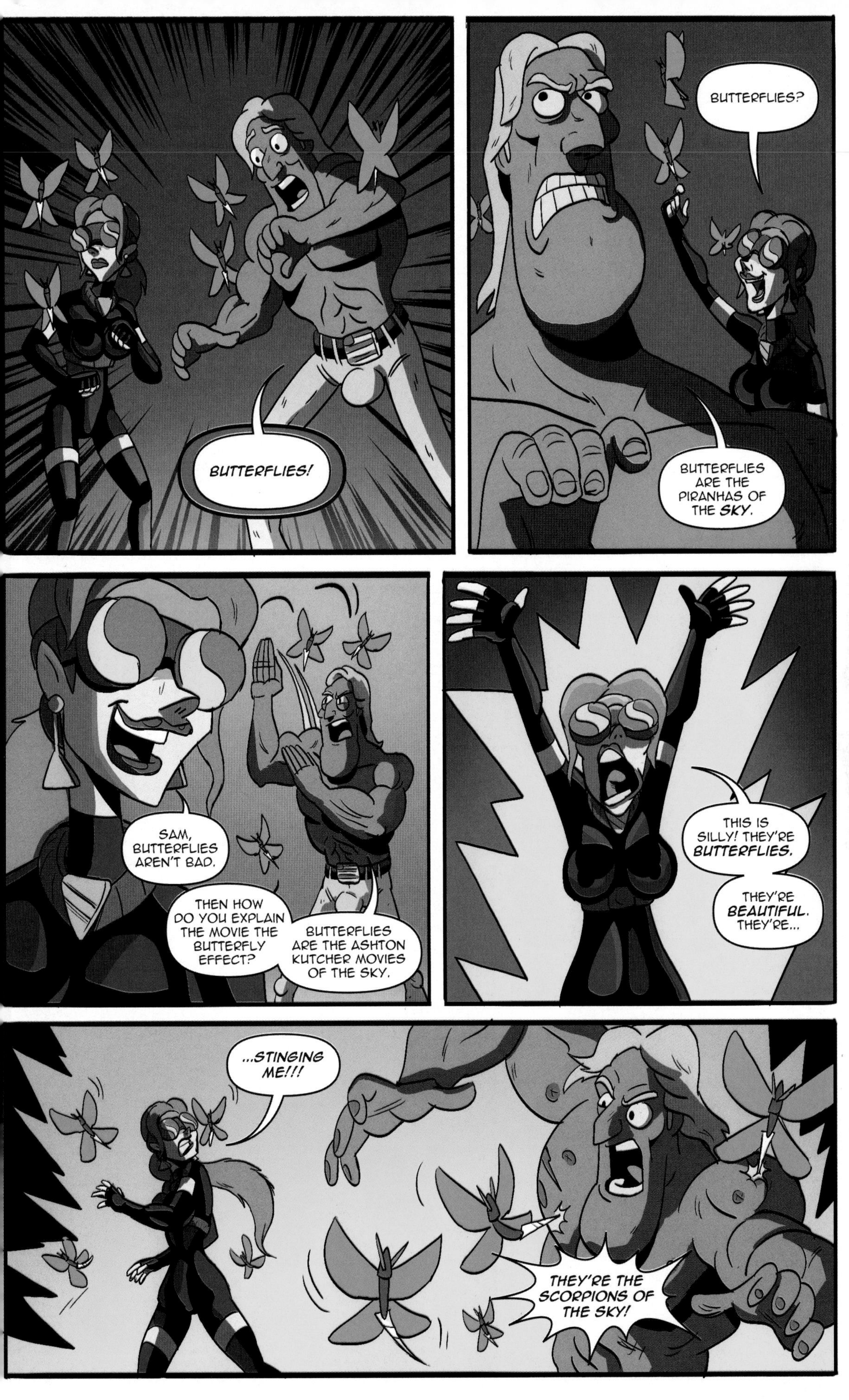
BUTTERFLIES!
BUTTERFLIES?
BUTTERFLIES ARE THE PIRANHAS OF THE SKY.
SAM, BUTTERFLIES AREN'T BAD.
BUTTERFLIES ARE THE ASHTON KUTCHER MOVIES OF THE SKY.
THEN HOW DO YOU EXPLAIN THE MOVIE THE BUTTERFLY EFFECT?
THIS IS SILLY! THEY'RE BUTTERFLIES.
THEY'RE BEAUTIFUL. THEY'RE...
...STINGING ME!!!
THEY'RE THE SCORPIONS OF THE SKY!

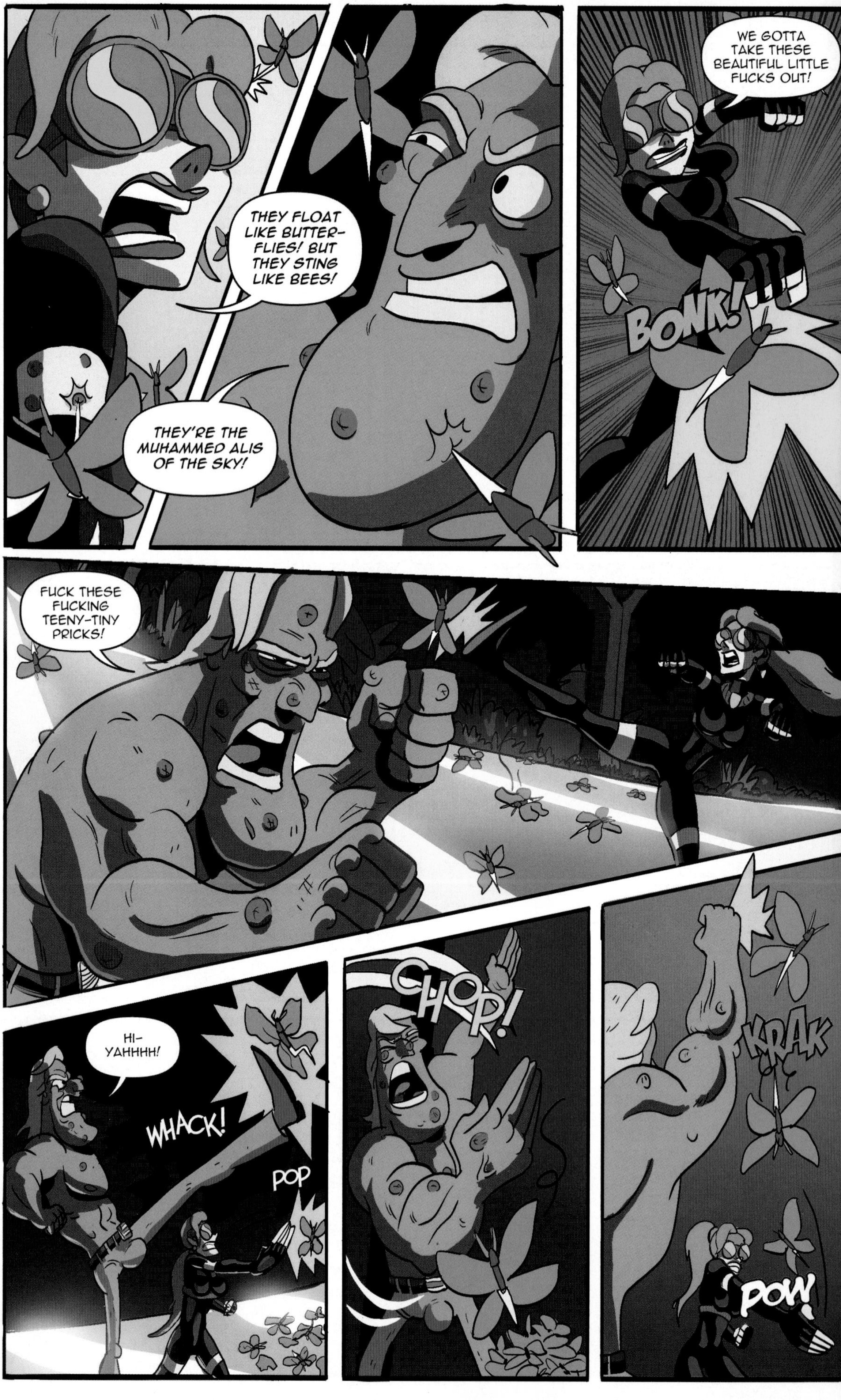
THEY FLOAT LIKE BUTTER-FLIES! BUT THEY STING LIKE BEES!
THEY'RE THE MUHAMMED ALIS OF THE SKY!
WE GOTTA TAKE THESE BEAUTIFUL LITTLE FUCKS OUT!
BONK!
FUCK THESE FUCKING TEENY-TINY PRICKS!
HI-YAHHHH!
WHACK!
POP
CHOP!
KRAK
POW!

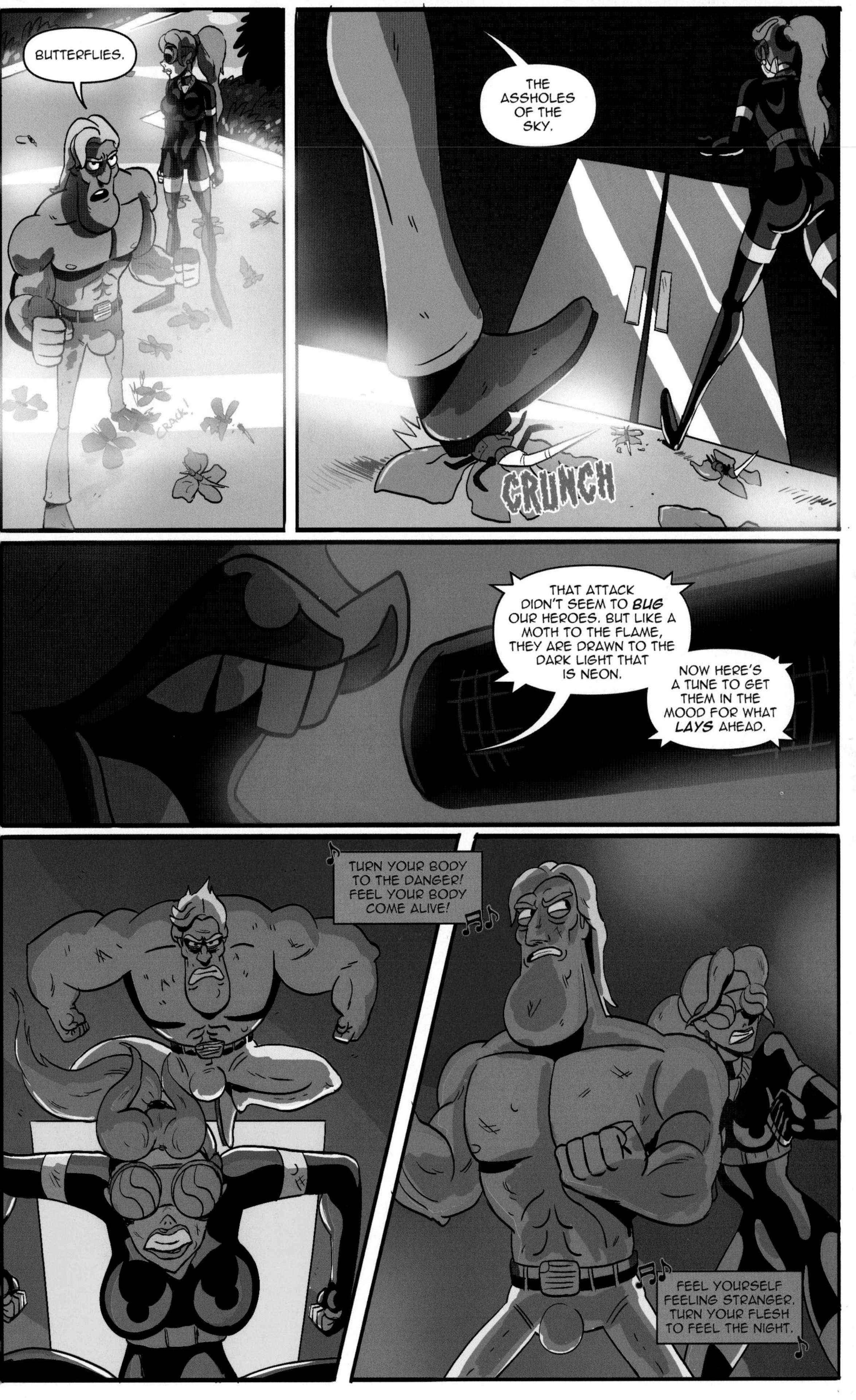
BUTTERFLIES.
THE ASSHOLES OF THE SKY.
CRACK!
CRUNCH
THAT ATTACK DIDN'T SEEM TO BUG OUR HEROES. BUT LIKE A MOTH TO THE FLAME, THEY ARE DRAWN TO THE DARK LIGHT THAT IS NEON.
NOW HERE'S A TUNE TO GET THEM IN THE MOOD FOR WHAT LAYS AHEAD.
TURN YOUR BODY TO THE DANGER! FEEL YOUR BODY COME ALIVE!
FEEL YOURSELF FEELING STRANGER. TURN YOUR FLESH TO FEEL THE NIGHT.

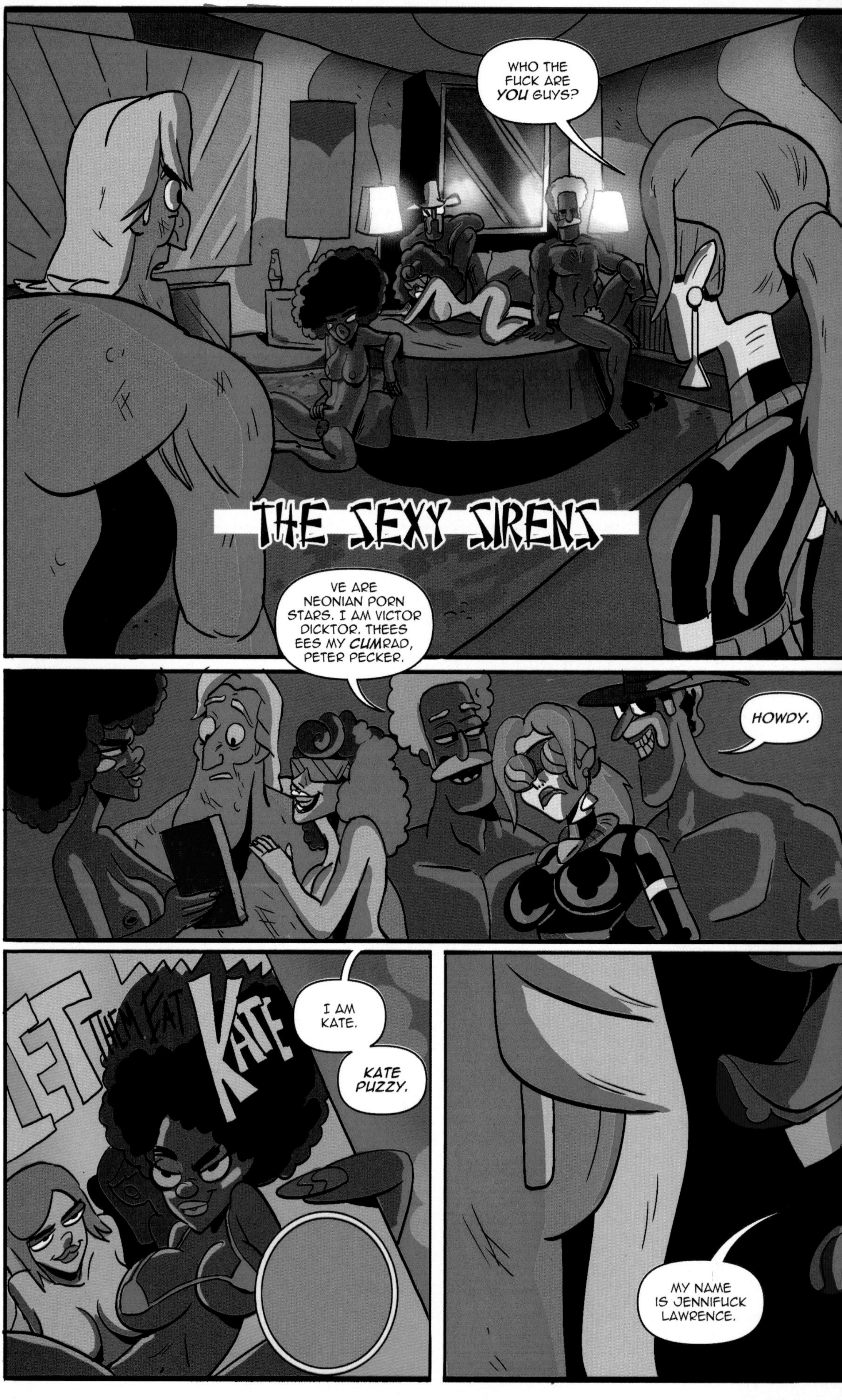
WHO THE FUCK ARE YOU GUYS?
THE SEXY SIRENS
VE ARE NEONIAN PORN STARS. I AM VICTOR DICKTOR. THEES EES MY CUMRAD, PETER PECKER.
HOWDY.
LET THEM EAT KATE
I AM KATE.
KATE PUZZY.
MY NAME IS JENNIFUCK LAWRENCE.

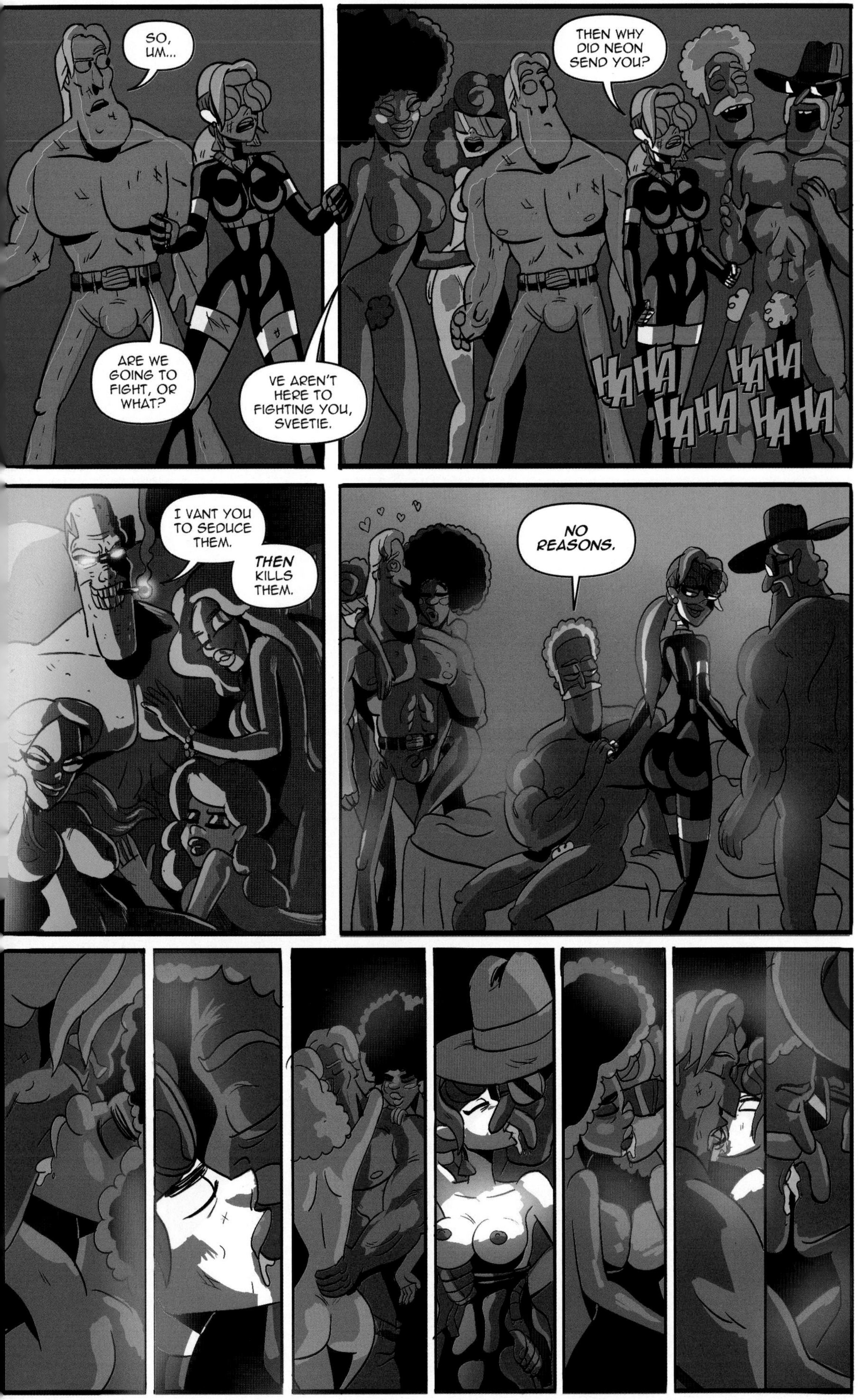
SO, UM...
ARE WE GOING TO FIGHT, OR WHAT?
VE AREN'T HERE TO FIGHTING YOU, SVEETIE.
THEN WHY DID NEON SEND YOU?
HAHA HAHA HAHA HAHA
I VANT YOU TO SEDUCE THEM.
THEN KILLS THEM.
NO REASONS.

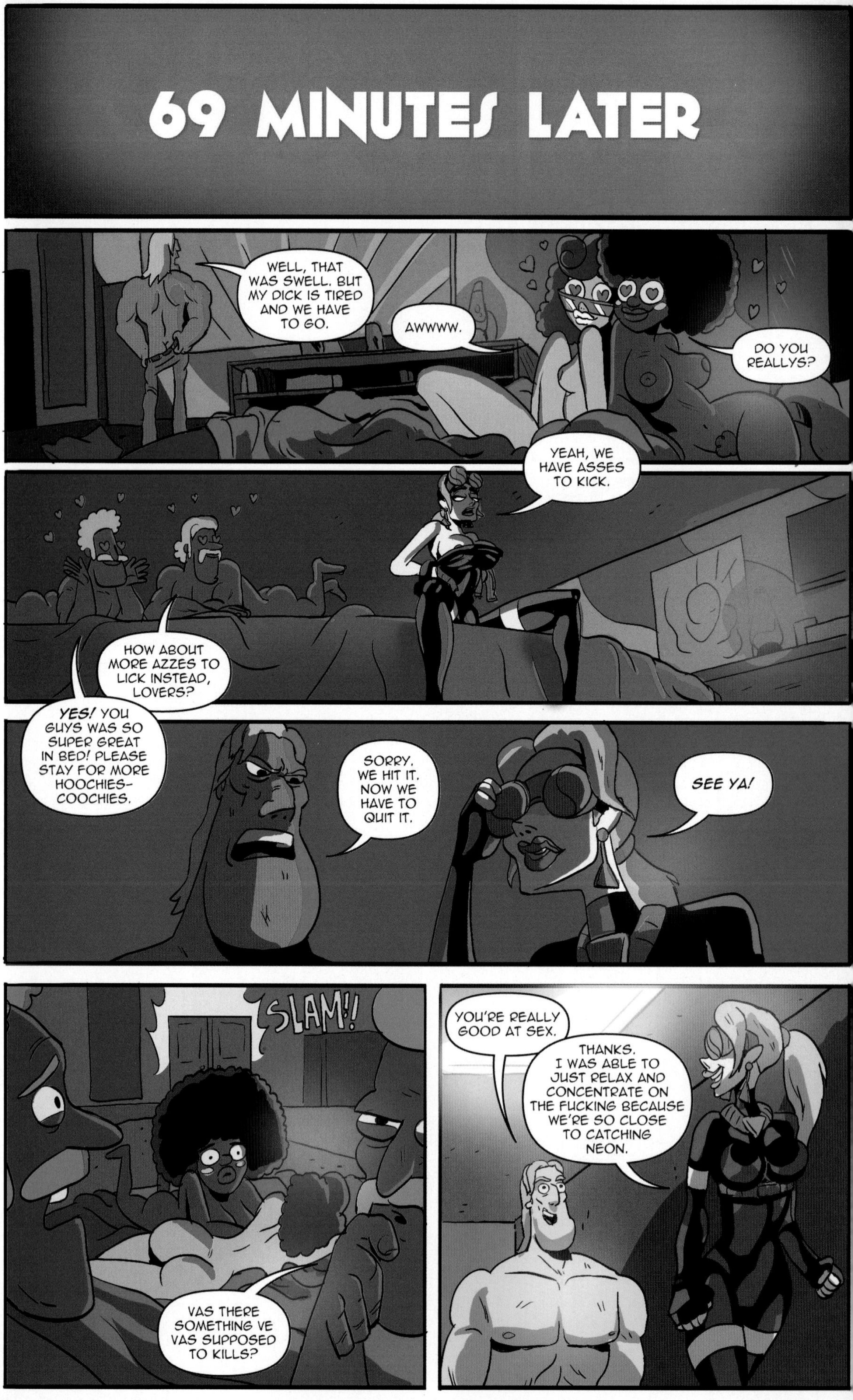
69 MINUTES LATER
WELL, THAT WAS SWELL. BUT MY DICK IS TIRED AND WE HAVE TO GO.
AWWWW.
DO YOU REALLYS?
YEAH, WE HAVE ASSES TO KICK.
HOW ABOUT MORE AZZES TO LICK INSTEAD, LOVERS?
YES! YOU GUYS WAS SO SUPER GREAT IN BED! PLEASE STAY FOR MORE HOOCHIES-COOCHIES.
SORRY. WE HIT IT. NOW WE HAVE TO QUIT IT.
SEE YA!
SLAM!!
VAS THERE SOMETHING VE VAS SUPPOSED TO KILLS?
YOU'RE REALLY GOOD AT SEX.
THANKS. I WAS ABLE TO JUST RELAX AND CONCENTRATE ON THE FUCKING BECAUSE WE'RE SO CLOSE TO CATCHING NEON.

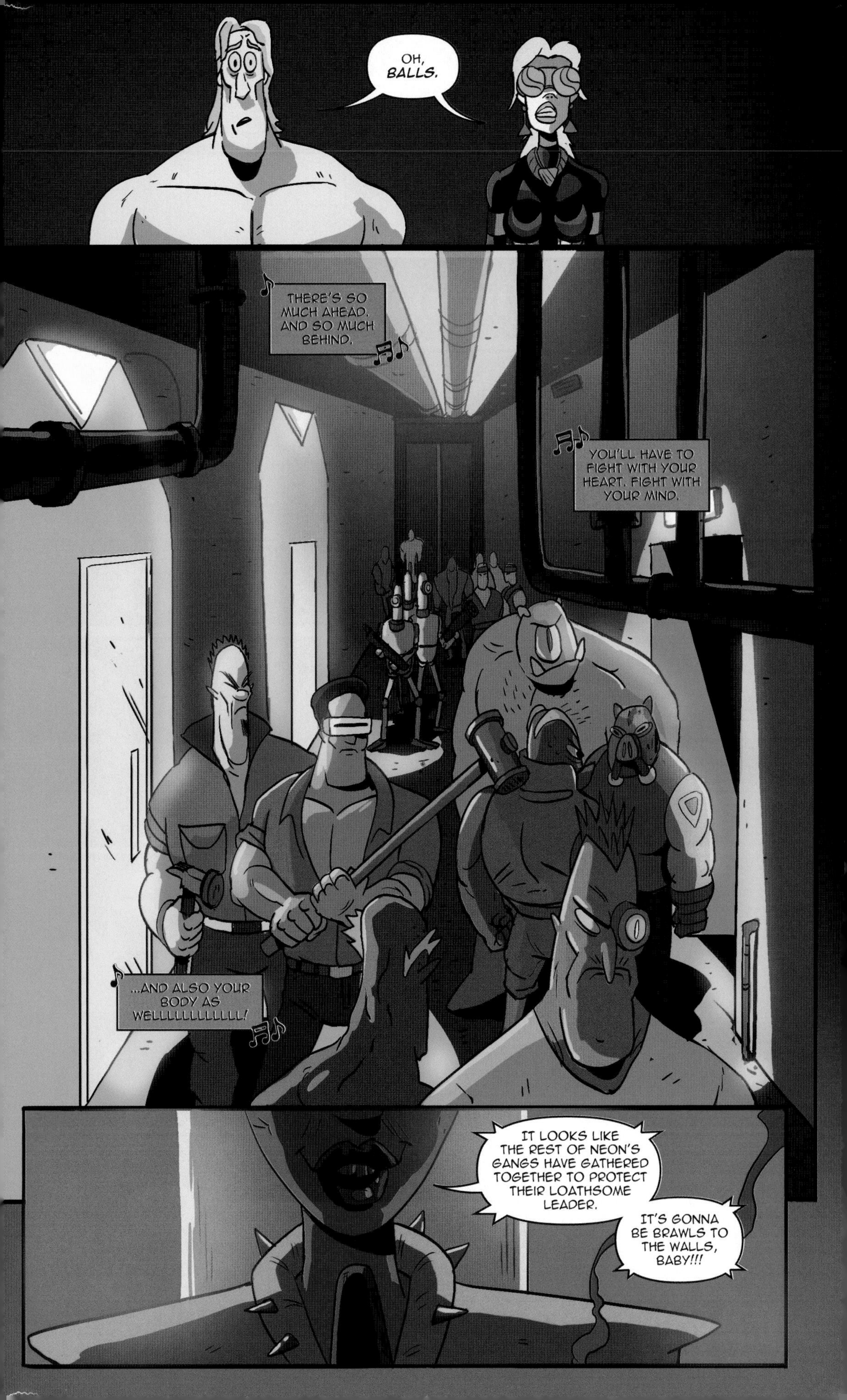
OH, BALLS.
THERE'S SO MUCH AHEAD. AND SO MUCH BEHIND.
YOU'LL HAVE TO FIGHT WITH YOUR HEART. FIGHT WITH YOUR MIND.
...AND ALSO YOUR BODY AS WELLLLLLLLLLLLL!
IT LOOKS LIKE THE REST OF NEON'S GANGS HAVE GATHERED TOGETHER TO PROTECT THEIR LOATHSOME LEADER.
IT'S GONNA BE BRAWLS TO THE WALLS, BABY!!!

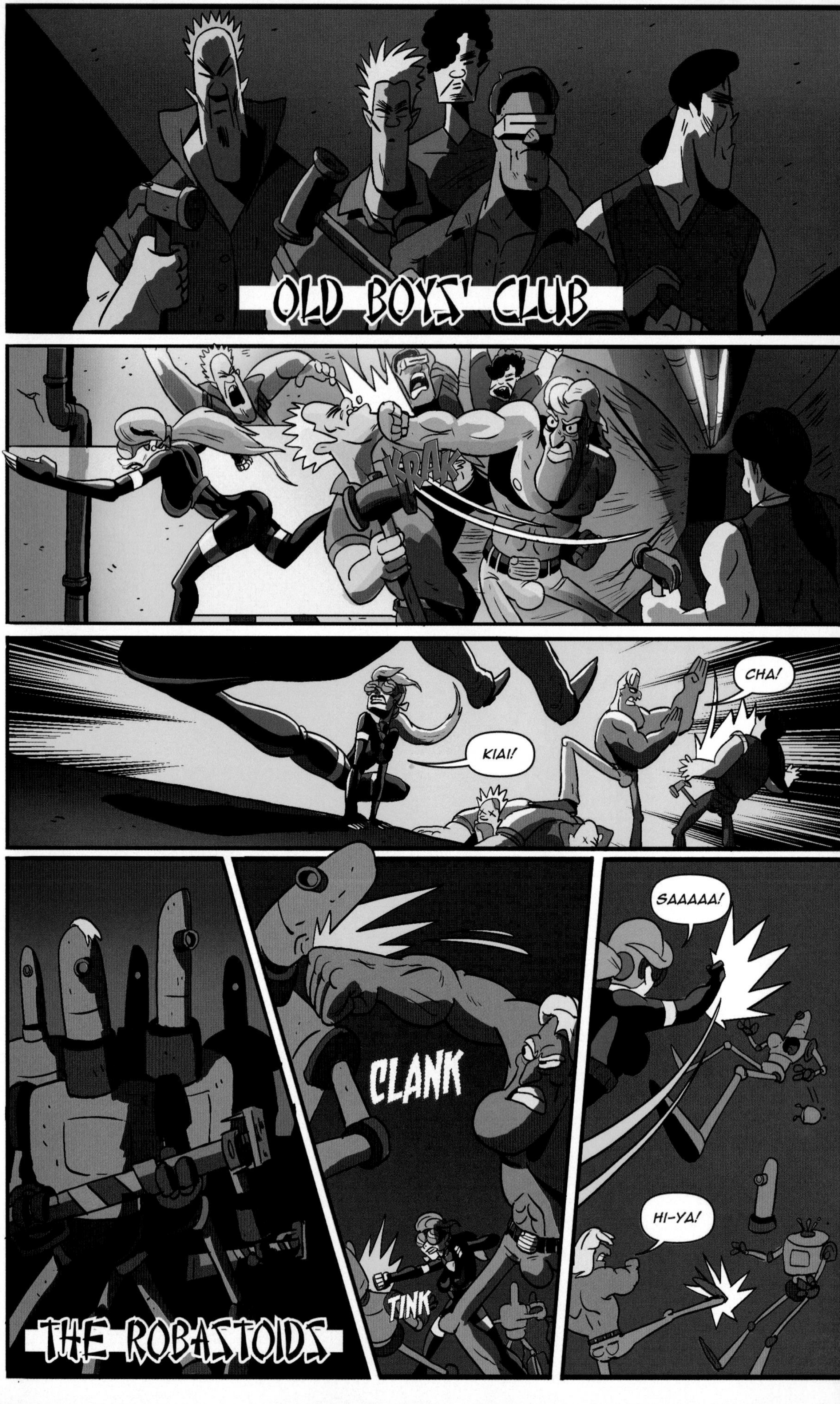
OLD BOYS' CLUB
KRAK
CHA!
KIAI!
THE ROBASTOIDS
CLANK
TINK
SAAAAAA!
HI-YA!

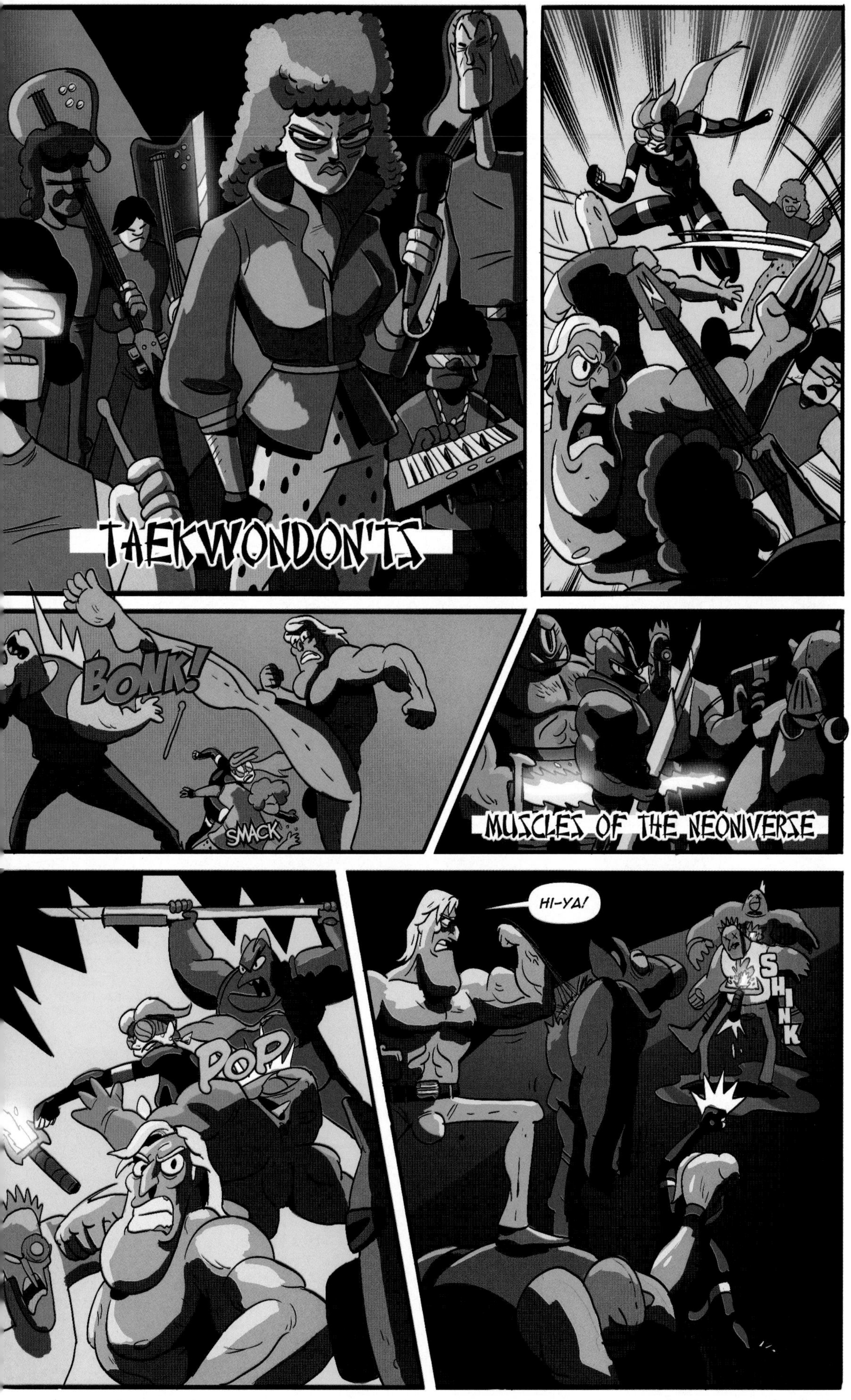
TAEKWONDON'TS
BONK!
SMACK
MUSCLES OF THE NEONIVERSE
POP
HI-YA!
SHINK

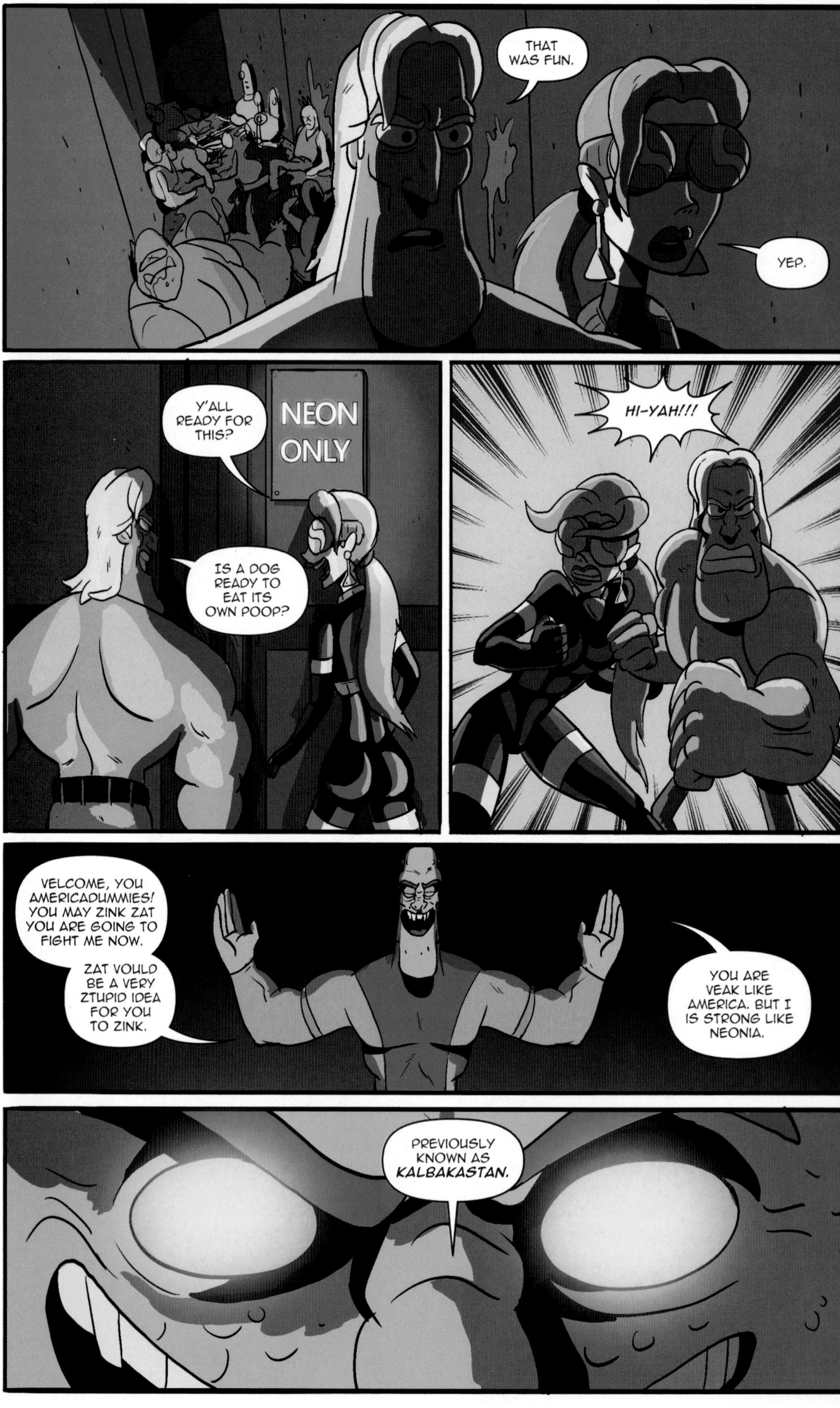
THAT WAS FUN.
YEP.
Y'ALL READY FOR THIS?
NEON ONLY
IS A DOG READY TO EAT ITS OWN POOP?
HI-YAH!!!
VELCOME, YOU AMERICADUMMIES! YOU MAY ZINK ZAT YOU ARE GOING TO FIGHT ME NOW.
ZAT VOULD BE A VERY ZTUPID IDEA FOR YOU TO ZINK.
YOU ARE VEAK LIKE AMERICA. BUT I IS STRONG LIKE NEONIA.
PREVIOUSLY KNOWN AS *KALBAKASTAN.*

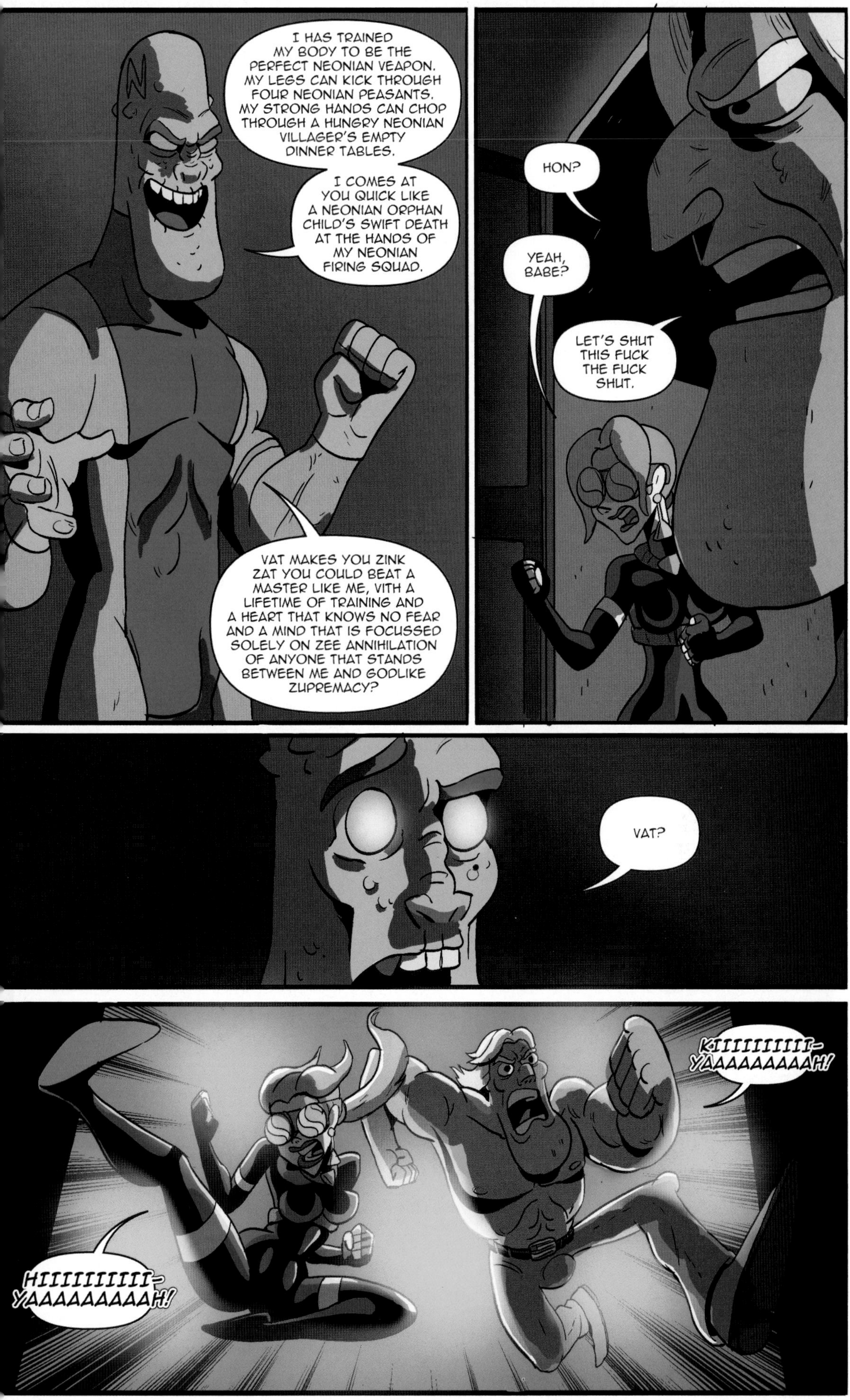
I HAS TRAINED MY BODY TO BE THE PERFECT NEONIAN VEAPON. MY LEGS CAN KICK THROUGH FOUR NEONIAN PEASANTS. MY STRONG HANDS CAN CHOP THROUGH A HUNGRY NEONIAN VILLAGER'S EMPTY DINNER TABLES.
I COMES AT YOU QUICK LIKE A NEONIAN ORPHAN CHILD'S SWIFT DEATH AT THE HANDS OF MY NEONIAN FIRING SQUAD.
VAT MAKES YOU ZINK ZAT YOU COULD BEAT A MASTER LIKE ME, VITH A LIFETIME OF TRAINING AND A HEART THAT KNOWS NO FEAR AND A MIND THAT IS FOCUSSED SOLELY ON ZEE ANNIHILATION OF ANYONE THAT STANDS BETWEEN ME AND GODLIKE ZUPREMACY?
HON?
YEAH, BABE?
LET'S SHUT THIS FUCK THE FUCK SHUT.
VAT?
KIIIIIIIIII-YAAAAAAAAAH!
HIIIIIIIIII-YAAAAAAAAAH!

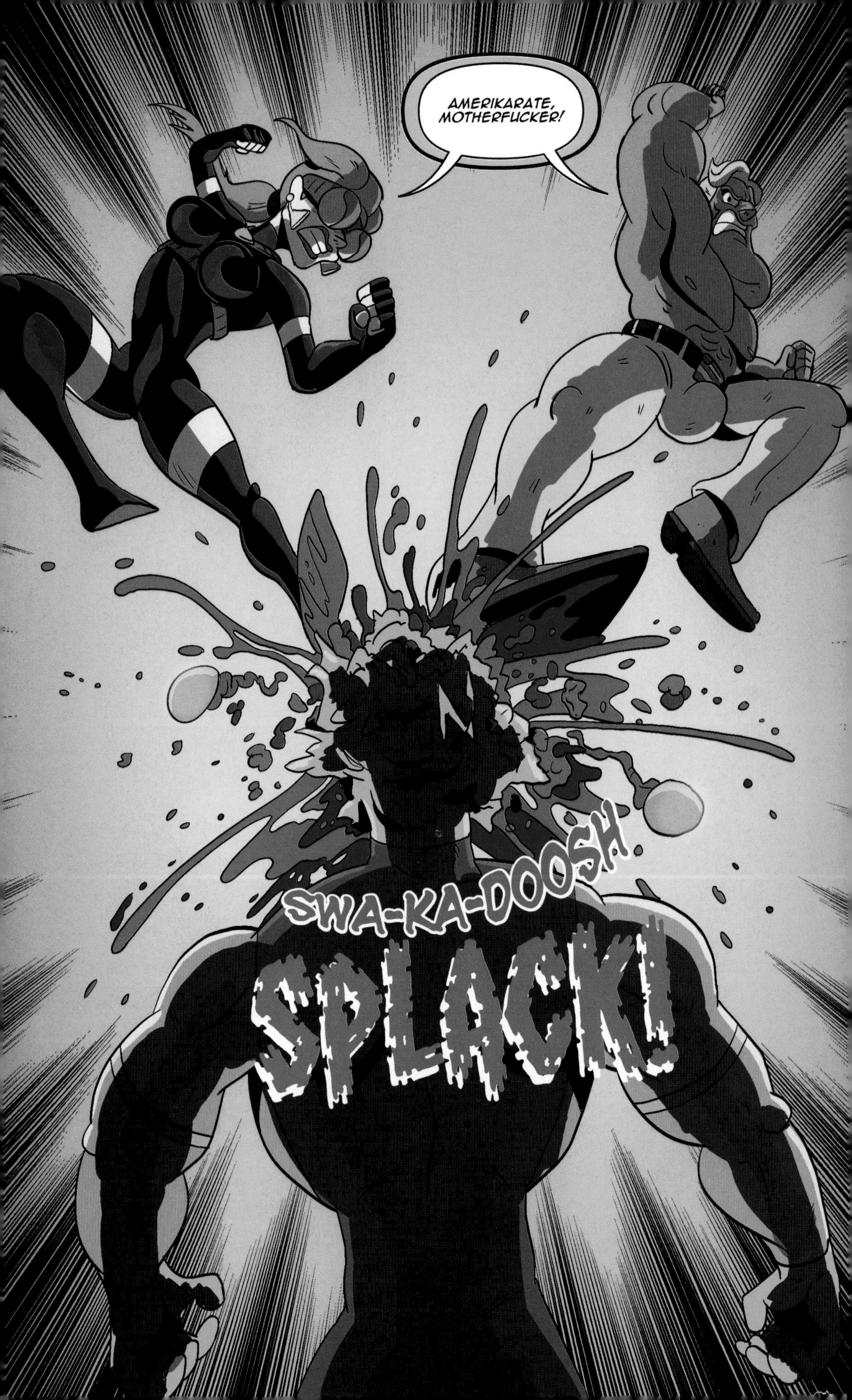
AMERIKARATE, MOTHERFUCKER!
SWA-KA-DOOSH
SPLACK!

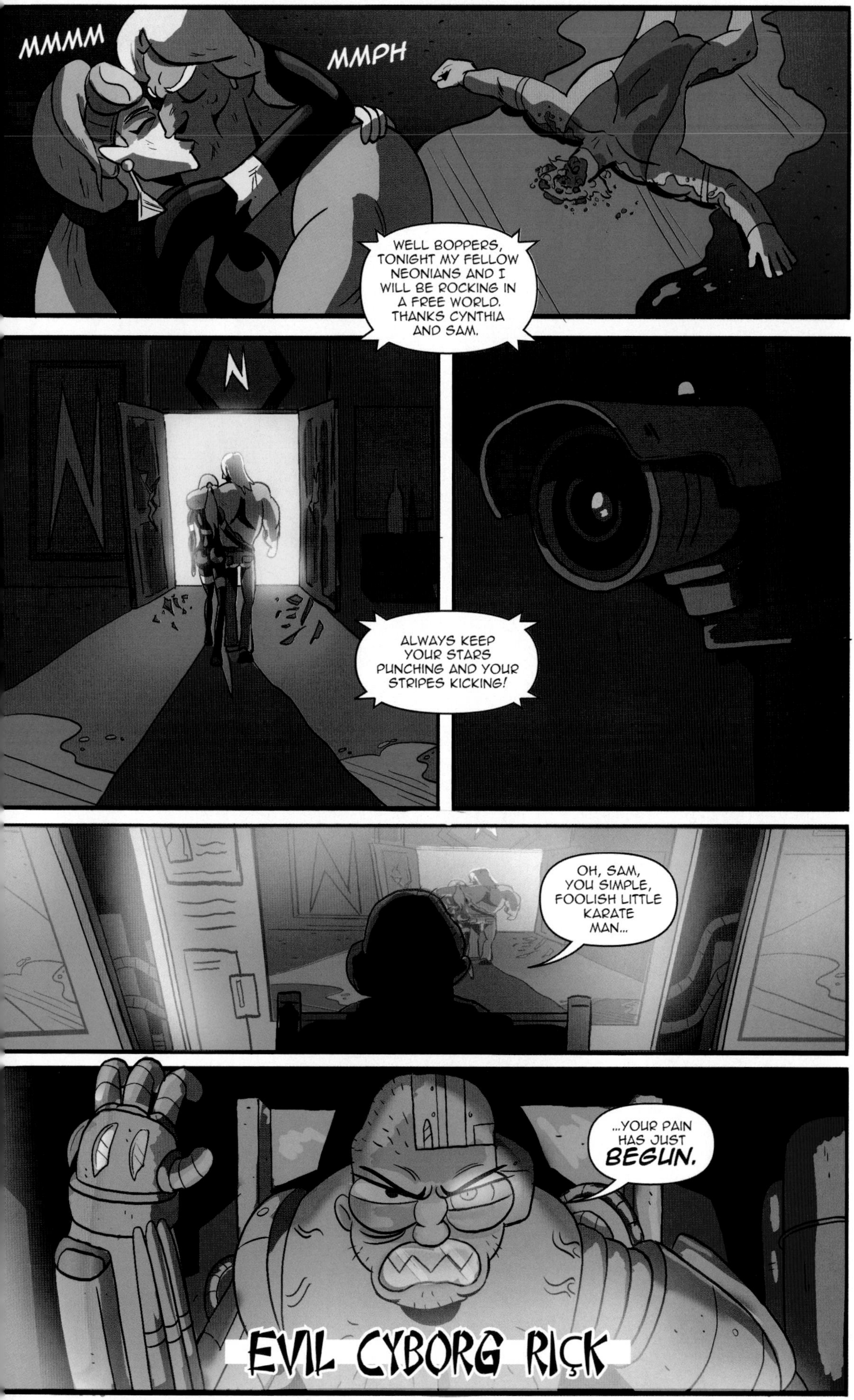
MMMM
MMPH
WELL BOPPERS, TONIGHT MY FELLOW NEONIANS AND I WILL BE ROCKING IN A FREE WORLD. THANKS CYNTHIA AND SAM.
ALWAYS KEEP YOUR STARS PUNCHING AND YOUR STRIPES KICKING!
OH, SAM, YOU SIMPLE, FOOLISH LITTLE KARATE MAN...
...YOUR PAIN HAS JUST BEGUN.
EVIL CYBORG RICK

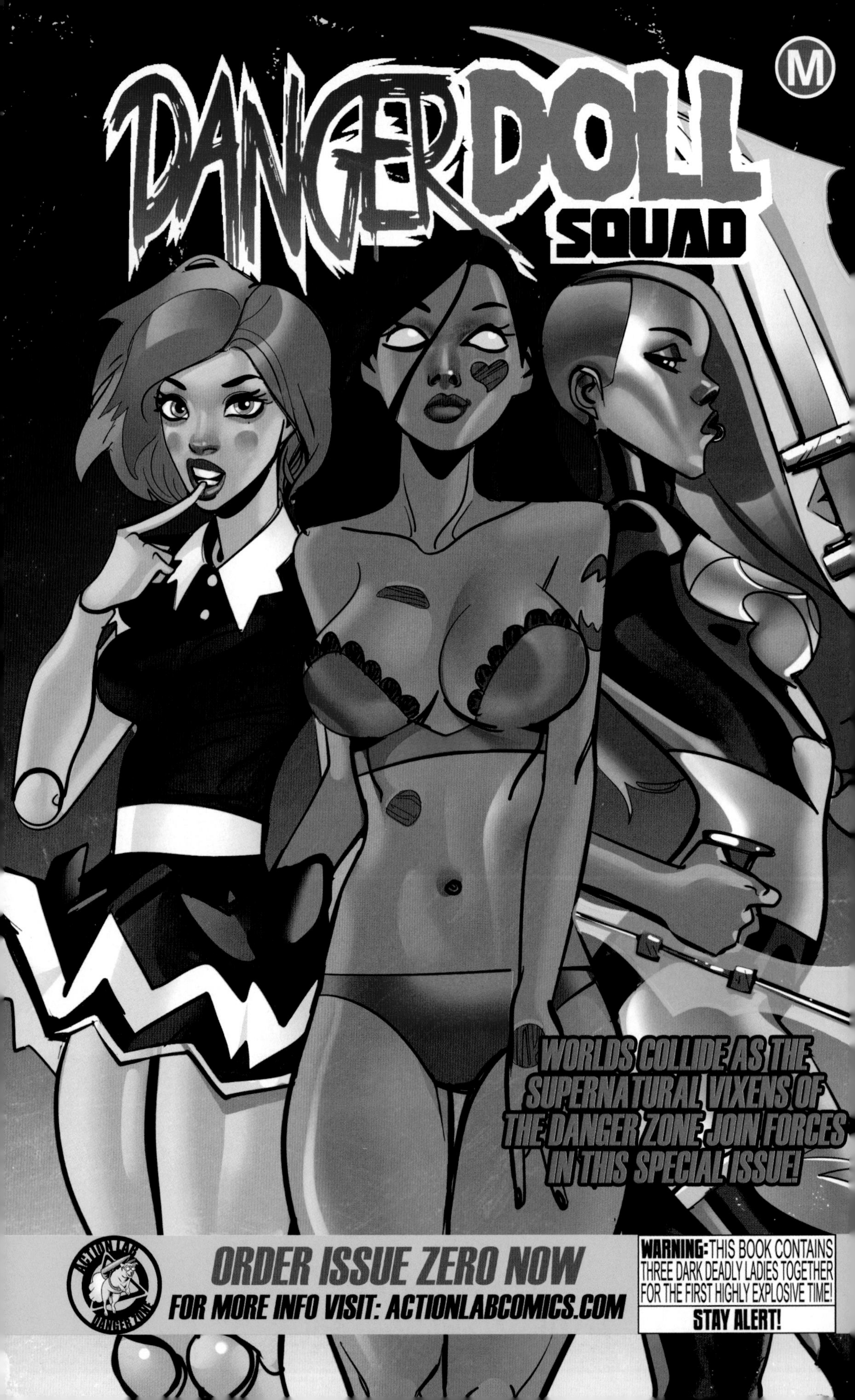
M
DANGER DOLL SQUAD
WORLDS COLLIDE AS THE SUPERNATURAL VIXENS OF THE DANGER ZONE JOIN FORCES IN THIS SPECIAL ISSUE!
ACTION LAB DANGER ZONE
ORDER ISSUE ZERO NOW
FOR MORE INFO VISIT: ACTIONLABCOMICS.COM
WARNING: THIS BOOK CONTAINS THREE DARK DEADLY LADIES TOGETHER FOR THE FIRST HIGHLY EXPLOSIVE TIME!
STAY ALERT!

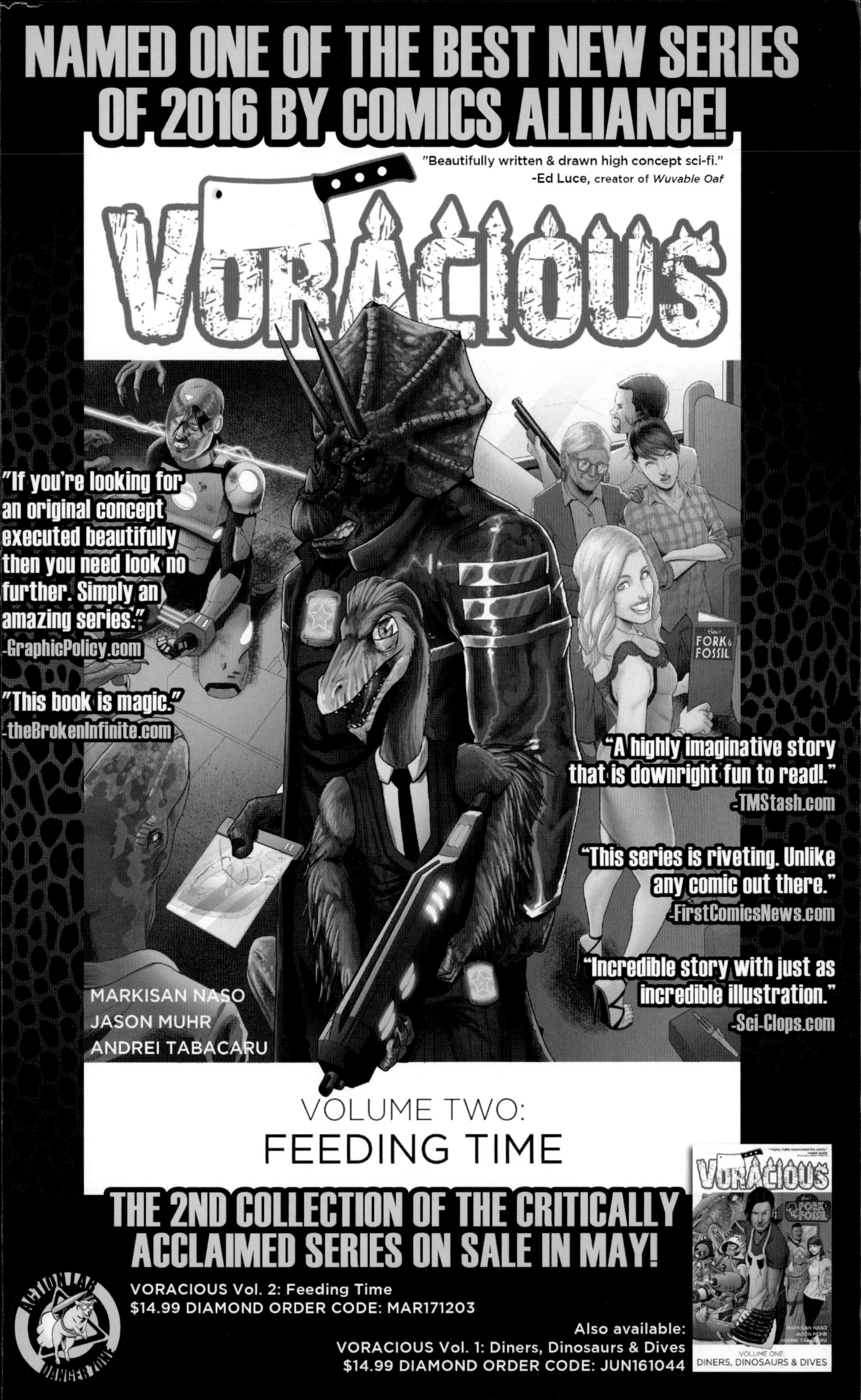

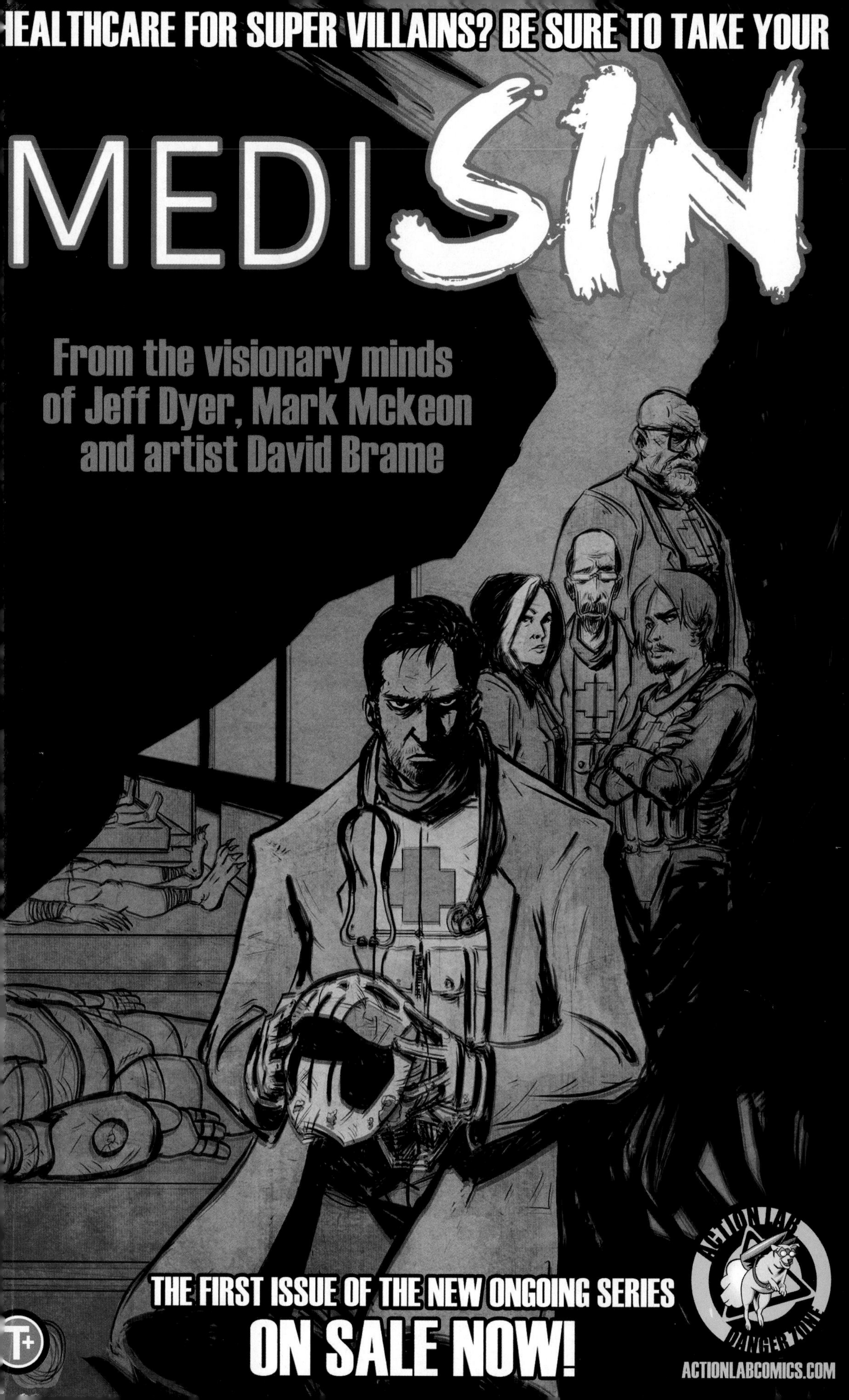
HEALTHCARE FOR SUPER VILLAINS? BE SURE TO TAKE YOUR
MEDISIN
From the visionary minds of Jeff Dyer, Mark Mckeon and artist David Brame
THE FIRST ISSUE OF THE NEW ONGOING SERIES
ON SALE NOW!
T+
ACTION LAB DANGER ZONE
ACTIONLABCOMICS.COM

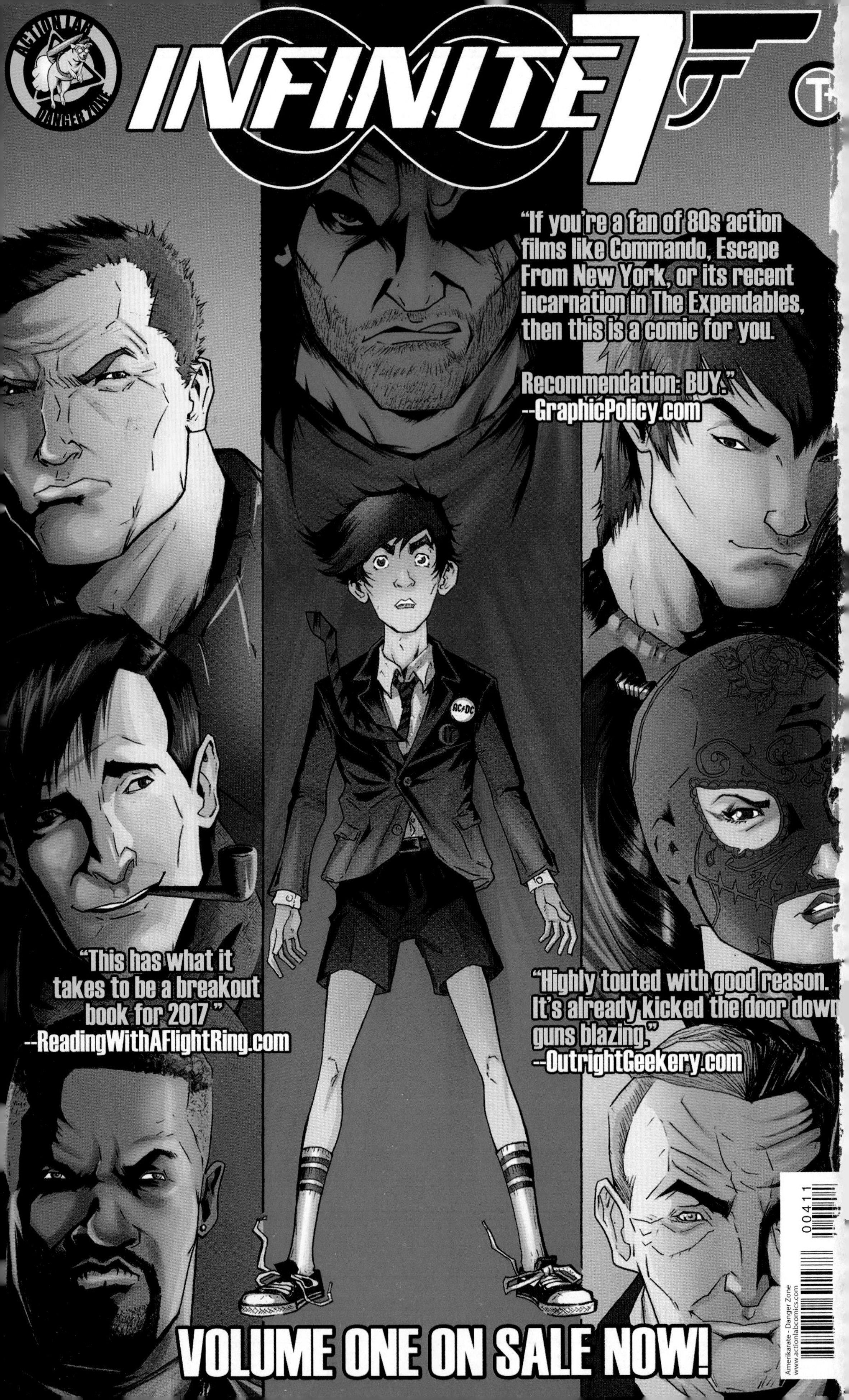
ACTION LAB
DANGER ZONE
INFINITE 7
"If you're a fan of 80s action films like Commando, Escape From New York, or its recent incarnation in The Expendables, then this is a comic for you.
Recommendation: BUY."
--GraphicPolicy.com
AC/DC
"This has what it takes to be a breakout book for 2017"
--ReadingWithAFlightRing.com
"Highly touted with good reason. It's already kicked the door down guns blazing."
--OutrightGeekery.com
VOLUME ONE ON SALE NOW!
Amerikarate - Danger Zone
www.actionlabcomics.com
00411